DEUTERONOMY

BELIEF

A Theological Commentary
on the Bible

GENERAL EDITORS

Amy Plantinga Pauw
William C. Placher[†]

DEUTERONOMY

DEANNA A. THOMPSON

WESTMINSTER
JOHN KNOX PRESS
LOUISVILLE • KENTUCKY

14 15 16 17 18 19 20 21 22 23—10 9 8 7 6 5 4 3 2

Book design by Drew Stevens
Cover design by Lisa Buckley
Cover illustration: © David Chapman/Design Pics/Corbis

Library of Congress Cataloging-in-Publication Data

Thompson, Deanna A., 1966-
  Deuteronomy / Deanna A. Thompson. — First edition.
    pages cm. — (Belief, a theological commentary on the Bible)
  Includes index.
    ISBN 978-0-664-23343-3 (hardback) — ISBN 978-0-664-26035-4
(paperback)
    1. Bible. Deuteronomy—Meditations. 2. Bible. Deuteronomy—
Commentaries. I. Title.
    BS1275.54.T46 2014
    222'.1507—dc23
                                                    2013041188

Contents

Publisher's Note

William C. Placher worked with Amy Plantinga Pauw as a general editor for this series until his untimely death in November 2008. Bill brought great energy and vision to the series, and was instrumental in defining and articulating its distinctive approach and in securing theologians to write for it. Bill's own commentary for the series was the last thing he wrote, and Westminster John Knox Press dedicates the entire series to his memory with affection and gratitude.

William C. Placher, LaFollette Distinguished Professor in Humanities at Wabash College, spent thirty-four years as one of Wabash College's most popular teachers. A summa cum laude graduate of Wabash in 1970, he earned his master's degree in philosophy in 1974 and his PhD in 1975, both from Yale University. In 2002 the American Academy of Religion honored him with the Excellence in Teaching Award. Placher was also the author of thirteen books, including *A History of Christian Theology, The Triune God, The Domestication of Transcendence, Jesus the Savior, Narratives of a Vulnerable God,* and *Unapologetic Theology.* He also edited the volume *Essentials of Christian Theology,* which was named as one of 2004's most outstanding books by both *The Christian Century* and *Christianity Today* magazines.

Series Introduction

Belief: A Theological Commentary on the Bible is a series from Westminster John Knox Press featuring biblical commentaries written by theologians. The writers of this series share Karl Barth's concern that, insofar as their usefulness to pastors goes, most modern commentaries are "no commentary at all, but merely the first step toward a commentary." Historical-critical approaches to Scripture rule out some readings and commend others, but such methods only begin to help theological reflection and the preaching of the Word. By themselves, they do not convey the powerful sense of God's merciful presence that calls Christians to repentance and praise; they do not bring the church fully forward in the life of discipleship. It is to such tasks that theologians are called.

For several generations, however, professional theologians in North America and Europe have not been writing commentaries on the Christian Scriptures. The specialization of professional disciplines and the expectations of theological academies about the kind of writing that theologians should do, as well as many of the directions in which contemporary theology itself has gone, have contributed to this dearth of theological commentaries. This is a relatively new phenomenon; until the last century or two, the church's great theologians also routinely saw themselves as biblical interpreters. The gap between the fields is a loss for both the church and the discipline of theology itself. By inviting forty contemporary theologians to wrestle deeply with particular texts of Scripture, the editors of this series hope not only to provide new theological resources for the church but also to encourage all theologians to pay more attention to Scripture and the life of the church in their writings.

We are grateful to the Louisville Institute, which provided funding for a consultation in June 2007. We invited theologians, pastors, and biblical scholars to join us in a conversation about what this series could contribute to the life of the church. The time was provocative and the results were rich. Much of the series' shape owes to the insights of these skilled and faithful interpreters, who sought to describe a way to write a commentary that served the theological needs of the church and its pastors with relevance, historical accuracy, and theological depth. The passion of these participants guided us in creating this series and lives on in the volumes.

As theologians, the authors will be interested much less in the matters of form, authorship, historical setting, social context, and philology—the very issues that are often of primary concern to critical biblical scholars. Instead, this series' authors will seek to explain the theological importance of the texts for the church today, using biblical scholarship as needed for such explication but without any attempt to cover all of the topics of the usual modern biblical commentary. This thirty-six-volume series will provide passage-by-passage commentary on all the books of the Protestant biblical canon, with more extensive attention given to passages of particular theological significance.

The authors' chief dialogue will be with the church's creeds, practices, and hymns; with the history of faithful interpretation and use of the Scriptures; with the categories and concepts of theology; and with contemporary culture in both "high" and popular forms. Each volume will begin with a discussion of *why* the church needs this book and why we need it *now*, in order to ground all of the commentary in contemporary relevance. Throughout each volume, text boxes will highlight the voices of ancient and modern interpreters from the global communities of faith, and occasional essays will allow deeper reflection on the key theological concepts of these biblical books.

The authors of this commentary series are theologians of the church who embrace a variety of confessional and theological perspectives. The group of authors assembled for this series represents more diversity of race, ethnicity, and gender than any other commentary series. They approach the larger Christian tradition with a critical respect, seeking to reclaim its riches and at the same time to acknowledge its shortcomings. The authors also aim to make available to readers a wide range of contemporary theological voices from many parts of the world. While it does recover an older genre of writing, this series is not an attempt to retrieve some idealized past. These commentaries have learned from tradition, but they are most importantly commentaries for today. The authors share the conviction that their work will be more contemporary, more faithful, and more radical, to the extent that it is more biblical, honestly wrestling with the texts of the Scriptures.

William C. Placher
Amy Plantinga Pauw

Acknowledgments

Even though the actual typing of this commentary has been a solitary exercise, the several-year-long process of theological reflection on the book of Deuteronomy has been a decidedly communal experience. From the four adult forums at Gloria Dei Lutheran Church in Saint Paul, Minnesota, to the Religion Colloquium at Hamline University in Saint Paul, I am indebted to the many, many readers, editors, and conversation partners who have taken time to ponder the theology and relevance of this "book of the law" for Christian communities of faith today. In particular I am indebted to dear friend and colleague Dr. Paul Capetz, who read, commented on, and encouraged me through early drafts, as well as to my parents, Reverend Mervin Thompson and Jackie Thompson, who also read, commented on, and encouraged me throughout the research and writing process. I am especially grateful for these readers' questions and comments; they kept my sights set on making sure this commentary addressed the world and the church beyond the academy.

I am also, always, indebted to my fabulous family: my daughters, Linnea and Annika Thompson Peterson, and my husband, Neal Peterson. Their ongoing support was integral in this project coming to fruition. My love and thanks to them all.

Abbreviations

LW   *Luther's Works*
NPNF[2]   *Nicene and Post-Nicene Fathers,* Series 2
PL   Patrologia latina

Introduction:
Why Deuteronomy? Why Now?

The word is very near to you; it is in your mouth
and in your heart for you to observe.
(Deut. 30:14)

After journalist David Plotz blogged his way through the Hebrew
Bible for the Web site Slate.com, Christian readers encouraged him
to blog the New Testament as well. Plotz explained that as a Jew,
he was hesitant to comment on Christian Scriptures. "Similarly,"
he wrote, "I'm not sure a Christian would [be] comfortable writing
about the Israelites and the God of the Hebrew Bible."[1]

It's understandable that Plotz would be reluctant to take up the
task of interpreting Christian Scripture. At the same time, his statement about Christians and the God of Israel suggests that the God
he's wrestling with in the Hebrew Bible is different from the one
Christians call God. Students of church history know that Plotz's
perspective echoes the views of second-century church bishop Marcion of Sinope. Based on his reading of the New Testament, Marcion concluded that the Creator God of the Old Testament was
other than (and inferior to) the loving, merciful God made known
in Jesus Christ. Armed with this conviction, Marcion called for the
separation of Christianity and its Scriptures from all things Jewish.
For Marcion it was imperative Christians understand the lawgiver

---

1. "Biblically Speaking: David Plotz discusses *Good Book*, his chronicle of reading every single
word of the Bible," Slate.com, March 4, 2009, www.slate.com/id/2212970/.

God of the Old Testament as utterly distinct from the New Testament God of love.

But the ancient church ruled against Marcion and his belief in separate gods and separate Scriptures for Christians and Jews. Marcion was deemed a heretic, the church emphasizing instead Christianity's dependence on Judaism and affirming that the Old Testament is indeed the church's book and that the God of the Ten Commandments is the same God incarnate in the Word made flesh.

Despite the church's official denunciation of Marcion's position, the history of Christian interpretation of the Old Testament is replete with Marcion-like treatments of the OT God and the biblical books of the Law. From ancient Christian allegorical readings of the Old Testament that ignore the import of the laws and stories for Jews and Christians to the current lectionary cycle that bypasses almost all OT legal sections, it's not surprising that Marcion's views are still very much in vogue.

Enter Deuteronomy, the quintessential OT book of the Law. As if the book's focus on law were not reason enough for Christians to sidestep the text, Deuteronomy also teems with references to a warriorlike God. What, then, are Christians to do with such a book, where most of its laws are seen as irrelevant to our contemporary context and many of its images of God make us squirm? It's tempting simply to agree with Marcion that this book should be left to our Jewish neighbors while we head for the greener pastures of the New Testament.

In striving to understand Deuteronomy as the Word of God for Christians today, we are helped by the distinction between the law and the gospel made by sixteenth-century theologian Martin Luther. For Luther and other theologians of the Reformation, the law signaled much more than commands given through Scripture. In Christians' encounter with God's Word, the Reformers believed, any text can speak to us as law—accusing and convicting us of the ways we fall short—as well as gospel, that is, the Word of God that saves. Luther believed that the faith in God's promises embraced by OT figures like Moses shares a fundamental similarity with the faith embraced by Christians in his own context. Theirs was an expectant faith in God's promises just as ours still is today. We will see that Deuteronomy's story of Moses and the chosen people of God offers gospel as well as law to its Christian readers.

To proclaim that Jews have the law and Christians have the gospel, then, is not only to propagate a mistaken view of Scripture, but it also risks paving a path toward anti-Jewish sentiment. If Christians believe that all we have inherited from Judaism is the law, then notions of Christian superiority are not far behind. It is vital that any contemporary Christian interpretation of Deuteronomy claim it as Christian Scripture in a way that does not deny that it was first, and still remains, Jewish Scripture. As biblical scholar Walter Brueggemann notes, even though Christians put the accent on fulfillment while Jews accentuate promise, tension between promise and fulfillment is common to both Testaments and both faiths.[2]

Therefore, Christian commentary on Old Testament books like Deuteronomy can benefit greatly from Jewish interpretations of the same Scripture. Understanding that Jews refer to Deuteronomy and the four biblical books preceding it as *torah* is an important first step. Since NT times, Christians have translated *torah* as "law," a necessary but insufficient name for the books of the Pentateuch. Translated more broadly, *torah* means guidance or instruction. Studying Deuteronomy, then, is not simply studying the law; studying Deuteronomy means attending to the instruction offered by a dying Moses to God's people as they prepared to enter the land God promised them.

Who wrote the book of Deuteronomy? Jewish and Christian thinkers in the ancient and medieval period claimed Moses as the author of the first five books of the Bible. Modern biblical scholarship, however, argues for multiple authors of the Pentateuch. Nineteenth-century biblical scholar Julius Wellhausen proposed a four-source theory that argues that Deuteronomy was written predominantly by a source he called "the Deuteronomist." While Wellhausen's four-source theory continues to enjoy strong support, uncovering the identity of the Deuteronomist remains an unsettled

2. Walter Brueggemann, *Theology of the Old Testament: Testimony, Dispute, Advocacy* (Minneapolis: Fortress Press, 1997), 111.

question. Seen as a school or a movement rather than an individual author, the Deuteronomist may have come out of priestly or prophetic circles or from within a group of wisdom teachers. Evidence exists to support each of these theories of authorship.

In terms of the dating of the text, most scholars agree that the book of Deuteronomy was composed somewhere between the eighth and fifth century BCE through a complex editorial process. This means that the text's audience would have been either the Israelites who lived under the divided monarchy of the kingdom of Israel in the north and the kingdom of Judah in the south or the Israelites who endured the turbulent years of the northern kingdom's destruction down to their exile in Babylon in 540 BCE. Scholars believe that Deuteronomy's theology directs itself to these contexts, for the Deuteronomist is intent on showing that an Israelite shift in allegiance away from worship of the one God will be responsible for their political downfall and loss of the land God promised them. Many scholars also suggest that chapters 12–26 in Deuteronomy (commonly understood as the "law code" section) is actually "the book of the law" found during the reign of King Josiah (cf. 2 Kgs. 22:8-20 ff.) in the seventh century BCE, where the king tears his clothes after hearing the book read aloud and calls Israel to reform and obey the words of the book.

In our contemporary reading of the book of Deuteronomy, then, we can see the Deuteronomist calling on a fractured and exiled Israel to remember their history, to remember their covenant with the God who claimed them, and to understand that this God's fidelity to the covenant brought them out of slavery and will lead them to the promised land. The four speeches given by Moses within Deuteronomy command Israel to listen, to hear again the story, to remember what their God has done for them, and to obey God's commands so that it will go well for them in the new land. Embedded within this Deuteronomic theology is also the harsh indictment against a people whose disobedience caused the loss of their land. But the text offers more than just judgment; it also points to glimpses of God's grace that offer hope to Israel for a life of blessing and eventual return to the land.

Hear Again the Story: The Significance of Retelling and Remembering

Most Christians likely know very little about Deuteronomy's retelling of Israel's life between its coming out of Egypt and its going into the promised land. When it comes to the Pentateuch, Sunday school stories of Adam and Eve, Joseph and his brothers, and Moses leading the Israelites out of Egypt probably are the first that come to mind. Unlike the pentateuchal books of Genesis through Numbers that brim with such stories, Deuteronomy is short on stories; in fact, it contains almost no action. The narrative is essentially a set of farewell speeches by Moses in which he retells the story of Israel's liberation from slavery, its wandering through the wilderness, and the covenantal relationship with Israel's God within which this history occurred.

And while contemporary Jews who attend synagogue hear the entire book of Deuteronomy read aloud each year (along with the other four books of the Torah), Christians typically hear little to none of Deuteronomy read aloud during worship. Those of us who attend churches that follow the lectionary hear nine short passages within the three-year cycle. For those churches selecting their own Scripture readings, Deuteronomy is often bypassed as well. Biblical scholar Ellen Davis mourns this contemporary Christian practice of ignoring large parts of the Old Testament and suggests that Christians suffer from a "loss of intimacy" with books like Deuteronomy. Davis believes that many OT books hold little authority for Christians because they're largely unknown and unread within Christian communities.[3]

Further, theological preoccupation in Christian circles with the creation-fall-redemption model of salvation history means that what occurs between "fall" and "redemption" often receives scant

---

3. Ellen Davis, "Losing a Friend: The Loss of the Old Testament to the Church," in *Jews, Christians, and the Theology of the Hebrew Scriptures*, ed. Alice Ogden Bellis and Joel S. Kaminsky (Atlanta: Society for Biblical Literature, 1990).

attention.[4] Thus Deuteronomy's recounting of God's foundational relationship with Israel, as well as Moses' setting forth laws that form the vision of what life should look like in the promised land, remain peripheral to what Christians consider the heart of God's story of creation and redemption.

> The placing of the history of deliverance (Exodus to Numbers) in a framework of the two books where blessing is the dominant theme [Genesis and Deuteronomy] is important because it shows that the arrangement of the Pentateuch, the Torah, expresses the close relationship between God's saving activity and the blessing he bestows.
>
> Claus Westermann, *Blessing in the Bible and the Life of the Church,* trans. Keith Crim (Philadelphia: Fortress Press, 1978), 30.

Our ignorance of books like Deuteronomy risks our missing out on insights from the theology embedded in Moses' retelling of Israel's story, which is the Christian story as well, since we claim to be spiritual descendants of Israel. Moses' speeches are cast as direct addresses; he speaks directly to the Israelites of *today* (no fewer than twenty-seven times throughout the book), telling those gathered before him about God's vision of blessing for their future in the promised land. Rather than simply a book of laws, Moses' retelling in Deuteronomy is more accurately described as a kind of "catechesis," that is, a passing down to the next generation the fundamentals of the faith as well as the parameters that frame a life lived in accord with the promises of God. Deuteronomy is Moses' final set of teachings to the whole of Israel. The children of Israel hear these final instructions as they reside temporarily in the plains of Moab, opposite Jericho, poised to enter Canaan. In this commentary we will work to discern the catechetical import of Moses' speech to the today of ancient Israel; just as importantly we will examine how Moses' direct address in that context speaks to the today of twenty-first-century Christianity.

We must also attend to the way Moses tells the Israelites the story

---

4. Neil B. MacDonald, *Metaphysics and the God of Israel: Systematic Theology of the Old and New Testaments* (Grand Rapids: Baker Academic, 2007), 160.

of their history in Deuteronomy. It is not simply a verbatim rehearsal of the story they already know. It is a retelling of Israel's story—the exodus being a central theme—for an exiled audience, a story for a people who had gained and then lost the land God promised them. Given that the reality of exile likely stands as a primary context for the hearers of Deuteronomy, Christians need to interpret Scripture like Deuteronomy with the knowledge that the world today is still engaged in the active production of exiles.[5]

Moses' words in Deuteronomy repeatedly emphasize the Israelites' straying from God; their disobedience is cited as the primary reason for their current state of exile (cf. 4:26–29). At the same time, at the heart of Deuteronomy's theology is an affirmation of the rich blessings of life lived in faithful covenantal relationship with God. The Deuteronomist insists that it *is* possible to move from the death of exile back to life in right relationship with God (cf. 30:11–20). Amidst the harsh judgment for Israel embedded in Moses' last words are whispers of hope for salvation for this exiled people. Such testimonies to hope remain faintly audible in today's exiled communities as well.

Deuteronomy as Covenantal Theology between Yahweh and Israel

The story of Deuteronomy is the story of a covenant people set in a unique and privileged relationship to Yahweh. Deuteronomy is the only book of the Pentateuch that contains rigidly monotheistic claims, such as in 4:35 where we hear that "there is no other besides [God]." In commentaries on the Pentateuch, scholars often prefer to talk of Israel's relationship to its God as monolatrous rather than monotheistic, where a single deity is worshiped without claiming it is the only deity (think about God's admonition to Israel in the First Commandment: "You shall have no other gods before me" [Exod. 20:3; Deut. 5:7]).[6] Yet a close reading of Deuteronomy reveals an

---

5. Brueggemann, *Theology of the Old Testament*, 77–78.
6. Laurel Schneider, *Beyond Monotheism: A Theology of Multiplicity* (New York: Routledge, 2008), chaps. 2–3.

on-going tension in the view of God as the only one and the view of God as the only one *for Israel* (e.g., see 32:8–9 where different peoples are allotted their own gods). While Walter Brueggemann acknowledges that it's not easy for a Christian theological reading of the Old Testament to embrace such an unsettled quality of the text, he nevertheless suggests that to resist such tensions is, "more than Christology, what Christian supersession looks like today."[7] Therefore, this commentary seeks to honor the unsettled rendering of the one God Yahweh within the Deuteronomic text.

The God of Deuteronomy is not only the God of Israel's ancestors, but as Moses repeatedly emphasizes, the defining event of the relationship between God and the ancient Israelites is God's liberating them from slavery in Egypt and propelling them forward toward the promise of their own land. In Exodus 19:3–6 we hear of the creation of the covenant between God and the people of Israel. In Deuteronomy, the terms of that covenant are expanded and defined, all the while anchored in the liberative character of Israel's God.

Accompanying the expanded discussion of what it means for Israel to be in covenantal relationship with God is Deuteronomy's deepening of the theme of Israel as God's chosen people (4:37) that is introduced in Exodus 19:5. The history of interpretation by Christian and Jewish readers regarding Israel's chosenness is vast and complex. From the time of ancient Christianity forward, the church has often been cast as the "new" or "true" Israel. Sixteenth-century Reformer John Calvin offers a representative Christian view of chosenness when he writes, "The meaning then is, as though he had said, 'Moses called formerly your fathers a holy nation, a priestly kingdom, and God's peculiar people; all these high titles do now far more justly belong to you [Christians].'"[8] Further, since the time of the Puritans, Americans have invoked the "chosen people" status and used it as sanctioning an American exceptionalism that has brought harm to many groups, from Native Americans to immigrants of various backgrounds. While we surely can benefit from reflection on what Israel's chosenness means for Christians today,

---

7. Brueggemann, *Theology of the Old Testament*, 111.

8. John Calvin, *Commentaries on the Catholic Epistles*, trans. and ed. John Owen (Grand Rapids: Baker, 1981), 73.

wholesale cooptation of Israel's distinction as God's covenantal partner—whether it be as Christians or Americans or both—neglects God's primary relationship with this small band of people, a reality that needs to matter to Christians of any age. In this commentary we will explore Israel's chosenness while attempting to avoid the supersessionist or exceptionalist attitudes that too often accompany Christian interpretations of the concept.

Why did God choose Israel as God's own treasured people? Deuteronomy emphasizes repeatedly that Israel did not become God's covenantal partner based on any merit of its own. Indeed, that a god of the ancient world would establish a covenant with a tiny band of people like Israel is a highly peculiar move. As Karl Barth has written, "Why is it that God inclined His heart to Israel? Only one reason: that the Lord loved you."[9]

This love of God about which Deuteronomy speaks is beyond mere emotion or attitude; it is an expression of God's inner nature and what Barth calls God's "unsentimental action."[10] God's love for Israel's ancestors, for the present generation, for those who will enter into and be exiled from the promised land, is a free and unmerited gift.

God's love for Israel led to the creation of a covenant with these particular people. It is important to note that a covenant relationship is two-sided; it suggests mutual rather than unilateral attention. This is why it is vital to understand the guidance and instruction offered in torah as set within the context of covenant. The laws that fill the pages of Deuteronomy are given to God's people so that they might be blessed, that they might live, and that it might go well with them in the land (5:33). The laws center around what life will be like in the land promised them by God as they live in response to what God has done for them.

But as central as the land is for Israel, the covenant God makes with Israel does not depend on possession of the land.[11] The laws set

---

9. Karl Barth, *Church Dogmatics*, IV/2 (London: T. & T. Clark, 2010), 151.
10. Ibid., 763.
11. Jeffrey Tigay, *The JPS Torah Commentary: Deuteronomy* (Philadelphia: Jewish Publication Society, 1996), xxvii.

the parameters for what covenantal living looks like in all its varied dimensions.

For Reformation theologians like Luther and Calvin, calling Deuteronomy the "book of the covenant" also adds a political dimension to the story. In order to live well, attention must be paid to questions of authority, to the ordering of communal life, to who rules and how, and to whom the community owes its loyalty and allegiance, all of which the book of Deuteronomy addresses.[12] Our task in this commentary is to attend to the ways in which the political dimensions of the laws interact with the social and theological dimensions and how those interplays affect our interpretation of the concepts of "covenant" and "law" today.

When we ponder how covenantal thinking should shape Christian thought and practice in our contemporary lives, we are drawn to the affirmation that Deuteronomy's preoccupation with the covenant relationship between God and Israel highlights the inescapable communal nature of the people's relationship with God. Jewish feminist scholar Judith Plaskow says it well: "There's no Jewish way to go off and have an individual relationship with God."[13] In the midst of Christian preoccupation with devotional readings of Scripture and a personal relationship with God, we are called to take notice of Deuteronomy's insistent presentation of the thoroughgoing communal relationship that exists between God and the people of Israel. Christians grafted

> When we read in Exodus and Deuteronomy of the delivery to Moses of the law . . . we are meant to understand that this is not simply a public occasion, but the establishment of what we would today call public policy. The Bible is for people, but more than that, it is understood to be for the ordering of the private and the public, the individual and the corporate affairs of a community of people.
>
> Peter J. Gomes, *The Good Book: Reading the Bible with Mind and Heart* (New York: Avon, 1996), 69.

---

12. Patrick Miller, *Deuteronomy,* Interpretation: A Bible Commentary for Teaching and Preaching (Louisville, KY: Westminster John Knox Press, 1990), 14.
13. Judith Plaskow, *Standing Again at Sinai: Judaism from a Feminist Perspective* (New York: HarperOne, 1990), 85.

into this covenant relationship are called to acknowledge that our relationship with God is not simply personal; it is also inescapably communal.

Why the Law Matters Today

The law is my delight.
(Ps. 119:77)

Deuteronomy, also known as the fifth book of the Law, has two Hebrew names, one taken from the first line of the book, "These are the words," and the other, from Deuteronomy 17:18, which talks of "a copy of the law." This second name was translated into the Greek *Deuteronomion,* meaning "second law," which eventually became the Latin and later the English name for the book. Ironically, the name "Deuteronomy" stems from a mistranslation of 17:18, which talks of a "copy" rather than the "second" law that it has come to be known.[14]

In light of the still-prevalent Marcionite views in communities of faith that the gospel replaces the law, Christians face an uphill struggle in articulating the value of scriptural law for Christians today. It is true that Deuteronomy's representation of the Ten Commandments continues to be important for Christians, as these commands remain central to Jews and Christians alike. Christian theologians have long understood the commandments' catechetical importance. Martin Luther, for instance, introduced his catechetical teachings with these words: "Every morning I read and say, word for word, the Ten Commandments, the Creed, the Lord's Prayer. . . . Let [them] be daily read and practiced in thought and speech."[15] Understanding that the torah provides guidance and that such guidance is crucial to the practice of Christian faith, Luther encouraged Christians to include meditation on such guidance as part of their daily practice.

---

14. Tigay, *JPS Torah Commentary,* xi.
15. Martin Luther, "The Large Catechism," in *Book of Concord: The Confessions of the Evangelical Lutheran Church,* by Robert Kolb, Timothy Wengert, and James Schaffer, 2nd ed. (Minneapolis: Fortress Press, 2000), http://bookofconcord.org/lc-1-intro.php.

And while many of the other statutes and ordinances set forth in Deuteronomy are not laws to which Christians—and in many cases, Jews—adhere (take the extreme example of the law for parents to stone a disobedient son to death in Deuteronomy 21:21), at the heart of Deuteronomy's laws stands the Shema, the command "You shall love the LORD your God with all your heart, and with all your soul, and with all your might" (6:5). This recitation remains central to Jewish prayer and worship. In Christian tradition, Jesus insists that the Shema remains "'the greatest and first commandment'" (Matt. 22:37). While Christians tend to focus on Jesus' disregard for some of the inherited laws of Jewish Scriptures, it is important to recognize Jesus as a torah-abiding Jew who understood the Shema as the greatest single commandment. In holding to some Deuteronomistic commands and not others, Jesus practiced a type of halachic interpretation, the Jewish practice of ongoing interpretation of scriptural laws for a new time and place. Part of our task here is to continue in the halachic tradition of Jesus with a contemporary Christian interpretation of Deuteronomy.

What does that mean for the other laws of Deuteronomy besides the Ten Commandments and the Shema? Many of the laws in chapters 12–26, for instance, seem relegated to an ancient community of an ancient time (and even with that contextualization some still seem highly problematic). Scholars note their similarity to ancient contracts, and most lay readers likely judge many of the statutes—such as the prohibition against wearing different types of fabric at the same time in Deuteronomy 22:11—to be irrelevant to our context.

> By electing Israel as a people, God inextricably intertwines God's work as Consummator with God's work as Creator. For better or for worse, God's consummating work must now engage the totality of the human condition, including its most private and its most corporate dimensions.
>
> R. Kendall Soulen, *The God of Israel and Christian Theology* (Minneapolis: Fortress Press, 1996), 123.

But there are several reasons why these laws still matter to twenty-first-century Christian readers. First, these laws, which represent the oldest parts of the text, are set within a larger narrative framework. The role played by the laws in the story gives us insight into the specific characteristics of life lived in covenantal relationship to God.

Second, how these laws were seen as preserving the life, health, and well-being (5:33) of Israel deserves our attention. To take just one example, we will be asking how the command to "choose life" (30:19) in its original context relates to choosing life today.

Perhaps the most important thing for Christians to understand about the law is this: keeping the commands is not intended to be an end in itself. At the heart of Deuteronomy's theology is the claim that keeping the commands is how the people receive blessing and remain intimately related to God; following the commands is how the community maintains its covenant ties. Therefore, following God's commands should be seen as cultivating intimacy with God. Even as we acknowledge the problematic biases of certain laws— such as the patriarchal framework underlying laws regarding women (e.g., Deut. 21:10–14; 22:13–30)—at the same time a number of the laws command special treatment of the most marginalized, limit the authority of leaders, and express consistent concern for how individual actions affect the community as a whole, all vital issues for God's people of any age.

For the Sake of the Alien, the Widow, the Orphan

> Central to Israel's own identity is that of
> strangers in the land of Egypt.

Living as strangers has too often been the experience of Jewish communities throughout history, and unfortunately it continues to be the experience of many ethnic minorities today. In the midst of the realities of living as strangers in a strange land, a key affirmation in Deuteronomy beckons our attention: that Deuteronomy's God does not gaze impartially on those strangers. Rather, as theologian Daniel Berrigan claims, "This God plays favorites—those favored by no one."[16] The concern expressed for the stranger is at the heart

16. Daniel Berrigan, *Deuteronomy: No Gods but One* (Grand Rapids: Wm. B. Eerdmans Publishing Co., 2009), 63.

of torah; therefore, the community of Israel is called to care for the stranger, widow, and orphan because God cares for them.

But Israel is called to do more than simply reach out to the stranger. As we see in Deuteronomy 31:12, the strangers themselves are summoned to the same requirements of listening to torah and acting on it as the rest of the community is called to do. In other words, the strangers are treated like integral members of the community. This ongoing and dogged concern with the welfare of the stranger is a hallmark of Israel's history. And God's people reflect God's concerns. We see that partiality is endemic to God's nature, and it is an inherent value for Israel's communal structure. At a time of national ferment over "the alien" (connoted by the term "illegal aliens" to reference immigrants) in our own society, Deuteronomy's powerful vision of inclusion of those at the edges of society should give us pause.

Even as we affirm the lavish care displayed in Deuteronomy for the most downtrodden, we cannot neglect the persistent tension in the text between the preferential treatment of the alien, the widow, and the orphan on the one hand and God's directing Israel to slaughter other tribes on their way to the promised land on the other.

God and Violence

It is likely that while readers of Deuteronomy are inspired by the text's provocative calls to care for the marginalized, most also find themselves at an impasse when it comes to reconciling the God who distributes such justice with the God who advocates vengeance not only against those outside Israel but also against the disobedient within Israel. Whether it is God's sanctioning the destruction of whole communities currently living in Canaan in chapter 7 or the haunting recitation of curses in chapter 32, Deuteronomy confronts us with violent dimensions of God's character that cannot be ignored.

Scholars point out that the text's words of war may tell us more about the time in which Deuteronomy was written than about the movement of Israel into the land of Canaan. Scholars also suggest that the metaphor of divine warrior is intended by the Deuterono-mistic writer to be more evocative than descriptive of God's character. Further, the divine warrior metaphor is just one among many used within Deuteronomy's text. The fact that God is imaged as a parent, an eagle, and a shepherd as well as a warrior helps us maintain a necessarily wide view of God's character. We are able to see, then, that God as warrior stands in direct tension with a number of these other images.

While such clarifications are important to note, they should not lead us to do what mainline Christians often do: ignore, discount, or bypass these terrifying texts. We can—and should—contextualize these passages, recognizing that it was a vicious time and that such passages reflect vicious realities. Indeed, it's tempting for us within contemporary mainline Christianity to assert that we're a long way from Jonathan Edwards's fiery Deuteronomy-based vision of God when he "comforts" his hearers by telling them that "it is nothing but [God's] mere pleasure that keeps you from being this moment swallowed up in everlasting destruction."[17] Surely we have moved beyond a puritanical, Deuteronomically inspired view of God?

Daniel Berrigan, for one, is not so sure. As he meditates on the Deuteronomistic text, Berrigan suggests that "a question haunts the seeking mind. Today, whom does our god resemble? Do we account ourselves believers in a better God than is here presented, better devotees than these ancestors, more human, compassionate, a thirst for justice?" As much as we might want to answer in the affirmative, Berrigan follows his question with a scathing response, insisting that "Christian history gives any such claim the lie."[18] With such piercing analysis comes the realization that the wrathful God cannot be so easily dismissed.

What is the relationship between God's love and God's wrath? While the biblical text declares, "God is love" (1 John 4:8), there is not a corresponding declaration that "God is wrath."[19] But Christians

---

17. Jonathan Edwards, "Sinners in the Hands of an Angry God," Christian Classics Ethereal Library, www.ccel.org/ccel/edwards/sermons.sinners.html.
18. Berrigan, *Deuteronomy*, 60.
19. D. A. Carson, "The Wrath of God," in *Engaging the Doctrine of God: Contemporary Protestant Perspectives,* ed. Bruce McCormack (Grand Rapids: Baker, 2008), 49.

also need to resist the persistent pull of Marcionism that calls for rejection of the angry OT God out of deference to the soft, loving Jesus. Indeed, H. Richard Niebuhr's famous statement about how liberal theology of the twentieth century led to a God without wrath and a Christ without the cross makes clear that violence and wrath are integral to the *Christian* story as well: "A God without wrath brought men without sin into a kingdom without judgment through the ministrations of a Christ without a cross."[20]

While many Christians want to distance themselves from such violent images of God, there are persons of faith who use such texts to support their claims that a holy war continues even today. Some Jewish fundamentalists believe there's an ongoing holy war about reclaiming the whole of the land of Israel for Jews alone. Some Christian fundamentalists agree that a holy war is being fought today but understand the land's role in a more provisional way. For Christian fundamentalists, the holy war is more often cosmic in scope—the battle is between God and the devil—and it foretells a cosmic war of good versus evil that God will wage—and God will win for Christ.[21] For such persons of faith the claims that God is a warrior are central to God's identity.

Where does this leave us with respect to God's violent acts in Deuteronomy? If we want to assert that God still speaks to God's people through Scripture today, we must also acknowledge that it takes hard work to interpret God's message for us. The God of Deuteronomy—indeed the God of the Bible in its entirety—is irreducibly compassionate and wrathful, just and vengeful, loving and destructive toward God's own creation.

We are left with the fact that there's no getting around God's wrath. But along with the acknowledgment that wrath is an aspect of God's nature, there's more to say. First, God's wrath should not be seen as wholly problematic. As liberation theologians have taught us, a God without wrath does not plan to do much liberating. Indeed, that God's anger is kindled when harm is done to the least among us

---

20. H. Richard Niebuhr, *The Kingdom of God in America* (Middletown, CT: Wesleyan University Press, 1988), 193.
21. Charles Kimball, *When Religion Becomes Evil: Five Warning Signs* (San Francisco: HarperOne, 2008), 156.

not only gives us hope that earthly injustices don't have the last word but also insight into God's compassionate nature.

Second, that the text reports God as saying, "Vengeance is mine" implies it's not ours.[22] Even in the midst of disturbing portraits of God in Deuteronomy, the text is unequivocal: vengeance is not to be Israel's. From the specified number of lashes—and no more—as appropriate punishment to fit the crime (cf. 25:2–3) to Israel's reported victories over other tribes, we glimpse calls for restraint amidst the harshness. No license is given to extravagant punishment, no validation of racial or ethnic superiority on Israel's part. The text repeatedly insists that it is not up to Israel to decide whom or when to fight—that decision is God's alone.

Third, Deuteronomy seems to advocate something similar to what Paul Tillich called Protestant principle: allegiance to anything other than what is ultimate—to anything other than God—leads to death. One of the most disturbing sections of Deuteronomy comes toward the end, where a terrifying litany of curses in chapters 28 and 29 outlines what will happen if Israel disobeys God, up to and even including God's blotting out their names from under heaven (29:20). As Tillich suggests, to follow anything else—whether it be wealth, coveting what is not yours, lust, and so forth—leads to death. "Choosing life" requires a life lived where God remains at the center.[23]

There is no easy resolution to the multiple portraits of the God of Deuteronomy. In the end, after all the curses and stories of God's wrath being visited on Israel and others, Deuteronomy concludes with passages that assert that the scales are tipped, however slightly, to life, to mercy, to grace. What permeates the final section of the book is the ongoing tension between the call to human obedience of God's commands and the promise that God will give the gift of obedience. That life—and obedience—are finally in God's hands means that life is first and last a gift, that the land promised the chosen people is a gift, that God stands with a little band of unknowns

---

22. Brueggemann, *Theology of the Old Testament*, 518.
23. Paul Tillich, *The Protestant Era* (Chicago: University of Chicago Press, 1959).

based on no merit of their own, and with the alien, the widow, and the orphan who are all beloved in the eyes of God.

According to Deuteronomy, our obedience itself can't bring about God's promised future—indeed, the text affirms that God will create a change in our hearts (Deut. 30:6)—nevertheless, the words and laws of Deuteronomy demonstrate that it does matter how we live. As people of God we are called to follow faithfully the will of God in our lives, and when we don't, it often feels like a curse. In the end, though, we are summoned to choose life, to choose God.

Death of Moses as Human Story

Finally, we cannot ignore that alongside Deuteronomy's call to choose life is the story of the death of Moses. That this final book of the Pentateuch is also Moses' final book has great bearing on how the text is interpreted. The story of Moses, the most important character of the Pentateuch and perhaps of the entire Old Testament, reaches its dramatic conclusion in Deuteronomy. And in the full sweep of the story, Moses, the resistant leader and one-time murderer, plays the role of liberator, reluctant prophet, teacher, and mediator between the people and their God.

At the climax of Deuteronomy's story of Moses lies chapter 34, where he dies without setting foot in the promised land. That his story ends without Moses' entry into the promised land has been viewed from numerous angles, sometimes interpreted as God's cruel joke on Moses, at other times viewed as a sign of failure for Moses or as punishment for his sins. From fourth-century theologian Gregory of Nyssa to the modern psychological interpretation of Sigmund Freud and the contemporary therapeutic handling of Moses as model of coping with crisis and disappointment by Rabbi Harold Kushner, the character of Moses has been a lightning rod for reflection on faith, obedience, human potential, and leadership. Within the American context, key historical figures like George Washington, Harriet Tubman, Abraham Lincoln, and, most recently and perhaps most profoundly, Martin Luther King Jr. have been called the Moses of their time, leading people from bondage into freedom. But the fact that Moses did not get to the promised land himself remains an insistent challenge to any tidy portrait of Moses or his protégés. Amid the broad range of interpretations of Moses' death outside the land, early-twentieth-century German writer Franz Kafka's stands as one of the most poignant:

> Moses is on the track of Canaan all his life; it is incredible that he should see the land only when on the verge of death. This dying vision of it can only be intended to illustrate how incomplete a moment is human life. . . . Moses fails to enter Canaan not because his life was too short but because it is a human life.[24]

Theological reflection on Moses as paradigmatic of the spiritual life, a life devoted to God, and at the same time a flawed, limited life with tragic dimensions to it, offers profound insight into the human condition. In the pages of Deuteronomy we find the dramatic conclusion to one of the most powerful stories of the Bible, one that speaks to the deeply human issues of limits, brokenness, and incompleteness along with evidence of faithful obedience to "choose life," as Moses implores the people to do in his final speech to them. Moses is not an ideal character; indeed, that his human failings mix with his successes is what draws us to his story and to the wider story that is Deuteronomy. Deuteronomy 30:14 implores us to keep the story in our mouth and in our heart as we strive to live in faithful obedience to God's living Word. May our reading and reflecting on Deuteronomy help us choose life in the midst of the constant threat of death.

24. Franz Kafka, *Diaries 1914–1923*, ed. Max Brod, trans. Martin Greenberg and Hannah Arendt (New York: Schocken, 1965), 195–96, as quoted in Dennis Olson, *Deuteronomy and the Death of Moses: A Theological Reading* (Minneapolis: Augsburg Fortress, 1994), 159.

1:1–4:49

Moses' First Speech:
Retelling Israel's Story

1:1–8
Resuming the Journey

The first chapter of Deuteronomy signals a different approach to telling the grand story of God's liberating, covenantal relationship with Israel than is used in the first four books of the Pentateuch. In Deuteronomy, the story of God's relationship with Israel is narrated primarily by Moses rather than by the omniscient narrator of Genesis, Exodus, Leviticus, and Numbers. In the opening verses of chapter 1, Moses stands before the Israelites in the wilderness and recounts for them the story of God's past faithfulness to them. This is not a neutral retelling of Israel's history; rather it highlights and clarifies the central theological theme of God's faithfulness found throughout Deuteronomy.

The setting is "beyond the Jordan in the land of Moab" (v. 5), a land inhabited by the descendants of Lot's son, Moab. The text notes that Moab is a mere eleven-day journey from Horeb (v. 2), which is the Deuteronomistic writer's name for Sinai, the mountain where Moses was called by God to lead Israel (Exod. 3:1–12) and the place

> Israel's testimony to Yahweh as a promise-maker presents Yahweh as both powerful and reliable enough to turn life in the world, through Israel and for all peoples, beyond present circumstances to new life-giving possibility. Yahweh's promises keep the world open toward well-being, even in the face of deathly circumstances.
>
> Walter Brueggemann, *Theology of the Old Testament: Testimony, Dispute, Advocacy* (Minneapolis: Fortress Press, 1997), 164.

where he received the Ten Commandments (Exod. 31:18). But the people listening to Moses' speech within the text—as well as the readers of Deuteronomy—know that despite their current proximity to Horeb, it actually took the Israelites forty years of desert wandering to arrive at their current location (v. 3). A central theme of this section and of the entire book is that Israel has not lived up to its side of the covenantal relationship it formed with God. This opening speech of Moses' repeatedly emphasizes Israel's rebellion, disobedience, and lack of trust in God's covenantal claims, which led them to their many years of wandering the wilderness.

In verse 5, the Deuteronomistic writer uses the verb *b'r*, which means "to expound" or "explain," to describe what Moses is doing in Deuteronomy with the law. As biblical scholar Robert Alter suggests, this one word also "provides a central rationale for the whole book."[1] The previous books of the Pentateuch have already set forth

> Moses, who once defined himself as "not a man of words," suddenly finds his voice, and his voice is remarkably similar to God's.
>
> Bruce Feiler, *Walking the Bible: A Journey by Land Through the Five Books of Moses* (New York: HarperCollins, 2001), 388.

the teachings of the law. But in Deuteronomy, the repetition of *torah* becomes connected to the textual character not just of the law within the book of Deuteronomy but also with *torah* as it refers to all five books of Moses. The laws that God initially gave Israel are supplemented in Deuteronomy with further explanation of what it looks like to fulfill the law in the context of a land Israel can claim as its own.

"'Resume your journey. . . . See I have set the land before you'" (vv. 6, 8). It is time for Israel to be on the move once again, up the east bank of the Jordan, headed toward Canaan, the land God has promised them. Moses insists that the time is now for the Israelites to live up to their side of the covenant they made with God and choose a life of obedience and blessing. Their location here is crucial; even as Israel is poised to enter a new future in a new land, these

---

1. Robert Alter, *The Five Books of Moses: A Translation with Commentary* (New York: W. W. Norton & Co., 2004), 880.

opening verses indicate that the Israelites can ill afford to forget their years in the desert or their years of enslavement before God freed them from Egypt. As Roman Catholic theologian Johann Baptist Metz discusses, memory is what gives human beings their historical identity. Metz writes, "Identity is formed when memory is aroused."[2] Moses' act of remembering and retelling Israelite history, as Israel stands between its future and its past, makes an important theological point about Israelite identity: Israel's relationship with the God who freed them from slavery *is* its identity, and after years of dishonoring that memory, it is time to remember, honor, and obey. Who they will be in the new land is bound tightly to who they were as God's chosen people, enslaved and then freed.

> **They may not have had the land, but they still transformed themselves into a nation. Moses was telling the people their past, building history into the character of the nation—the DNA you might call it—so that when they conquered the Promised Land, their spiritual unity was already in place.**
>
> Avner Goren, in conversation with Bruce Feiler, in *Walking the Bible: A Journey by Land through the Five Books of Moses* (New York: HarperCollins, 2001), 390.

The arc of Moses' long struggle to lead this tiny band of people in remembering and honoring their past ends in Deuteronomy's final chapter with his death on Mount Nebo, before he or anyone in Israel enters the land God has promised Israel. But here, in the opening chapters of the book, this central character of the Old Testament speaks to the people about their past, their present, and their future, leaving them with everything they need to become the people God calls them to be.

1:9–18

Expanding the Leadership

It is noteworthy that just after Moses' rousing call to Israel to "resume [their] journey" toward Canaan, he immediately turns his

---

2. Johan Baptist Metz, *Faith in History and Society: Toward a Fundamental Practical Theology* (New York: Seabury, 1980), 66.

attention toward expanding the leadership of Israel beyond himself. As we discussed in the introduction, the impending death of Moses before Israel enters the promised land is a theme that runs through the entire narrative. In this section, Moses' move to expand the leadership marks the beginning of the transition of power that will be completed with his death.

Before shifting our attention to Moses' expansion of leadership, however, it is important to notice the reference to blessing in verses 10–11. The claim "The Lord your God has multiplied you" confirms the fulfillment of God's promise to Abraham in Genesis 15:5 and 22:17.

That God has been faithful to Israel in the past is a recurring theme throughout Deuteronomy. The words of Moses in verse 11, "'May the LORD, the God of your ancestors, increase you a thousand times more and bless you as he has promised you!'" suggest God's

> I will indeed bless you, and I will make your offspring as numerous as the stars of heaven and as the sand that is on the seashore.
>
> (Gen. 22:17a)

faithfulness in the past will also continue into the future. Further, that the Pentateuch begins with blessings recited throughout the book of Genesis and ends with Deuteronomy, where blessing again is a dominant theme, says that God's saving activity of the exodus is set within the larger framework of God's blessing for God's people.[3]

Moses' expansion of the leadership within Israel and the transition of power begin with Moses' sharing the role of adjudicator of the disputes within Israel. In verses 12–18, we hear again the story of how Israel came to have judges as the Deuteronomistic writer recasts the stories of the judges from Exodus 18 and Numbers 11. While the three accounts of the story are similar in many ways, the differences offer clues about the theological agenda put forward in the book of Deuteronomy.

In Exodus 18, the story of the judges contains an important additional character not mentioned in Deuteronomy: Moses'

---

3. Claus Westermann, *Blessing in the Bible and the Life of the Church,* trans. Keith Crim (Philadelphia: Fortress Press, 1978), 30.

father-in-law, Jethro. In the Exodus version, Jethro visits Israel's wilderness encampment and observes Moses playing the role of sole adjudicator of disputes for all the Israelites. Jethro tells his son-in-law, "'You will surely wear yourself out. . . . The task is too heavy for you; you cannot do it alone'" (Exod. 18:18). Jethro urges Moses to find trustworthy men from among the Israelites who can help bear the burden of hearing the many cases of the Israelites. In Exodus, Moses heeds Jethro's warning and selects "able men from all Israel" (18:25) to serve as judges.

> To stand in a living tradition, then, is to participate in a dynamic process of interpretation—one that moves between received heritage and the realities and challenges of the present world in order to express a continuing and vital orientation or identity. . . . A contemporary interpretation must do no more and no less than engage the community's experiences of the distinctive realities of the present, yet stand in a meaningful measure of continuity with the originals.
>
> Douglas F. Ottati, *Jesus Christ and Christian Vision* (Minneapolis: Fortress Press, 1989), 36.

A second version of the story appears in Numbers 11, where the Israelites are camped out close to Egypt and spend their days waxing nostalgic for the good old days of living in slavery in Egypt, where at least they were given fish to eat (Num. 11:4–6). In the Numbers version, Moses is the one complaining about the burden of leading this disgruntled group: "'I am not able to carry all this people alone, for they are too heavy for me'" (11:14). In response to Moses' plea, God proposes that Moses gather seventy elders of Israel upon whom God will "'take some of the spirit that is on [Moses] and put it on them'" (11:17), allowing them to share the burden of adjudication with Moses. Moses follows God's instructions and appoints the judges.

In Deuteronomy we hear the story a third time, and the differences in this version give us insight into the theological commitments behind Deuteronomy's re-presentation of Israel's history. Biblical scholar Martin Noth, author of the widely accepted Deuteronomistic History theory that argues for a Deuteronomistic author for Deuteronomy through Kings, proposed that the Deuteronomist often used a heavy editorial hand with the historical sources to which he had access. In this version the fact that there are too many Israelites (and too many disputes) for Moses to be the sole judge is offered as evidence of God's rich blessings on Israel (v. 10). In contrast to the other two versions, Deuteronomy's Moses is neither an overwhelmed adjudicator nor a complaining, reluctant leader. Instead he is portrayed as wise, respected, and in charge. He himself summons the tribes to elect fair judges, and the Israelites support him. In Deuteronomy, Moses is Israel's wise and trusted leader, but his time has come to share the responsibility of leading Israel. That the book opens with Moses directing the election of judges also indicates the importance of life in the new land being ordered justly.

1:19–33
Israel's Rebellious Refusal to Enter the Land

In Moses' recounting of Israel's history in Deuteronomy, we hear that God instructed the Israelites to travel from Horeb, where they received the Ten Commandments, to Kadesh-barnea, a place located in the hill country of the Amorites (v. 19). It is significant that Moses tells the people they must go and take possession of the land God has promised them while they are camped at Kadesh-barnea, for Kadesh represents an important place of failure for the Israelites. It is there that Miriam dies (Num. 20:1); it is there that Moses is reprimanded for striking the rock without invoking the name of the Lord (Num. 20:9–12); and it is there that Moses seeks permission to take Israel on the move through Edomite land and God rejects his request (Num. 20:14). This is the place where the entire generation of Israelites perished before they could stand before Moses at the edge of the promised land. These images of failure at Kadesh haunt the rest of chapter 1.

Verses 22–33 also offer a retelling of Numbers 13–14, and once again, Deuteronomy's distinct accents in the story offer further insight into several key themes of the narrative. These verses continue to cast Moses as the faithful interpreter of the Lord's covenantal promise to Israel. Here Moses tells the people, "'See, the

LORD your God has given the land to you: go up [from Kadesh-barnea], take possession, as the LORD, the God of your ancestors, has promised you'" (v. 21). Not only is Moses' faithfulness stressed, but God's fidelity is emphasized as well. It is up to Israel to live in faithful obedience in response.

In the Greek and Roman mythologies, the past is re-presented as an everlasting foundation. In the Hebrew and Christian view of history the past is a promise to the future; consequently, the interpretation of the past becomes a prophecy in reverse.

K. Löwith (*Meaning in History*, 1949), as quoted in Jürgen Moltmann, *The Theology of Hope: On the Ground and the Implications of a Christian Eschatology* (Minneapolis: Fortress Press, 1993), 109.

After these reminders of God's abiding care of Israel, Deuteronomy's telling of the sending of spies from Kadesh, located just south of the promised land, into Canaan diverges significantly from its first telling in Numbers. In the Numbers version, God proposes that Israel send spies into Canaan. In Deuteronomy, the people propose the spying plan. In both stories, though, the spies return to Israel's camp affirming the goodness of the land—"It is a good land that the LORD is giving us'" (Deut. 1:25). It is also the case that in both stories the Israelites express reluctance about going into the land. But in the Numbers version, the size of the inhabitants of Canaan lead Israel to complain, and they express a desire to be back in Egypt. Their complaints in turn make God angry, which prompts Moses into negotiating with God on Israel's behalf. In Deuteronomy, which is likely first written during the time of exile in the late seventh century but later revised by postexilic, sixth-century authors, Moses' speech stresses the people's rebellious character, a major point of emphasis for Israelites living during and after the exile: "You were unwilling to go up. You rebelled against the command of the LORD your God; you grumbled in your tents . . ." (vv. 26–27). In Deuteronomy's version of the story, Moses again displays a confident response to the people that differs from the pleading he does with Israel in the Numbers account. The Moses of Deuteronomy calmly reassures the people of God's faithfulness: "'The LORD your God, who goes before you, is the one who will fight for you, just as he did for you in Egypt before your very eyes, ... where you saw how the LORD your God carried you, just as one carries a child'" (vv. 30–31). This beautiful and powerful parental imagery of God and God's care for Israel is also noteworthy and accentuates the Deuteronomic theme of God's fidelity to Israel.

In this final book of the Pentateuch, Moses' retelling of the stories offers an added layer of complexity to understanding Deuteronomy's theology. Moses' role as mediator between God and the people of Israel is taken to new heights: not only do the words of Moses inform the people of God's will, but his words actually mediate God and God's presence. Second-century theologian Origen comments on the new dynamic at work in Deuteronomy:

> And here this other fact will not appear to be without significance: that it is Moses who hears from God all that is written down in the law of Leviticus, whereas in Deuteronomy it is the people who are represented as listening to Moses and learning from him what they could not hear from God.[4]

In Deuteronomy, Moses is at once staggeringly significant and also perilously close to the end of his life and his leadership of the people. His farewell speeches in Deuteronomy impart to the Israelites the vision, the laws, and the statutes that should govern them when they move into God's gift of the land. But later, in chapter 27, we learn that Moses will leave behind more than just the memory of his speeches; in his stead, Israel will use a book where "all the words of this law" are recorded very clearly (27:8).

1:34–45
The Cost of Rebellion

Similar to the Numbers account of the aftermath of the spy story, this section highlights that Israel's doubting and questioning of God's faithfulness will result in the generation freed from slavery in Egypt not living to see the promised land. Once again Deuteronomy's

---

4. Origen, *On First Principles* 4.3.12, http://www.newadvent.org/fathers/04124.htm.

accent is on the people's rebellion against Moses and their failure to obey God's commands. In these verses the Israelites in the wilderness are referred to as "this evil generation," and God says to Moses, "'Not one of these . . . shall see the good land I swore to give to your ancestors'" (v. 35). So those who stand before Moses "today" at the edge of the land of Canaan are not the ones who were freed from Egypt and wandered in the wilderness. And yet the descendants of the disobedient Israelites, we see in Deuteronomy, share in the responsibility of their ancestors. In Moses' retelling of this history, the memory of the sins of the past remains with Israel "today" and influences its current identity.

The sins of Israel's past affect not only those Israelites poised to enter the promised land, but they affect Moses as well. In fact, Israel's disobedience is so great, Moses tells the people, "Even with me the LORD was angry on your account, saying, 'You also shall not enter there'" (v. 37). This is one of several reasons given in Deuteronomy as to why Moses will not be allowed into the land. That the people's disobedience contributed to Moses' inability to reach this long-sought goal is testimony to the costliness of Israel's rebellion. In addition, this statement is the first of several that create symmetry between the beginning of this story and the ending, with the death of Moses before Israel enters the land promised to it by God. In this passage in chapter 1, as well as in Deuteronomy 3:26, Moses' impending inability to enter the land is laid at the feet of a disobedient Israel. Israel's refusal to follow God's commands costs not just Israel but its trusted leader as well.

While the Numbers story focuses heavily on Moses' pleading with God for mercy—and on God's acquiescence to Moses' request (cf. Num. 14:13–25)—Deuteronomy depicts the people as listening to Moses and admitting their sin, only to prepare themselves to fight their way into the land. But in Deuteronomy, Moses—who is the only one actually privy to God's intention for Israel—tells them to hold back, insisting God does not want them to fight. Predictably, however, the Deuteronomy narrative documents Israel's disregard of Moses'—and God's—words and their subsequent decisive loss in battle: the Amorites, a people who occupied much of the land in and around Canaan, chased them "as bees do" and "they beat [Israel] down" (v. 44). Moses' rehearsal of Israel's failure to obey and failure to win in battle emphasizes Israel's disobedient and turbulent past and sets the stage for them to make another choice "today."

1:46–2:15
Back to the Wilderness

Here the text is direct and to the point: Israel's disobedience led to its banishment to the wilderness, not once but multiple times. This section is heavy with imagery of God as divine warrior, a God who is completely in charge of any and all on-the-ground warfare. Moses speaks of how Israel wandered through territories of various other groups, through the lands of the descendants of Esau—Edom—and the land of Moab, all of which are located southeast of Canaan in what is today called the Transjordan. Even though Moses acknowledges that these other clans feared Israel, he emphasizes that God told him, "Be very careful not to engage in battle with them, for I will not give you even so much as a foot's length of their land" (2:5). The Deuteronomistic writer wants to make clear that Israel's military success is utterly dependent on their obedience to God's commands. What 2:5 also highlights is that God has given land not just to the Israelites but to other peoples as well. God will give Canaan over to the Israelites, the Deuteronomist proclaims, but the land they cross through to get there belongs to their kin (the descendants of Esau, Moab, and Ammon are descendants of Lot; cf. Gen. 19:30–38), and they cannot win it by waging war.

The emphasis here is on God's sovereign control not just of Israel but also of the entire landscape and all the people inhabiting it. Moses reminds Israel again about God's fidelity to them: "'These

> As the Hebrew name for the book, *mishne tora*, indicates, Deuteronomy is a "copy of the Torah," a retelling of the law. Accordingly, Moses reviews the Israelites' trek through the wilderness, recapitulates the laws, and generally reminds the Israelites of their responsibilities as a people. In effect, he leads a public reeducation of his people, a mass seminar on the desert floor.
>
> Bruce Feiler, *Walking the Bible: A Journey by Land Through the Five Books of Moses* (New York: HarperCollins, 2001), 389.

forty years the LORD your God has been with you: you have lacked nothing'" (2:7). In particular the Deuteronomist wants his audience to remember that Israel is under God's care in all that they do, from the battlefield to the bedroom, as we will hear more about later in the text (cf. Deut. 22:14–30).

The Deuteronomic narrative now confirms what had been stated earlier: that all the Israelites who were freed from Egypt and wandered in the wilderness have died out. And yet the Israelites who stand before Moses today are not cast simply as observers of this history; rather, they are participants in it. As theologian Johann Baptist Metz claims in his work *Faith and History in Society*, memory makes demands on individuals and communities.[5] Moses' recollection of how God led the Israelites to the place where they now sit calls on Israel to live in faithful response to that history.

2:16–3:22
Marching as to War

Moses tells the people that God calls them to ready for battle. Moses then reminds the people that God has also destroyed other peoples living in these lands to make way for the descendants of Lot and of Esau, just as God will do for Israel (2:9–12). The intensity of this first speech of Moses increases when he quotes God's words to Israel: "'This day I will begin to put the dread and fear of you upon the peoples everywhere under heaven; when they hear report of you, they will tremble and be in anguish because of you'" (v. 25). The stage is set for Israel's impending battles as they head north toward Canaan.

The story in 2:26–35 of Israel's defeat of King Sihon—ruler of the Amorites whose land in the Transjordan included the capital city of Heshbon—appears first in Numbers 21. Both versions begin with Israel's approach to King Sihon, informing the king that if he allows Israel to pass through his land, he and his people will not be harmed. In the Numbers account, the king simply refuses, and Israel moves in and overtakes them. The Deuteronomy version shares the same

5. Metz, *Faith in History and Society*, 109.

outcome as the Numbers text but with an additional twist: the king refuses to let Israel pass through because God "hardened his spirit and made his heart defiant in order to hand him over to you" (v. 30). This small but significant detail serves to deepen the portrait of God as the one who controls all warfare—in addition to everything else. God then instructs Moses to "take possession" of King Sihon's land. Israel follows God's command, leaving not a single survivor (v. 34). Moses reminds the people that their victory is not of their own doing but is only because the warrior God who led them in battle is their God, the One who "will neither abandon [them] nor destroy [them, the One who] will not forget the covenant" (4:31) made with Israel's ancestors.

A fate similar to King Sihon's is assigned to King Og, the king of Bashan whose territory Israel had to enter before crossing the Jordan, and much of the rest of chapter 3 chronicles Israel's steady victories as they inch closer to the land. Moses' speech intends to make sure the Israelites do not forget who is in charge or why victory has been theirs: "'Your own eyes have seen everything that the LORD your God has done to these two kings; so the LORD will do to all the kingdoms into which you are about to cross. Do not fear them, for it is the LORD your God who fights for you'" (3:21–22).

FURTHER REFLECTIONS
The Warrior God

One of the most challenging aspects of the book of Deuteronomy is the vivid, repeated depiction of God as a divine warrior who hardens the hearts of Israel's enemies and leads the Israelites into war against other human beings, sanctioning battles where no one who is not an Israelite survives. It is stories like the defeat of King Sihon and his people that tempt Christians to set aside this OT text and focus on passages from the New Testament where God in Christ refuses to pursue the path of violence.

But Deuteronomy is also Christian Scripture, and we must address head on this deeply unsettling portrait of a God who sanctions slaughter of human beings purportedly made in God's own image. While there's no easy resolution, there are several things we can and must say:

First, it is important to note that the Deuteronomist is ultimately more interested in making a theological point than being historically accurate. Central to the story is the claim that Israel's failures as well as its successes in terms of battle are all in God's hands. We are also reminded that these stories about God as divine warrior are likely intended for a context of exile; it is an Israelite community dispossessed of the land and hearing that when they fulfill their role as God's covenant partner, they will succeed militarily and prosper in all other aspects of life. The community's despairing situation in exile serves as a constant reminder that they strayed from God's commands. According to Deuteronomic theology, exilic existence comes about through Israel's willful disregard for God's commands.

> Critical interpretation of the Bible is an essential way that Christians practice the virtues of humility, charity, and patience in a distinctly intellectual mode.
>
> Ellen Davis, "The Soil That Is Scripture," in *Engaging Biblical Authority: Perspectives on the Bible as Scripture*, ed. William P. Brown (Louisville, KY: Westminster John Knox Press, 2007), 37.

To assert that divine warrior imagery is more about theology than it is about history, however, does not resolve the problem that the actions God endorsed for the Israelites would today be considered war crimes: the divine call for carefully planned, carefully executed massacres cannot be glossed over. Why was there a "need" for Israel to wipe out whole other communities? As we move through the Deuteronomic narrative, we will see time and again the writer's strong concern over Israel's being led astray to worship idols and to disobey God. The groups of people living both outside of and within the land of Canaan follow different religious practices, and from the vantage point of exile, the hearers of Deuteronomy understand they turned away from the worship of God toward the gods worshiped by others. So again we note the heavy editorial spin to this text: that Israel's current situation goes back to the perceived failure of Israel to annihilate all the groups that occupied the land Israel came to inhabit.

As mentioned in the introduction, Deuteronomy's presentation of God as divine warrior stands in direct tension with its persistent focus on the alien, widow, and orphan in Israel's midst. The stories throughout Deuteronomy of holy war also stand in tension with Israel's foundational story of God's promise to and covenant with them. From the articulation of the covenant with Abraham and Sarah onward, God's words to Israel proclaim that Israel's ancestors and their descendants are chosen "so that [they] will be a blessing ... and in [them] all the families of the earth shall be blessed" (Gen. 12). There is no way around such tension; it remains at the heart of the Deuteronomistic theology.

3:23–29

It Won't be Moses Leading Israel into the Land

Even though we hear Moses say in 1:37 that he will not—on Israel's account—be allowed into the promised land, he nevertheless takes advantage of his intimate relationship with God and expresses to God directly his strong desire to "cross over and see the good land beyond the Jordan" (3:25). We learn quickly, however, that Moses' wish will not be granted. Indeed, God responds to Moses' plea with anger, insisting Moses refrain from speaking of this issue again.

Why is Moses denied this request? Throughout the book of Deuteronomy several reasons are given. In this particular passage, we hear once again that it is Israel's fault that Moses will not be able to cross over to Canaan (3:26). Moses informs his followers that Joshua will be the one to lead the people into the land God has promised them (1:38; 3:28). Moving in the text from Moses' prohibition to enter the land to the claim that Joshua will

> When we think of Moses, we think of his triumphs. . . . But Moses was a man who knew frustration and failure in his public and personal life at least as often and as deeply as he knew fulfillment.
>
> Harold Kushner, *Overcoming Life's Disappointments: Learning from Moses How to Cope with Frustration* (New York: Anchor Books, 2006), 4.

lead Israel into the land gives us another indication of how Moses is giving up his central role as leader and teacher.

It is important to note that the Pentateuch concludes with Israel—just like Moses—not yet able to reach the promised land. Though Moses dies while Israel eventually enters the land, the narrative arc of the Pentateuch sets down when Israel is still waiting to enter.

FURTHER REFLECTIONS
Why a Pentateuch and Not a Hexateuch?

That not just Moses but all of Israel is kept outside the promised land at the end of the Pentateuch is of utmost theological significance. This fact demonstrates that the original story of Israel includes neither the conquest of Canaan nor the possession of the land that God has promised them. Biblical scholars Gerhard von Rad, Martin Noth, and others have debated whether Deuteronomy's material is more closely connected to the book of Joshua (should we speak of a "hexateuch"?) and even beyond (hence the term "Deuteronomic History" when describing Deuteronomy through Kings). But as Jewish scholar Jeffrey Tigay asserts, as central as the land is for Israel, the covenant God makes with Israel does not ultimately depend on possession of the land.[6] Theologically speaking, the incompleteness of Israel's journey to God's promised future at the close of the Pentateuch has eschatological significance for both Jews and Christians. Jürgen Moltmann admits that the insight of the Old Testament is that "history is what happens between promise and fulfillment."[7] All Jews and Christians stand in that history between the now and the not yet, looking forward to the day when God's promised future will be fully realized.

---

6. Jeffrey Tigay, *The JPS Torah Commentary: Deuteronomy* (Philadelphia: Jewish Publication Society, 1996), xxvii.

7. Jürgen Moltmann, *A Theology of Hope: On the Ground and the Implications of a Christian Eschatology* (New York: Harper & Row, 1967), 78.

4:1–15

Called to Keep the Commands

This section contains the dramatic conclusion of Moses' first speech. In his commentary on Deuteronomy, Gerhard von Rad wonders, "Who would expect Moses, after he had just reported the command to go up to Pisgah [on Mount Nebo] in order to die there, now to launch out into a detailed introduction to his recital of the law?"[8] This sermonic section highlights the crucial catechetical role Moses plays in the life of Israel.

Indeed, Moses sets the scene for his passing down—and elaborating on—the set of guidelines and instructions that shape and define the parameters of Israel's anticipated life in the land God is giving them. Biblical scholars have noted how the structure of this chapter resembles treaty structures of the ancient Near East. And within this structure reminiscent of a treaty, Moses insists that the statutes and ordinances in Deuteronomy should be understood to be in the service of the life and well-being of the entire community.

> I have stated that all Christians, and especially those who handle the word of God and attempt to teach others, should take heed and learn Moses aright.
>
> Martin Luther, "How Christians Should Regard Moses," in *Martin Luther's Basic Theological Writings*, ed. Timothy F. Lull (Minneapolis: Fortress Press, 1989), 147.

We should also remember that even though the laws given in Deuteronomy by the Deuteronomic writer are intended to govern Israel's new life in the promised land, wilderness is and remains the context for all pentateuchal law. The law is given in the wilderness in anticipation of enjoying God's full blessing in the new land. We are also cognizant that those who hear Moses' claim that the commands are given "so that [they] may live" (v. 1) likely do so in the midst of the deadly conditions of exile. As Robert Alter and other biblical scholars suggest, the Deuteronomist likely formed this text in a period after the neo-Assyrian empire (911–609 BCE) had instituted a policy of deporting subjugated populations like the Israelites

---

8. Gerhard von Rad, *Deuteronomy: A Commentary* (Philadelphia: Westminster Press, 1966), 48.

in order to make room for colonizers in the conquered land.[9] For life in the wilderness, for life in the promised land, for life in exile, Moses gives the Israelites the tools not just for survival but for flourishing. That these commands support a rich life is a repeated refrain throughout the rest of this speech and the remaining Deuteronomic text.

> The God of the Exodus must be the God of the Exile if he is to remain the God of the future and not simply the God of memory.
>
> Paul Ricouer, *From Text to Action: Essays in Hermeneutics,* vol. 2, trans. Kathleen Blamey and John B. Thompson (Evanston, IL: Northwestern University Press, 1991), 92.

Chapter 4 marks a shift from the more descriptive quality of chapter 3 to a more persuasive, sermonic tone in the remainder of the chapter and first speech of Moses. Calls to follow the law laid out in Deuteronomy are set within this larger narrative of Moses' speaking to Israel, teaching them the value of the law that they will teach to their children and their children's children (4:9).

In 4:2, Moses insists Israel should "neither add anything to nor take away anything" from the instruction he is about to set forth. The Deuteronomist is likely addressing concerns that Deuteronomy is offering a less-than-faithful revision of the foundational laws of God's covenant with Israel, for there is tension between the significant expansion of laws given in Deuteronomy and Moses' injunction neither to add nor take away as they leave their wilderness existence and prepare to settle in the land God is giving them. Within the story line of Deuteronomy, Moses' expanded exhortation on what it means to live in covenantal relationship with God comes at the point where this band of former slaves is poised to settle in the land God has promised them. There is real need for more than the basic, foundational commands; a settled society needs and benefits from regulations governing the wide range of issues that living within a society involves.

Nevertheless, this phrase "neither add anything to nor take away" encourages reflection. In his own commentary on Deuteronomy,

9. Alter, *Five Books of Moses,* 902.

Martin Luther anticipates readers' responses to Moses' apparent rigidity regarding the commands laid out in Deuteronomy: "But you will say [in response to Moses' comment]: 'Then why have so many additional books of the prophets been added?'" Luther continues by listing the commands given by Joshua and David, stating that such actions were simply continuations of what Moses said, and what Moses said, Luther insists, came from God, the One who "remains true" regardless of whether anything is added to or subtracted from the commands.[10] In Luther's view, then, because of this faithfulness to God, Moses' own verbal expansion on the foundational commands of God do not constitute adding to or taking away from but simply further clarification of the divine commands for a new context.

Moses quickly moves from calling Israel to keep the commands to reminding them of what happened to those Israelites who turned from God and worshiped Baal of Peor (4:3; the location is called "Beth-peor" in 3:29), located in the Transjordan not far from Hesban. Baal, a title bestowed on a variety of fertility and nature gods, is given specific content here. As Israel is poised to transition from nomadic to settled living, Deuteronomy portrays a Moses whose concern over the temptation for Israel to worship a fertility god is on the rise. Jewish philosopher Martin Buber writes, "What met YHVH [God] on the threshold of the Promised Land is therefore nothing less than the spirit which holds sway at the initiation of settled tilling of the soil. Where a man settles in order to win blessings of the soil from out of its midst . . . there he finds the domain of Baal."[11] Thus the temptation to turn to idols was a concern tied intimately not just to the culture of Canaan but also to the land itself.

In verses 6–8 Moses expands even more on how adherence to the commands goes far beyond the task of simply following certain requirements. Just as ancient treaties contained a list of blessings that would follow from adherence to the conditions of the treaty, so too does Moses articulate the benefits that will come to an Israel

---

10. Martin Luther, *Luther's Works,* vol. 9 (Saint Louis: Concordia Publishing House, 1960), 52.
11. Martin Buber, *Moses: The Revelation and the Covenant,* trans. Michael Fishbone (Amherst, NY: Humanity Books, 1998), 193.

faithful to the statutes. Living according to God's commands, Moses insists, will produce a "'wise and discerning people'" (4:6) who will be noticed by other nations for it. This verse offers a glimpse into Deuteronomy's embrace of the wisdom tradition of ancient Israel. From Moses' wise decision to have each tribe select its own discerning judges to adjudicate the claims of the community (1:13) to his call for judges to refuse bribes and rule justly, Deuteronomy binds together obedience to God's commands with the concepts of wisdom and justice. While parts of Deuteronomy resemble the structures of ancient treaties, the emphasis on wisdom and justice within the text suggests that Israel's laws possess a quality of justice not often seen among other nations (v. 8).

> The fear of the LORD is the beginning of wisdom,
> and the knowledge of the Holy One is insight.
>
> (Prov. 9:10)

Giving a still-deeper description of what life according to the commands of God means for Israel, Moses teaches the Israelites that holding fast to life according to the commands means holding fast to the Lord their God. Verse 7 talks of the fact that no other nation has a "god so near" as the "LORD our God." This intimacy with God through obedience to commands came alive for me during a conversation with a rabbi who told me that she kept kosher "in order to remember that eating is a sacred act." "Our actions bind us to God," she told me. The rabbi's approach to keeping kosher sheds light on how we might interpret the commands of Deuteronomy: these laws are significant not simply in some secondary way; rather the commands are fundamental to how members of the community as a whole remain devoted to God.

Moses' admonition for Israelites to "take care and watch [themselves] closely" (v. 9) so that they will neither forget nor let slip this call to observe all the statutes and ordinances is unique to Deuteronomy (see also 4:15) and suggests that such obedience will never be easy.[12] In addition, it is incumbent upon the hearers of Moses'

---

12. J. Gary Millar, *Now Choose Life: Theology and Ethics in Deuteronomy* (Grand Rapids: Wm. B. Eerdmans Publishing Co., 1998), 163.

speech to pass these teachings on to their children and their children's children (v. 9b). The admonition in verse 9, when linked with the warning that Israel's child and children's children "will soon utterly perish from the land" if they "become complacent" or "act corruptly" (vv. 25–26), reveals the Deuteronomist's deep mistrust of human nature and his skepticism about whether Israel will actually live as they should. Such lack of trust in human ability to do what we ought is, of course, a central tenet in Christian anthropology as well. As theologian Reinhold Niebuhr said, "The temptation to sin lies . . . in the human situation itself." For Niebuhr, we are bound by the contingencies of our finitude yet also able to transcend them, and this transcendent capability makes us anxious. In our anxiety, Niebuhr asserts, we seek to transmute our finiteness into infinitude, our weakness into strength, and our dependence into independence.[13] The Deuteronomist portrays the Israelites as constantly struggling with the command to obey God over against the temptation to believe that following their own desires will lead them to flourish in the new land.

In verse 10 God calls on Moses to assemble the people. Christian theologians like fourth-century bishop Cyril of Jerusalem have made connections between such assembling of the Israelites to what the Christian church is called to do. Cyril writes, "Well is the church named *ecclesia* ["assembly"], because it calls forth and assembles all men. . . . In Deuteronomy God says to Moses, 'Assemble the people for me; I will have them hear my words, that they may learn to fear me.'"[14] Note that the people are to fear as well as hear. In this passage of Deuteronomy, the assembled people of God meet God through a consuming fire; indeed, Moses recounts for Israel that God established the covenant with them in the midst of this fire. Moses' detailed description of Israel's fiery encounter with God represents a change in the narrative. Up until chapter four Moses' summary of Israel's history had been sparse on the details. But here in verses 11–14, when the story of Sinai is retold, rich description is given to

13. Reinhold Niebuhr, *The Nature and Destiny of Man: A Christian Interpretation*, vol. 1 (New York: Scribner's Sons, 1949), 250.
14. Cyril of Jerusalem, *Catechetical Lecture* 18.24, http://www.newadvent.org/fathers/310118.htm.

the terror and the awesomeness of Israel's experience of God. Notice the juxtaposing imagery: Israel approaches the mountain, which was "blazing up to the very heavens" and simultaneously "shrouded in dark clouds" (v. 11). God speaks out of the fire, declaring to Israel the covenant, giving them the Ten Commandments. God's message comes to Israel out of the fire. At the same time, God remains opaque, even in the midst of this revelation.

Theologians across the centuries have reflected much on God's persistent hiddenness even in the midst of revelation. In the Middle Ages, mystical reflections often gravitated toward God's mysterious, hidden character. One anonymous medieval writer uses the cloud imagery seen here in Deuteronomy as a basis for his meditation on our persistent ignorance of God:

> Do not suppose that because I have spoken of darkness and of a cloud I have in mind the clouds you see in an overcast sky.... This isn't what I mean at all so forget this sort of nonsense. When I speak of darkness, I mean the absence of knowledge. If you are unable to understand something. . . are you not in the dark as regards this thing? You cannot see it with your mind's eye. Well, in the same way I have not said "cloud" but *cloud of unknowing*. For it is a darkness of unknowing that lies between you and your God.[15]

This medieval reflection on the limits of human knowledge of God helps illumine for us the possibility of simultaneous intimacy with the divine even in the midst of a deep, and even turbulent, fearsome unknown.

The true vision and knowledge of what we seek consists precisely in *not* seeing, in an awareness that our goal transcends all knowledge and is everywhere cut from us by the darkness of incomprehensibility.

Gregory of Nyssa, *The Life of Moses*, trans. Abraham Malherbe and Everett Ferguson (Mahwah, NJ: Paulist Press, 1978), 95.

---

15. Anonymous, *Cloud of Unknowing*, in *The Essential Writings of Christian Mysticism*, ed. Bernard McGinn (New York: Modern Library, 2006), 266.

4:15–24
Worshiping God Alone

The Deuteronomist understood that when faced with God's hiddenness in the midst of divine revelation, we humans are tempted to turn to images that we think resemble the divine. As a teacher, Moses anticipates this very human strategy, addressing it directly in verses 15–19. In the list of images prohibited by God in these verses, a close reading of the text reveals a recitation in reverse of the first creation story (cf. Gen. 1:1–2:4). The hearkening back to the creation account, where we are told that each aspect of God's creation is good, suggests that creation's goodness is not at issue—in fact, creation is nothing other than a blessing that God has allotted to "all peoples everywhere" (v. 19). What Moses warns Israel about in this passage is their—and indeed all of humanity's—predisposition to confuse the likenesses of created things—whether it be maleness or femaleness, birds or fish, or the sun, moon, or stars—with God, who alone is worthy of worship. While creation is good, Moses' message is clear: Israel's allegiance should only be to this God, the one who "brought [them] out of the iron smelter, out of Egypt" (v. 20) to become God's treasured people.

The imagery here is noteworthy in its connection to the imagery in 4:11–12 where God is depicted as speaking through fire. This fiery God is also the one who brought Israel out of the iron smelter—a fiery furnace that uses combustion to mold the iron—to mold and make Israel into God's own treasured people. Israel's existence, we see once again, is utterly dependent on God. To serve any image or likeness other than God is to serve what Karl Barth has called the "No-God,"[16] a practice that distances God's people not merely from God but from wisdom and life as it is meant to be lived in the land God promised to provide.

---

16. Karl Barth, *Epistle to the Romans*, trans. Edwyn C. Hoskyns (New York: Oxford University Press, 1968), 40.

> A god is that to which we look for all good and in which we find refuge in every time of need. . . . That to which your heart clings and entrusts itself is, I say, really your God.
>
> Martin Luther, "The Large Catechism," in *Book of Concord: The Confessions of the Evangelical Lutheran Church,* by Robert Kolb, Timothy Wengert, and James Schaffer, 2nd ed. (Minneapolis: Fortress Press, 2000), http://bookofconcord. org/lc–1-intro.php.

FURTHER REFLECTIONS
God and Idolatry

Throughout the book of Deuteronomy—and throughout the entire Old Testament—Israel's idolatrous behavior is an ever-present theme. The prophet Isaiah chastises Israel for worshiping an image made out of wood, saying, "No one considers, nor is there knowledge or discernment to say, 'Half of it I burned in the fire; I also baked bread on its coals. . . . Now shall I make the rest of it an abomination? Shall I fall down before a block of wood?'" (Isa. 44:19). In the many stories spanning the Old Testament, Israelites betray a particularly human predilection to, as Luther suggests, give their hearts and entrust themselves to that which is not God.

Writing against the looming destructive force of Nazi ideology in the twentieth century, Karl Barth notes a danger implicit in such divine claims to exclusivity: "No sentence is more dangerous or revolutionary than that God is One and there is no other like Him. . . . It was on the truth of the sentence that God is One that the 'Third Reich' of Adolf Hitler made shipwreck. Let this sentence be uttered in such a way that it is heard and grasped, and at once 450 prophets of Baal are always in fear of their lives."[17] The danger inherent in claims to God as the only one worthy of worship is that any human

> Even religious devotion, which literally means the dedicating or consecrating of oneself by a vow, can become an idol. We can become so focused on our love of God that we demean other people in the process. The English language once reflected this ambiguity; until the middle of the nineteenth century, to "devote" could also mean to curse, or consign to the power of evil.
>
> Kathleen Norris, *Amazing Grace: A Vocabulary of Faith* (New York: Riverhead Books, 1998), 89.

17. Karl Barth, *Church Dogmatics,* II/1 (Edinburgh: T. & T. Clark, 2004), 444.

call for ultimate allegiance and loyalty to that which is not divine risks being exposed as idolatrous. With this dangerous wager, Barth was able to unmask Nazi claims as dangerous ideological illusions of truth and power and might.

As we see repeatedly in the chapters of Deuteronomy, Moses' persistent concern regarding the Israelites and their imminent entry into the land God promised them is the concern that the Israelites will turn their backs on God to pursue various ideologically tainted religious goals like military might, materialistic accumulation, and moralistic pride. We will explore these dangers in more depth in the pages to come.

> Here Moses faces his final choice: will he stand up to God and fight for his just reward, or will he accept God's decision and prepare Israel for their future? . . . The leader chooses his followers. He will spend the remainder of his days teaching the people what they must know. As he guides his people toward Mount Nebo, Moses knows that the peak from which he will see the Promised Land will be his final spot on earth. What will the man of few words choose as his final words? What will his farewell message be?
>
> Bruce Feiler, *America's Prophet: How the Story of Moses Shaped America* (New York: HarperCollins),18.

In 4:21, we hear once again that God's anger toward Moses is ultimately Israel's fault. Because of Israel's actions, Moses will not be permitted to reach the promised land. Here again Israel's disobedience—rather than anything Moses himself did—is given as the reason Moses is kept out.

FURTHER REFLECTIONS
An Angry, Jealous God

Descriptions of God's character throughout Deuteronomy and the Old Testament are punctuated with references to God's anger and jealousy. Theologically speaking, it is vital that we understand divine anger and jealousy within the wider context of God's love and devotion to Israel and to the whole created order (cf. Gen. 9:8–17). Contemporary theologians attend to the importance of God's anger,

> For his anger is but for a moment; his favor is for a lifetime.
>
> (Ps. 30:5)

particularly when they address God's relationship to situations of oppression and injustice. Liberation theologians remind us of the positive role of God's wrath. For a God without wrath does not plan to do much liberating.

These attributes are the necessary underside of God's love, devotion, and favor. It is also important to note, as we see in Psalm 30:5, that God's wrath is often cast as momentary while God's favor outlasts the anger, the wrath, and the jealousy.

Throughout the Old Testament, the notion of God's jealousy is integrally related to the command to have no other gods before God. In Exod. 34:14, for instance, the Israelites are instructed to worship "no other god, because the LORD, whose name is Jealous, is a jealous God." God's jealousy is related to God's passion for Israel (cf. Isa. 9:7). According to biblical scholar Patrick Miller, that God's self-description includes the attribute of jealousy "is God's way of saying 'I will have nothing less than your full devotion, and you will have nothing less than all my love.' It is the kind of attribute that belongs to a marriage relationship, where there is proper covenantal jealousy."[18] God's anger and jealousy over Israel's straying from its relationship with God bespeaks a passion and a zeal for God's beloved people and a fervent desire on God's part to be in right relationship with Israel.

> God punished Israel so often, and yet always received it again when it returned afterwards. . . . Hence, in order to arouse this repentance and to condemn despair, He adds the sweetest and most faithful promise. . . . "The Lord your God is merciful. He will not forsake or destroy you; nor will He forget the covenant He swore to your fathers." In this way He shows at the same time what true repentance is, namely, a burning thirst for mercy in the affliction of conscience. For to them alone is sweet mercy offered, not to the hypocrites."
>
> Martin Luther, *LW* 9:59–60.

---

18. Patrick Miller, *Deuteronomy*, Interpretation: A Bible Commentary for Teaching and Preaching (Louisville, KY: Westminster John Knox Press, 1990), 76.

4:25–31
The Exile Foreseen

The original hearers of this first speech by Moses undoubtedly recognized their current situation in Moses' foretelling of the exile: "You will soon utterly perish from the land that you are crossing the Jordan to occupy; you will not live long on it" but will be scattered among other nations and will serve other gods (vv. 26–28). In the midst of a desperate exilic context, where Jews from the kingdom of Judah lived in exile under the Assyrian regime in Babylon, the Israelites were meant to hear a strong judgment in the text from their God: that they were exiled because they turned away from their God.

Moses' predictions of the scattering of Israel were surely evocative to the hearers of this text, likely recalling for them the deportations of Israelites occurring during the sixth century BCE. We see again in verse 28 that the most egregious transgression by Israel was idolatry, the charge of serving other gods.

> To think of exile as beneficial, as a spur to humanism or creativity, is to belittle the mutilation. . . . Think instead of the uncountable masses for whom UN agencies have been created, of refugees without urbanity, with only ration cards and agency numbers.
>
> Edward Said, "The Mind of Winter: Reflections on Life in Exile," *Harpers*, September 1983, 50.

But in the midst of a situation that reeks of death, Moses offers a glimpse of hope: after the awful situation they no doubt endure in exile, Moses reassures the people of God, "You will return to the LORD your God and heed him" (v. 30). How will this come to pass? Again Moses is clear that Israel's future return to God will not be due to any righteousness on their part; rather, he tells them, "You will return . . . because the LORD your God is a merciful God, he will neither abandon you nor destroy you; he will not forget the covenant with your ancestors that he swore to them" (v. 31). This claim is what Martin Luther calls "the sweetest and most faithful promise": that God is merciful.

The section concludes not with a focus on disobedience but with a reassurance characteristic of the Deuteronomistic writers: despite Israel's turning away, "God is merciful, and will never abandon

[them] or destroy [them], nor forget the covenant made in person with [their] ancestors" (vv. 29–31).

FURTHER REFLECTIONS
Exilic Existence

> Any Christian theology that seeks to take the Old Testament seriously must ponder well that the core of faith, for Christians as for Jews, is situated in the matrix of exile.
>
> Walter Brueggemann, *Theology of the Old Testament: Testimony, Dispute, Advocacy* (Minneapolis: Fortress Press, 1997), 77.

> If, as the New Testament indicates, extending certain phases of the Old [Testament], God calls his people to prophetically critical relationship to the structures of power and oppression, then the alliance between Rome-as-Empire and Church-as-Hierarchy, which the fourth and fifth centuries gradually consolidated, is not merely a possible tactical error but a structured denial of the gospel.
>
> John Howard Yoder, "The Disavowal of Constantine: An Alternative Perspective on Interfaith Dialogue," in *Royal Priesthood: Essays Ecclesiological and Ecumenical,* ed. Michael G. Cartright (Grand Rapids: Wm. B. Eerdmans Publishing Co., 1994), 245.

Exile is a significant category of experience for both Jews and Christians. Much of the OT texts are written out of and for the context of Israel's exile. Psalm 137:1 captures the sense of despair that often accompanies exilic existence: "By the rivers of Babylon—there we sat down and there we wept when we remembered Zion." In contemporary theological circles, exile remains a significant category given the ever-present global realities of massive dislocation of peoples. It is not only a condition faced by the Israelites of the ancient world but also a state of being for people continuing up to the present day, from the Tibetans exiled from their homeland by the Chinese to Syrian citizens living in refugee camps after fleeing the intensifying civil war in 2012–2013. Christian concern for the realities of exile, then, is shaped not simply by the realities faced by an ancient Israelite people; the condition of exile also had profound effects on the formation of ancient

Christianity and has continued to affect its incarnations in the world ever since.

Modern theorists like Edward Said have recently broadened the scope of the category to include social, psychological, and political exile as well as its physical manifestations. Scripture from both Testaments calls Christians to work to unmask those forces that force God's people into exile of various kinds. Indeed, such work is central to incarnating the gospel in the world.

4:32–40
Israel's Covenantal Relationship: Rooted in God's Love

Deuteronomy is the first biblical book to state explicitly that "there is no other" besides the God of Israel (4:35, 39). Assertions of monotheism are rare in the Pentateuch; that they only appear here suggests an evolving view of God within these first books of the Bible. The claim that there is no one besides God is embedded in this lengthy recitation of God's identity as the liberating God of Israel. The rhetoric of this passage soars, asking the Israelites to consider whether "anything so great" as their story of God's choosing them to be God's people and delivering them out of the bonds of slavery and oppression has ever happened to any other nation of people. Indeed, for Israel there is no one other than this liberating, redeeming God.

While 4:35 and 4:39 suggest a strongly monotheistic view of God, other Deuteronomic passages are not as clear. At the beginning of the Decalogue in Deuteronomy 5:7, for instance, the command is to have no other gods before God, which seems to tacitly support the existence of other gods. Even more explicitly, the Song of Moses in

> The oneness of God is given as an aspect of the power and liberative character of the One God. . . . What is being excluded here is not plurality but the possibility of thinking of oppressive powers as truly divine. The liberator God is God from before the Creation to the end of history, by when all the powers will be shown once and for all to be non-existent and powerless.
>
> Editorial, *Monotheism: Divinity and Unity Reconsidered*, ed. Erik Borgman, Maria Clara Bingemer, and Andres Torres Queiruga (Norfolk, VA: Canterbury Press Norwich, 2009), 8.

Deuteronomy 32:8 claims that God intended for other peoples to worship other gods:

> When the Most High apportioned the nations,
>   when he divided humankind,
> he fixed the boundaries of the peoples
>   according to the number of gods.

To say that Hebrew Scripture presents a consistent, strictly monotheistic view, then, is simply not supported by the text. Even within Deuteronomy, the biblical view of monotheism is unsettled. While 4:35 offers a thoroughgoing monotheistic view of the God of Israel, we will soon see other passages in Deuteronomy that depict more of a "monolatrous" view of Israel's God where a single deity is worshiped without claiming it is the only deity. The apostle Paul also sets forth a monolatrous view of God when he writes to the Corinthians, "Indeed, even though there may be so-called gods in heaven or on earth—as in fact there are many gods and many lords—yet for us there is one God" (1 Cor. 8:5–6a). It is important to acknowledge the tensions that exist in the text between a monotheistic and monolatrous view of God and to attend to that tension in our contemporary interpretation of the text.

In verse 37 Moses offers an explanation of why God chose Israel to be God's covenant partner. He states it succinctly: "Because he loved your ancestors, he chose their descendants after them." Reformer John Calvin picks up on the theme of God's love for Israel, stressing the unmerited nature of Israel's deliverance from slavery and their special status before God:

> Moses desires to shew that whatever good things God has conferred upon His people are gratuitous, by which circumstance he commends God's grace the more. He had said that by unusual favor this nation was taken from the midst of another; and he now adds that this was done on no other account but because God had embraced Abraham, Isaac, and Jacob with His love, and persevered in the same love towards their posterity. But we must remark that by the word *"love"* is expressed that favor which springs of mere generosity, so as to exclude all worthiness in the person beloved. . . . We now understand

the meaning of Moses, that the deliverance of the people was only to be ascribed to God's goodness. He thus amplifies this blessing by another circumstance, viz., that God had preferred to great and mighty nations this ignoble people, whose own proper worthiness could not have acquired His favor.[19]

That God's love of Israel is unmerited is a persistent theme of Deuteronomy. And the love of God given to Israel is connected throughout Deuteronomy to the command to serve this God who labored on Israel's behalf to set the Israelites free from bondage and death. In response to God's love and liberating action on their behalf, Israel is called upon, once again, to "keep his statutes and commandments . . . so that [they] may long remain in the land that the LORD [their] God is giving [them]" (v. 40). Once again, we see that memory of Israel's past gives the Israelites their identity for the "present" as they prepare to enter the land.

4:41–49

Transition to Second Address

Verses 41–49 offer a brief hiatus from the words of Moses to allow for some narration of Moses' actions. First, in verses 41–43, the Deuteronomist retells part of the story from Numbers 35:9–14, where Moses sets aside three cities of refuge for members of the community who unintentionally kill another person. These cities (and as Numbers mentions, three additional cities in the land of Canaan as well) serve as places of refuge for those who would otherwise likely be victims of retributive acts by relatives of the one killed. Having cities set aside for asylum, then, function in the ancient world to discourage acts of vengeance. This practice of setting cities aside resurfaces in Deuteronomy 19:1–7. Here again we see an emphasis on compassion throughout the text for those at the margins of Israelite society.

---

19. John Calvin, commentary on Deuteronomy 4:32–40, *Harmony of the Law*, vol. 1 (Grand Rapids: Christian Classics Ethereal Library, 1998), 337, http://www.ccel.org/ccel/calvin/calcom03.v.viii.html?bcb=right.

5:1–11:31

Moses' Second Address: Reiterating the Role of Rules

5:1–21
Let's Review: The Ten Commandments, Again

Deuteronomy 5:1–5 marks the beginning of Moses' second address, a speech that concludes in chapter 11. He calls all Israel together to hear again the story of receiving the Ten Commandments. Yet again we observe that Moses' speech is not intended to be a verbatim rehearsal of Israel's past; rather his sermon is addressed directly to the people standing before him, and practically speaking, to those Israelites who hear the commands in their exiled context. Rather than merely reporting on past events, Moses insists, "Not with our ancestors did the LORD make this covenant, but with us, who are all of us here alive today" (5:3). The covenant, then, has more than historical significance; it is binding on those who hear it "today." Interestingly Moses continues informing these descendants of those who wandered in the wilderness that "the Lord spoke with [them] face to face at the mountain [at Sinai], out of the fire" (5:4).

This introductory section to a re-presentation of the Ten Commandments is at once a reenactment and a foreshadowing. The reenactment comes with some important twists, however. Take Moses' claim in verse 4 that God speaks to Israel face to face. Such a claim

> Promise and command, the pointing of the goal and the pointing of the way, therefore belong immediately together.
>
> Jürgen Moltmann, *The Theology of Hope: On the Ground and the Implications of a Christian Eschatology* (New York: Harper & Row, 1967), 120.

stands in tension with the depiction of Israel's being confined to the foot of Mount Sinai when this story is first told in Exodus 19. In the very next verse, Deuteronomy 5:5, a qualification is made: Moses explains that he stood between Israel and the Lord because Israel was afraid. What do we make of this section's claims to Israel's seeing God face to face and Moses' simultaneous claim to serving as mediator between God and Israel in this telling of the story?

> While Deuteronomy unfolds as a sort of *Reader's Digest* condensation of the preceding four books, the language is different, more sanctified. The tone would be familiar to anyone who attends [Jewish] services today.
>
> Bruce Feiler, *Walking the Bible: A Journey by Land Through the Five Books of Moses* (New York: HarperCollins, 2001), 414.

Both accounts agree that Israel remains at the base of Mount Sinai (or Horeb, depending on the story); Moses' role as intermediary is also maintained in both stories. At the same time, the Deuteronomist emphasizes Israel's role as living witness to God's great epiphany at Sinai. This reference to seeing God face to face also foreshadows the dramatic tribute to Moses at his death in the final chapter of Deuteronomy. In 34:10, the Deuteronomist proclaims that Israel has never seen a prophet like Moses, "whom the LORD knew face to face." What does it mean for the Deuteronomist to say that Moses sees God's face, especially given that in the story of Moses' encounter with God in the burning bush, Moses "hides his face," afraid to look at God (Exod. 3:6b)? Twentieth-century Jewish philosopher Emmanuel Levinas formulated a philosophy of the face, a perspective rooted in OT encounters with the face of God. Levinas writes, "To my mind the Infinite comes in the signifyingness of the face. The face *signifies* the Infinite. . . . When, in the presence of the Other, I say 'Here I am!', this 'Here I am!' is the place through which the Infinite enters into language. . . . The subject who says 'Here I am!' *testifies* to the Infinite."[1] In Deuteronomy, we do not see the Moses who was overwhelmed by the burning bush. Instead we get a mature Moses, one whose intimate, face-to-face contact with God translates

1. Emmanuel Levinas, *Totality and Infinity: An Essay on Exteriority* (Pittsburgh: Duquesne University Press, 1969), 105–6.

> Revelation is understood from the standpoint of the promise contained in the revelation.... Yahweh's revelation manifestly does not serve to bring the ever-threatened present into congruence with his eternity. On the contrary, its effect is that the hearers of the promise become incongruous with the reality around them, as they strike out in hope towards the promised new future.
>
> Jürgen Moltmann, *The Theology of Hope: On the Ground and the Implications of a Christian Eschatology* (New York: Harper & Row, 1967), 100.

"the Infinite" into words of hope for a future of abundant life in the land. Facing God, Moses understands what the people need to do to flourish. Afraid of God's face, the people hear but often do not take to heart what they must do to follow God's commands.

As they rely on Moses to mediate the Infinite, what is it the Israelites of "today" hear? Nothing less than the utterance of the divine name. Integral to the revelation of God's own identity is God's role as the One "who brought [Israel] out of the land of Egypt, out of the house of slavery" (v. 6). It is important to understand that the Decalogue begins not with a commandment or a prohibition but with God's self-revelation as a liberating God who upholds Israel's right to freedom. Further, God's identity as liberator of Israel is essentially bound up with Israel's obligation to follow these particular commands.

> For [Moses,] God's dominion over the people and the inner cohesion of the people are only two aspects of the same reality. From out of the words, "I, YHVH, am thy God who brought thee out of the land of Egypt" which flood into his expectant spirit, gush forth all the remaining ones in a stream that is not to be stayed.
>
> Martin Buber, *Moses: the Revelation and the Covenant,* trans. Michael Fishbone (Amherst, NY: Humanity Books, 1998), 135.

FURTHER REFLECTIONS
The Decalogue

Second-century Clement of Alexandria was the first Christian theologian to use the term "Decalogue" to refer to what today are popularly known as the Ten Commandments. The term derives from the Greek words *deka* and *logoi*, which are translations of the Hebrew *'eshr mylym* and literally mean "ten words," the designation given to these words in Exodus 24:12 and Deuteronomy 4:13; 10:4. Since the original meaning is the "ten words" rather than "ten command- ments," many scholars contend that the Decalogue is distinct from other types of legal instruction given in the Pentateuch. Rather than following up each of the commands with a description of a pun- ishment or a reward, most of the ten words of the Decalogue are not immediately linked to specific consequences. As is made clear in the introduction to the Decalogue in Deuteronomy 5:2–3, these ten words are to be understood within the context of a covenantal relationship between God and the people of God. The words pro- vide the foundation through which that covenant is understood and lived out.

While the Decalogue is distinct in terms of its relationship to other laws presented in the Old Testament, it shares commonalities with law codes of the ancient Near East. One of the most famous early law codes, the Code of Hammurabi, is the earliest known example of a ruler—in this case, King Hammurabi (1795–1750 BCE)—making public a body of laws so that those under his rule might know what was expected of them. Before that time, law was essentially at the whim of the ruler. Some four hundred years later, Moses gave his tiny band of wanderers another set of commands to live by. And while similarities exist between the Decalogue and other ancient codes like that of Hammurabi, the Decalogue is not attributed to a king or any other earthly ruler. It comes from God and does not change with leaders, prophets, or kings. These words were not just meant to be carved into tablets (Exod. 31:18, Deut. 4:13); or simply to be placed in the ark of the covenant and carried by the Israelites wherever they went and laid in the Holy of Holies in the Tabernacle (Exod. 25:16); or just set inside the temple in Jerusalem (1 Kgs. 8:6, 9). These words were meant to be inscribed on the hearts of the people of God (cf. Deut. 11:19; 30:6).[2]

Most Jews and Christians know that there are two versions of the Decalogue in the Pentateuch, the first in Exodus 20:2–17 and the second in Deuteronomy 5:6–21. The striking similarities of the

---

2. Joan Chittister, *The Ten Commandments: Laws of the Heart* (Maryknoll, NY: Orbis Books, 2006), 8–9.

two presentations suggest that even when the context shifts—when there's a monumental relocation from wilderness to settled land—these commandments are fundamental, basic parameters for a flourishing community. While the Decalogue as presented in Deuteronomy is almost entirely a verbatim representation of the Exodus 20 version, the few differences once again clue us in to some of Deuteronomy's distinctive theological accents. In the Exodus version—which most scholars agree is the older version—it is Yahweh who delivers the words to the Israelites at Sinai. In Deuteronomy's version, the words come from Moses and make up an important part of his second speech to the Israelites on the plains of Moab. The few differences between the two versions of the commandments serve to highlight God's investment in Israel's evolving future that moves from the wilderness context to the context of life in the land God promised.

Even though there is consensus that there are ten words presented by the Exodus and Deuteronomy texts, there has long been discrepancy regarding how the words—or commands—are enumerated. The most significant variation exists regarding the First Commandment. Where exactly does it begin, and what exactly does it include? It depends on where you go to find the answer. The Jewish Talmud says that the divine utterance—"I am the LORD your God, who brought you out of the land of Egypt, out of the house of slavery" (Exod. 20:2; Deut. 5:6)—is itself the first word, suggesting again that "words about covenantal relationship" rather than "laws" or "commands" might be the more accurate description. According to the Talmud, the Second Commandment is Exodus 20:3–6 (or Deut. 5:7–10), which includes the command to "have no other gods" before Yahweh as well as to "not make for yourself an idol."

Most Christian listings of the Ten Commandments begin instead with "you shall have no other gods before me" (Exod. 20:3; Deut. 5:7). Just what else is included in that First Commandment varies, however. While Roman Catholics claim that Exodus 20:2–5 (Deut. 5:6–9) is the First Commandment, which includes the affirmation of the divine name as well as the "no other gods" command, one of the most influential theological voices on the Decalogue, Augustine, leaves out the invocation of the divine name and claims instead that Exodus 20:3–6 (Deut. 5:7–10) is the First Commandment (making the Talmud's Second Commandment into the First). To complicate matters further, Orthodox Christians and most Protestants (including Reformed, Anglican, Presbyterian, Methodist, and Baptist) see two commandments in Augustine's one: for them the First Commandment is still "no other gods," and the Second Commandment is, "you shall not make for yourself an idol. . . ." (Exod. 20:4–6; Deut. 8–10).

After such great variation regarding the First and Second Commandments, even though the numbering is different, the main focus of each subsequent commandment—whether it be on the Sabbath, parents, or adultery—is not contested again until the final commandments about bearing false witness and coveting that which is the neighbor's. The following list of commandments, with the first number representing the Augustinian tradition (the tradition followed by Roman Catholics and Lutherans) and the second number representing Orthodox Christians and most Protestant groups (who, starting with the Third Commandment, follow the Talmudic numbering), illustrates the consensus regarding the content of most commandments:

2 or 3: "You shall not make wrongful use of the name of the LORD your God" (Exod. 20:7a; cf. Deut. 5:11a);

3 or 4: "Remember the Sabbath day, and keep it holy" (Exod. 20:8; cf. Deut. 5:12);

4 or 5: "Honor your father and your mother" (Exod. 20:12a; cf. Deut. 5:16a);

5 or 6: "You shall not murder" (Exod. 20:13; cf. Deut. 5:17);

6 or 7: "You shall not commit adultery" (Exod. 20:14; cf. Deut. 5:18);

7 or 8: "You shall not steal" (Exod. 20:15; cf. Deut. 5:19); and

8 or 9: "You shall not bear false witness against your neighbor" (Exod. 20:16; cf. Deut. 5:20).

Continuing to follow the Talmudic numbering, Orthodox Christians and most Protestants assert that the Tenth Commandment concerns the coveting of anything that is the neighbor's (following the list in Exod. 20:17). Roman Catholics follow Augustine, who looks to Deuteronomy 5:21a, "Neither shall you covet your neighbor's wife," for the ninth commandment, and Deut. 5:21b–21c, "Neither shall you desire your neighbor's house, or field, or male or female slave, or ox, or donkey, or anything that belongs to your neighbor," for the tenth. The Lutheran Confession follows Augustine in that the Ninth and Tenth Commandments both deal with coveting, but Lutherans follow the order of the listings in Exodus 20:17, with the neighbor's house being the focus of the Ninth Commandment and everything else being the focus of the Tenth.[3]

While the different approaches to numbering the commandments is worth reviewing, the much more significant issue is the importance of the commandments for the Israelite hearers of Deuteronomy and how that informs Christian hearers of this text today. As mentioned earlier, the Decalogue instructs the Israelites on how to live in covenantal relationship with God, the one who brought them out of slavery into freedom (Deut. 5:6). The Decalogue is at the heart of the vision of life as it should be for Israel. How does this fundamental importance of the Decalogue for the Israelites relate to its importance for Christians?

According to the Gospel of Matthew, Jesus understood following the Decalogue to be fundamental to faithful living. In his conversation with the rich man who asks him what he should do to inherit eternal life, Jesus responds by saying, "'If you wish to enter into life, keep the commandments'" (Matt. 19:17). "'Which ones?'" the man asks. Jesus responds with a list that covers the second table of the Decalogue (Matt. 19:18–19). Those who know the rest of this exchange remember that adherence to these commands is not all there is to inheriting eternal life—indeed, when pushed further by the rich man, Jesus tells him to sell all that he has. On hearing this, the disciples ask Jesus who will be able to meet such stringent criteria, and Jesus responds, "'For mortals it is impossible, but for God all things are possible'" (19:26). Faithful living, according to Matthew's accounting of Jesus' words, then, involves following the commandments as well as relying on the grace of God.

---

3. Yiu Sing Lucas Chan, *The Ten Commandments and the Beatitudes: Biblical Studies and Ethics for Real Life* (Lanham, MD: Rowan & Littlefield, 2012), 241.

Historically speaking, theologians have long held up the Decalogue as vitally important to the Christian life of faith. Theologians like Augustine and Thomas Aquinas understood the Decalogue as not just part of the Old Law but as standing for the entire Old Law.

Even as theologians have referred to the commands as laws, ever since Augustine they have had a prominent place in the catechetical instruction of the church, a fact that points to their enduring importance to Christian faith. Aquinas, for instance, correlated several commandments together according to different levels of love for neighbor. Even more significant, though, was his turning negative commands into positive ones: the commandment against stealing, according to Aquinas, is actually a command to protect the property of the neighbor.[4] Both Luther and Calvin also wrote comprehensively on the commandments, insisting that they are central to a Christian life of faith. For Luther, following the commandments is what follows from faith. His approach in his Small Catechism is similar to Aquinas's approach—the commands are not simply prohibitions but also need to be understood in the context of positive ways to respect the neighbor.[5] In other words, the ways of being set forth in the Decalogue are how a faithful people *will*—rather than must—act toward God and neighbor.

In her recent meditative reflections on the relevance of the Ten Commandments for contemporary society, Benedictine Sister Joan

> I understand by the word "law" not only the Ten Commandments which set forth a godly and righteous rule of living, but the form of religion handed down by God through Moses. And Moses was not made lawgiver to wipe out the blessing promised to the race of Abraham. Rather, we see him repeatedly reminding the Jews of that freely given covenant made with their fathers of which they were the heirs.
>
> John Calvin, *Institutes*, 2.7.1, as cited in *A Theological Guide to Calvin's Institutes: Essays and Analysis (Calvin 500)*, ed. David W. Hall (Phillipsburg, NJ: P&R Publishing, 2008), 186.

---

4. Ibid., 24.
5. Martin Luther, "Small Catechism," *Book of Concord: The Confessions of the Evangelical Lutheran Church*, by Robert Kolb, Timothy Wengert, and James Schaffer, 2nd ed. (Minneapolis: Fortress Press, 2000), 345-76, http://bookofconcord.org/lc-1-intro.php.

Chittister offers powerful insights on how these words can (and should) continue to shape our living today. Chittister suggests that more important than posting them publicly outside state or county courthouses is to understand how the commandments provide guidance on moral and compassionate ways of living in the world today. Rather than being made for a court of law, these "ten words" are concerned most fundamentally with dispositions, which are ultimately unenforceable. For what would it mean to prosecute the "coveting" of something our neighbor has? How would we monitor "remembering" the Sabbath? According to Chittister, "the point is that the Ten Commandments are laws of the heart, not laws of the commonwealth. They are laws that are intended to lead to the fullness of life, not simply to the well-ordered life."[6]

It is interesting to note that even though the Decalogue was consistently highlighted in Christian catechesis along with the Lord's Prayer and the Apostles Creed, the commands are certainly less prominent in Christian worship than they have been in the past. Biblical scholar Patrick Miller points to past practices of Lutheran churches, where the Ten Commandments were read prior to the confession of sin and to Anglican churches where the priest would read the commands and the congregation would respond with "Lord, have mercy."[7] Miller's observation begs the question: How will the ten words of the Decalogue become "laws of the heart" for contemporary Christians if scant attention is paid them by the contemporary church? Once again we are reminded of many Christians' lack of familiarity with numerous Old Testament texts. Let's examine how the ten words of the Decalogue in Deuteronomy present a vision for a full life—not just for ancient Israel but also for contemporary Christians who are called to be active followers of the Decalogue as well.

The recitation of the commandments begins in Deuteronomy just as it does in the Exodus telling: moving directly from the proclamation of God's identity to the command that Israel have no gods before

6. Chittister, *The Ten Commandments*, 10.
7. Patrick D. Miller, *The Ten Commandments* (Louisville, KY: Westminster John Knox Press, 2009), 11.

this God whose identity was just proclaimed: "I am the LORD your God, who brought you out of the land of Egypt, out of the house of slavery; you shall have no other gods before me" (Deut. 5:6 and Exod. 20:2). The list of commands in Deuteronomy continues to follow the Exodus account in its prohibition against idolatry, referencing again the ban on representing God with any created form. That the Decalogue begins with claims about God's identity, the nature of faithful worship, and prohibitions against idolatry suggests, according to Christian ethicist Yui Sing Lucas Chan, that such issues are not simply theological but ethical as well. Chan points out that "while the commandment does not deny the presence of other powers, it reminds the Israelites about the temptation of turning to these powers or realities and choosing them as the ultimate center of their lives."[8] Once again we're back to Luther's claim that it is that to which our heart clings that is truly our god. Many theologians talk about the ordering of the commands being hierarchical in nature, which in this case suggests that if life is centered around something other than God, it's not possible for the rest of our habits and practices to be ordered rightly. It is noteworthy, too, that the law code section of Deuteronomy (chaps. 12–26) also begins with laws and statutes about proper worship of "the LORD your God" and includes strong prohibitions against worshiping God through any of the idolatrous practices of those who had been living in Canaan (cf. 12:29–32). The law code is in large part an explication of how these words from the Decalogue are to be lived out in the new land.

Just as in the Exodus version of the Decalogue, God is referred to here as a jealous God, and this first commandment includes a sanction—a vow to punish children for the sins of their parents to the fourth generation. Similar claims are made elsewhere in the Pentateuch (e.g., Exod. 34:7 and Num. 14:18). Significant also are the reprisals later in Deuteronomy regarding this issue: in 7:9 the emphasis is on God's faithfulness to those who follow the commands "to a thousand generations." In contrast, Deut. 24:16 is striking in its insistence that children will not be punished for parents' crimes but only for their own sins. These competing pronouncements on

---

8. Chan, *Ten Commandments and the Beatitudes*, 46.

punishment for the sins of one's ancestors betray an internal scriptural tension that is not easily resolved. What we can say is that amid the tension here again, the scales are tipped toward God's faithfulness and mercy in the midst of human sinfulness.

In addition to linking idolatry to punishment of children in the commandment above, the command in 5:11a—"You shall not make wrongful use of the name of the LORD your God"—is the only other command linked to a specific punitive sanction.[9] In 5:11b, we hear that "the LORD will not acquit anyone who misuses [the LORD's] name." This command both reaffirms the holiness of God's name as well as instructs on its proper use. While this commandment often gets reduced in contemporary parlance to not invoking God when one curses, the wording of the NRSV translation helpfully encourages a broader interpretation. More than simply refraining from claiming, "Oh my God!" when something surprising happens, this commandment encourages reflection on the many ways in which God's name can be wrongfully put to use. The biblical text offers many examples of how God's name is profaned. Take, for example, the explanation in the book of Ezekiel of how ancient Israelite disobedience to the commands profanes the name of God. Ezekiel hears a voice from the temple that says, "Mortal, this is the place of my throne and the place for the soles of my feet, where I will reside among the people of Israel forever. The house of Israel shall no more defile my holy name . . . they were defiling my holy name by their abominations that they committed" (Ezek. 43:7–8). These verses demonstrate that violation of this command comes not just through words but also through deeds.

Related to biblical examples of how God's chosen ones repeatedly make wrongful use of God's name, Joan Chittister suggests that it is often the "pious ones" more than the "sinners" who are in danger of ignoring this commandment. We need only to think of the church's long and problematic history of invoking the name of God to support oppression of God's own children. A particularly repugnant example of this can be seen in the slave ships named "Jesus" that brought African women and men to American shores. Chittister writes, "To take

9. Miller, *Ten Commandments,* 85–86.

God's name in vain—to make God responsible for who we hate and who we hurt and how we cease to think and who becomes our god and conscience—is to make God the doer of our evil."[10] Chittister also points out that in refusing to speak the divine name, Jews have decided not to risk it. The temptation to misuse God's name is such a powerful one that the Jews have found it better to refrain from saying the name altogether. Since Christians aren't likely to forego invoking the divine name, it seems that proper respect of God's holiness should lead to humility in claiming God as champion of any of our political, religious, or social groups and causes.

As in the Exodus telling, most of the commands in Deuteronomy are presented as prohibitions: "You shall not . . ." Such basic negations serve, as Gerhard von Rad has suggested, as "signposts on the margins of a wide sphere of life."[11] The accent is on the freedom given to this band of former slaves—freedom within the bounds of allegiance to a liberating God. The next signpost on the margins of life is the commandment that speaks to a central aspect of how Israel is to count time. In the middle of the list of commands lies the command to honor the Sabbath; put simply, it commands Israel to take time to rest.

While many Christians and Jews living today may view "a day off" as time we cannot afford to take in our fast-track lives, this passage asks that we see this call to rest as a radical gift, as it undoubtedly was to those living in ancient society—and indeed, to those living throughout much of world history. It is vital to understand that most members of ancient society labored without rest. To be given permission to rest on the seventh day was nothing short of revolutionary.

The Sabbath is also a command that, when followed, orders the priorities of the community. While most Christians do not maintain the same day of the week for Sabbath observance as ancient Israel, they have nevertheless emphasized the significance of the Sabbath for orienting oneself toward God. As John Calvin wrote,

---

10. Chittister, *The Ten Commandments*, 32.
11. Gerhard von Rad, *Old Testament Theology: Essays on Structure, Theme and Text*, vol. 1, ed. Patrick Miller (Minneapolis: Augsburg Fortress, 1992), 194.

Thus, the first way to keep the Sabbath as we should is to give up the things that seem good to ourselves. Instead we must rest. How are we to rest? We must stand still so that our minds don't wander to our own inventions. I say, we must continue quietly in obedience to God. . . . Now, if we are so unruly that we must always keep our arms and legs in action and be continually doing what we think is best, surely this breaks the bond that is between us and God. It separates us and estranges us from him as much as is possible.[12]

The inclusion of the daughter and the female slave shows that women are to stop working on the Sabbath. Is the wife not mentioned because "a woman's work is never done" and the wife still has to work? But if the wife worked, so would the daughter and the maidservant. Quite the contrary, the omission of the phrase "and your wife" shows that the "you" that the law addresses includes both women and men, each treated as a separate moral agent.

Tikva Frymer-Kensky, "Deuteronomy," in *The Women's Bible Commentary*, ed. Carol A. Newsom and Sharon H. Ringe (Louisville, KY: Westminster John Knox Press, 1998), 54.

The main difference between the Exodus and the Deuteronomy versions of the Sabbath command comes in the Deuteronomist's explanation of the command in 5:12–15. While the description of the Sabbath in Deuteronomy is identical to the Exodus version (cf. Exod. 20:8–10), the divergence begins with an elaboration in the Deuteronomy version about a Sabbath for the slaves in Israel so that they may rest "as well as [Israel]" (v. 14b). Rather than linking the command for Sabbath to God's rest on the seventh day of creation as is done in Exodus 20, Moses here invokes the stream to which Martin Buber referred earlier: all that Israel is commanded to do flows out of its identity as covenant partner with a liberating God. Why give your slaves rest? "Remember," is Moses' response. "Remember that you were a slave in the land of Egypt, and the LORD your God brought you out from there" (5:15). The disposition of such humane treatment of slaves anchors Deuteronomy's vision of justice and its keen

---

12. John Calvin, "On the Sabbath, Part I," *Great Sermons*, vol. 1 (Uhrichsville, OH: Barbour Publishing,1998), 183,186.

attention to the conditions of the least among the Israelites. And we note again: this way of structuring communal life would have been quite distinct from the surrounding ancient Near Eastern tribes.

In addition to serving as a commandment for "today," the Sabbath also offers a glimpse of the world to come. In his book on the Sabbath, Jewish Rabbi Abraham Heschel tells of a rabbinic legend where God tells the Israelites that if they keep the commands, they will receive as a gift what is most precious to God. When they ask God what is most precious, God replies, "The world to come." When the people ask God for a sign of the world to come, God responds by saying, "The Sabbath is an example of the world to come."[13]

The eschatological character of the Sabbath also comes through in one of the few places where Deuteronomy's recitation of the Ten Commandments diverges from the Exodus rendition. In the command to honor one's parents, Moses introduces the command just as God reportedly gave it in Exodus: mothers and fathers are honored "so that [their] days may be long." But Moses' retelling here includes a short expansion. Parents are also to be honored so "that it may go well with [them]" in the land God has promised (5:16b). Again Israel is called to follow these commands not simply because God desires it but because such commands are foundational to the structure of a just and well-functioning society. As Moses continues teaching an expanded version of these foundational commands in chapters 6–28 that follow, we will see how right relationships between parents and children figure prominently in such teachings.

The command to honor one's father and mother is linked to the command to remember the Sabbath in that it is also stated in the affirmative. Given that Israel was a patrilineal society, interpreters often highlight that the mother is included along with the father as one to be honored. Although men had more rights than women in Israelite society, this commandment is consistent with other laws in the Pentateuch (e.g., Exod. 21:15, 17; Deut. 21:18; 27:16) where mother and father are acknowledged equally with respect to laws regarding their children. To include a word about honoring parents

13. Abraham Heschel, *The Sabbath: Its Meaning for the Modern Man* (New York: Farrar, Straus & Giroux, 2005), 72.

in the Decalogue also highlights the fundamental importance of the family in Israelite society.

The importance of honoring and obeying parents is emphasized in the New Testament as well. The author of Ephesians makes explicit reference to this commandment in 6:1–3: "Children, obey your parents in the Lord, for this is right. 'Honor your father and mother'—this is the first commandment with a promise: 'so that it may be well with you and you may live long on the earth.'" In Deuteronomy, the command is followed not just by a promise of long life but also with a promise for flourishing life in the land. As biblical scholar Patrick Miller observes, the command suggests a kind of reciprocity—that parents shall be cared for by their children and that the children will receive the blessing of a long and good life in the land God has promised them. Miller also offers an important observation—that this command to care for one's parents is not contingent on love between parents and children or on the quality of the relationship.[14] Old Testament and New Testament versions of the command are clear: our parents deserve our respect. Indeed, disobeying parents is often understood in biblical terms as a serious threat to the social order (cf. Mic. 7:6). In Christian catechetical practices, then, this command has often been used to instruct children about how they should behave toward their parents.

Here's where it becomes important to acknowledge that each of the ten words of the Decalogue is at once simple and complex. In terms of the command to honor one's father and mother, we must ask, What about abusive parents who harm their children? If "honoring" is synonymous with "obeying," clearly adherence to this command can be the cause of great harm. The Hebrew word used for "honor" in Deuteronomy 5:16 is *kabbed,* the same verb used to describe how the Israelites should act toward the divine (cf. Mal. 1:6). Thus many interpreters point to this as evidence that honoring one's parents is analogous to honoring God, which seems to suggest that following parental authority is divinely sanctioned. While there are numerous instances where parental respect is given high regard in Scripture and significant negative consequences are prescribed

14. Miller, *Ten Commandments,* 207.

when such regard is neglected (cf. Exod. 21:15, 17; Deut. 21:18–21), it is also important to highlight that there is ample scriptural evidence to suggest that honoring God and parents has room for critical questioning and protest. The words of David's psalms are full of protests as well as praise for God. Indeed, the protest of Psalm 22—"My God, my God, why have you forsaken me?"—are words that Jesus speaks from the cross. Further, as Patrick Miller points out, the intent behind honoring and listening to one's parents (cf. Prov. 23:22–25) is "on the good consequences for the child who honors and heeds; in this [Proverbs] text the proper respect and listening of the child will have positive outcomes for the parents, who will rejoice and be glad as they see [their children] act wisely."[15] Thus as a law of the heart, this command is not about blind obedience to abusive parents. Rather it is a call to all of us to realize that we are indebted to those who brought us into the world and that we have a responsibility to honor those who have guided and cared for us as we've grown into adulthood.

In reflecting on what honoring our parents might look like in our society today, many of us might be tempted to point to the very different social structure that existed in ancient Israel compared to what exists in twenty-first-century American society. Honoring one's parents in ancient Israel might seem to have been much more easily done, as extended families often lived together or in close proximity. In a society where many of us live far from parents, honoring them is necessarily different. But if we dig more deeply into this commandment, thinking about it not simply in terms of external actions but also as a "law of the heart," as Chittister suggests, what does it mean to honor our parents?

In the Jewish tradition, rituals practiced for centuries demonstrate the special value given to parents. When a person from the Jewish tradition passes away, the kaddish prayer is said daily for eleven months. When this person is also a parent, the prayer is said one day less "to signify that the very act of parenthood is itself a holy and meritorious act that renders the fullness of the normal penitential period following death unnecessary. Parenting, we learn, transcends

15. Ibid., 197.

the value to the children alone. It is a holy gift for the sake of the whole community."[16] It is important to ask ourselves how we—both individually and corporately—fulfill the spirit of the command to honor our parents.

The Exodus and Deuteronomy accounts of the giving of the Decalogue both state that the ten words were written by God on two tablets (Exod. 31:18; Deut. 4:13). Commonly referred to as the "two tables," it is understood that the words on the first table are focused on honoring and serving God while the words of the second table—words that follow from the first table—are concerned with loving the neighbor. As Patrick Miller notes, this command is the first on the list of things not to do to harm the neighbor.[17] The command against killing (or murdering, as it says in the NRSV) is by no means unique to ancient Israel—indeed, such prohibition is very common to both ancient and contemporary societies.

At the same time, we all know that a literal interpretation of "You shall not kill" has never been followed, be it inside or outside Israel. This command is in need of further clarification, for there are multiple places in Deuteronomy—indeed throughout Scripture as a whole—where killing is permissible (e.g., Deut. 20:12). As ethicist Chan notes, the commandment "clarifies that life is sacred but not absolute—that is, it does not mean under no circumstances can life be taken by legitimate authority in society."[18] If we view the law code in Deuteronomy 12–26 as an explication of the Decalogue for settled life in the land, we can look to 19:1–22:8 as specifically focused on articulating how this command against murdering should be lived out by the Israelite community.[19] As we will see later in the commentary on those verses, this section of the law code details guidelines for what should be done when one person unintentionally kills another person (19:4–13), what rules of warfare should be followed to limit the loss of life during war (chap. 20), how to deal with a person found murdered, and how to deal with rebellious children. As Miller notes, killing a person has wide ramifications,

16. Chittister, *The Ten Commandments*, 50.
17. Miller, *Ten Commandments*, 222.
18. Chan, *Ten Commandments and the Beatitudes*, 86.
19. Miller, *Ten Commandments*, 230.

and much attention is given in Deuteronomy and beyond to those ramifications.

But embedded in that same section of the law code are also positive affirmations about how to treat the neighbor. This is why, for Jewish and Christian interpreters alike, the "law of the heart" of this commandment is ultimately about care of the neighbor. Whether it is making sure that your neighbor's stray ox or sheep is safely returned to the neighbor (22:1–2) or that your roof is safe enough so that a person couldn't fall and be injured while on top of it (22:8), or even to offer guidance on proactive care for nonhuman community members, like a mother bird, who might be in danger (22:6), the concern is for the neighbor. This is why in his commentary on this commandment John Calvin insists that it contains "the requirement that we give our neighbor all the help we can."[20] Living a life dedicated to God, then, is played out in a life dedicated to protecting the neighbor.

The next command, that one should not commit adultery, is fundamentally about the protection of the neighbor as well. It is ironic to observe, however, how few people in the Old Testament actually keep the command. Indeed, it is the most prominent metaphor used when describing Israel's wayward relationship to God (cf. Hos. 2:2–23). While gender is not explicitly mentioned in this command, there were different standards for men and women in ancient Israel. Men could have more than one wife (e.g., Abraham takes another wife named Keturah in Gen. 25:1); men could sleep with women to whom they were not married (e.g., Abraham slept with Sarah's servant, Hagar). Once again the law code in chapters 12–26 helps us understand the differences. For men, adultery was sleeping with another man's wife, and the punishment was death (cf. Deut. 22:22). A married or engaged woman who has sex with another man was condemned to death (22:22–24). Interestingly, though, premarital sex between unmarried men and women was not treated with the same seriousness (cf. 22:28–30). What this shows us is that the concern is not first and foremost about sexual activity; rather the

---

20. John Calvin, *Institutes of the Christian Religion*, ed. John T. McNeill, trans. Ford Lewis Battles (Louisville, KY: Westminster John Knox Press, 2001), 2.8.9, as quoted in Miller, *Ten Commandments*, 264.

concern seems to be more about the importance of the marriage relationship and its central role within the community. As is clear from the stories about adulterous relationships recounted in the Old Testament (the story of David and Bathsheba in 2 Sam. 11–12 being perhaps the most prominent one), such actions often spawn tragic consequences (such as David's orchestrating the death of Bathsheba's husband, Uriah, in 2 Sam. 11:17, and the death of David and Bathsheba's son in 2 Sam. 12:18). Such actions lead to the opposite of a full life in community. Instead they threaten to destroy the fabric of community.

That this commandment is ultimately about respecting the neighbor's marriage relationship means that all of us are called to interact with the neighbor in a context wider than the parameters of our own desires. The human temptation of the self to turn in on itself takes us back to the most important commandment(s) in the Decalogue: to have no other gods before God and to make no idols for yourself. Committing adultery is ultimately a selfish act. What this "word" commands, Chittister suggests, is "to truly care about the people we say we love. Not to use them. Not to exploit them. Not to ignore them. Not to patronize them. Not to manipulate them for our own satisfaction."[21] This way of framing the prohibition against adultery allows us to see the expansive potential of the commandment when viewed not just as a law of the body but also of the heart.

The next commandment in the Decalogue is the one prohibiting stealing (5:19). The law code in chapters 12–26 gives numerous guidelines on how to refrain from stealing. From directing the Israelites not to charge interest in loans given to another Israelite (23:19) to "not withholding the wages of poor and needy laborers" (24:14), the code offers a vision for what not stealing should look like in ancient Israel. That "not stealing" needs to be understood as a law of the heart as well as a command regarding property, food, or other possessions is illustrated well by what is perhaps the most famous Christian account of stealing: Augustine's pear tree story. In his *Confessions*, Augustine tells the story of stealing from a pear tree with some of his friends when he was young. According to Augustine,

21. Chittister, *The Ten Commandments*, 80–81.

that he stole pears is not the main problem; rather it is what the act says about his own heart that is the problem. He and his friends steal the pears not because they are hungry but because the pears didn't belong to them: "I loved my error, not that for which I erred but the error itself."[22]

The affirmative reading of this command, then, is not just to refrain from taking what is not yours. If we understand this word as a law of the heart, the words of Deuteronomy help us see that it is ultimately a law of sharing what one has with others, as we see clearly in the injunction in Deuteronomy 24:19–21, where Israelites are to leave a portion of their harvest in the fields to share with their neighbors. The text is quite specific about which neighbors this portion is for: "the alien, the orphan, and the widow" (24:19). Fulfilling the spirit of this command, then, moves us far beyond the young Augustine's self-absorption to focus on others in need of communal support, a recurring theme in Deuteronomy.

The next commandment prohibits bearing false witness against one's neighbor. It is also one that reappears later in both Deuteronomy 17:2–7 and 19:15–21. In both of the later passages, the concern is that in order for an Israelite accused of a crime to be granted due process, there must be more than one witness who can testify that a transgression was committed (cf. 17:6). As it says in 19:15, "a single witness shall not suffice." Indeed, bearing false witness against the neighbor, the text is clear, is an evil that shall be purged from Israel's midst (17:7b; 19:19), and punishment shall be forthcoming (19:20). Why was "bearing false witness" such a big deal back in ancient Israel? And what does it mean for us today?

Narrowly understood, the commandment's concern is with justice in legal matters. There was a persistent concern in ancient Israel that persons not be wrongly convicted of acts they did not commit. Understood more broadly, though, the implications of this word from the Decalogue go far beyond telling the truth in legal proceedings. Yet again, this commandment is really about how to treat the neighbor within a society where neighbors are respected. In his commentary on the Ten Commandments, John Calvin acknowledges

---

22. Augustine, *The Confessions* 2.4. 9, http://www.ourladyswarriors.org/saints/augcon2.htm.

human beings' persistent disregard for this commandment. He writes, "Very few are found who do not notoriously labor under this disease: such is the envenomed delight we take both in prying into and exposing our neighbor's faults."[23]

If the commandments are not just for individuals but also intended to form the foundation of a moral and compassionate society, then it is clear that the understanding of the neighbor should not be limited to persons who live next door but be extended to all members of the community. This nonspatial understanding of neighborliness takes on even more significance in an age of virtual relationships via the Internet. For good and for ill, human relationships are increasingly created, maintained, and discontinued through online communities like Facebook and Twitter. Indeed, "cyber bullying," the act of spreading cruel words about another person online, might be the newest form of bearing false witness against the neighbor. Young people have taken their own lives after rumors about them have spread via social media or after others have posed as romantic partners and then cruelly broken off the relationship. Calvin describes our human predilection to harm one another with our words as the "disease of evil-speaking," cautioning us to be aware that such a disease is not confined to what comes out of our mouths (or through our fingers). It is a malignancy that spreads to the mind as well. When we say something harmful about the neighbor, the action harms us, too. Still more, it poisons our communities.

The differences regarding commands against coveting in the Exodus and Deuteronomy versions of the Decalogue contribute

> **Stealing is one thing, but lying is another. Stealing takes from someone something they have. Lying takes from people what they are: their reputations, their understanding, the quality of their lives. And the really interesting thing is that it takes those things from the one who lies as well as from the one who is lied about.**
>
> Joan Chittister, *The Ten Commandments: Laws of the Heart* (Maryknoll, NY: Orbis Books, 2006), 4–5.

---

23. Calvin, *Institutes* 2.8.9.

to differing views of what constitutes the Ninth and Tenth Commandments. While in Exodus the final commandment begins with the neighbor's house and continues with a list of all other things of the neighbor's the one should not covet (Exod. 20:17), in Deuteronomy the author singles out coveting the neighbor's wife with its own paragraph (Deut. 5:21a) distinct from the paragraph about coveting the house, field, slave, animals, or anything else a neighbor might "own" (5:21b–21c). Why the difference between the two versions? On the one hand, some scholars suggest that separating out the neighbor's wife in Deuteronomy highlights that she's considered property—perhaps the most important property—of a male neighbor. On the other hand, other scholars propose that the wife's separation from the house, field, and so on sets the wife apart as distinct from those other possessions. In both lists, the fundamental issue here is about desiring what is not yours.

One of the dynamics we have been exploring through this commentary on the Decalogue is the relationship between the actions that are encouraged or prohibited by each "word" versus the inner disposition the word encourages. In these prohibitions against coveting, the accent seems to be on the inner disposition—to be content with what you have—more than on a particular action. When we look at other places in Scripture where coveting is addressed, however, we find that it is often linked directly with the act of taking what is not yours. In Micah 2:2, for instance, the prophet condemns the wealthy who "covet fields, and seize them." In Deuteronomy 7:25 Moses commands the Israelites not to covet the gold and silver of the people inhabiting the land "and take it for [themselves]." What these passages help us see is that when we covet what is not ours, it's a small step to acting on it. Augustine's example of stealing pears is relevant here as well—from his retelling of the story, we understand that it's the inner disposition he is most concerned about. Rather than being content with what he already has, Augustine is consumed with wanting what is not his and doing what is prohibited, and he famously admits a restlessness as he searched constantly for what would satisfy his desirous appetite.

"Our hearts are restless until they rest in You," are words from

Augustine's famous prayer. In the last sections of the *Confessions,* he writes about how his desire was satiated when he desired God most of all. In other words, desire is not itself a bad thing. *What* we desire is the primary issue. In his commentary on the commands against coveting, Patrick Miller points us to Deuteronomy 14:26, where Moses directs Israelites to spend the money in the new land "on whatever [they] desire" and tells them that they should eat before the Lord, rejoicing together with members of their households. Miller writes, "The world is full of things pleasant and desirable that the Lord God has provided for our enjoyment. In the context of what God has provided for our desire the specific rules God gives for our daily life, desire is to be enjoyed. . . . From the beginning, desire for the things of this world for our enjoyment is both what it means to be human and what it means to be a member of the covenant community."[24] Within the boundaries of loving God before all others and protecting all that is the neighbor's, we are encouraged to enjoy the good gifts of creation and community God has provided. Far more than being simply a list of prohibitions for us to follow, the Ten Commandments continue to offer wisdom and edification for us today.

> [Moses] not only gave the law, but was there when men were to fulfill it. When things went wrong, he explained the law and reestablished it. Yet this explanation of the fifth book really contains nothing else than faith toward God and love toward one's neighbor, for all God's laws come to that.
>
> Martin Luther, "Preface to the Old Testament," in *Martin Luther's Basic Theological Writings,* ed. Timothy Lull (Minneapolis: Fortress Press, 1989), 121–22.

5:22–33

Moses as Mediator

Following the clear demarcation of the Ten Commandments, Moses returns to the evocative imagery of God's hiddenness in fire, clouds, and darkness. Confronted with such terrifying displays of power, the

24. Miller, *Ten Commandments,* 413.

people are afraid. They ask, "'For who is there of all flesh that has heard the voice of the living God speaking out of fire, as we have, and remained alive?'" (5:26). In the midst of their fear, the Israelites come to a realization: Moses seems to be able to survive such an experience. "'Go near,'" the people implore him. Be our mediator. Report back to us what God wants us to hear, "'and we will listen and do it'" (v. 27). Moses makes it clear that the people have called on him to serve as mediator between the people and God. Once again we see that it is only Moses who sees the face of God, the only one who speaks the words of God.

In 5:28, Moses invokes God's words yet again. He reports on God's affirmation of the people's understanding of where things stand: that human beings do risk death by being in the presence of God and that in Moses the people have exactly what they want and need: a mediator. We are quickly reminded, however, that contrary to what the people might have claimed, they will not follow the commands. "'If only they had such a mind as this, to fear me and to keep all my commandments always, so that all might go well with them and with their children forever!'" God complains to Moses (v. 29).

But from the vantage point of the story line in Deuteronomy, there is still hope for the current generation of Israelites. Moses tells the people that God commissions him to go and teach the commandments, statutes, and ordinances "so that [they] may live, and that it may go well with [them]." Moses offers hope, but the decision to obey still rests with Israel. He mediates between God and the people, but the people, we hear again and again in Deuteronomy, choose to disobey God and turn from following the commands God has set out for them.

The book of Deuteronomy concludes with claims about Moses that give us pause: we hear that *never since* Moses has there been a prophet like him in Israel; that he was *unequaled* in his service of God and in his leadership of Israel out of Egypt to the edge of the promised land. The concluding verses of chapter 5 highlight Moses' exceptional status as unparalleled leader of Israel and mediator between the people and God.

6:1–9

The Heart of the Law and the Covenant

Chapter 6 is the pivotal chapter on which the remainder of Deuteronomy rests. Chapters 1–4 recount the story of God's faithfulness in the past whereas chapters 6–28 focus on the commandments and laws to guide the Israelites' action in the present and near future. Moses' words at the beginning of chapter 6 signal the importance of what follows: not only will he give *the* commandment that Israel is to keep, but he will also deliver teachings on "the statutes and ordinances" that follow from this central commandment. The command Moses will give has become known as "the Great Commandment" not only to Jews but to Jesus (who, of course, was also a Jew) and his followers (cf. Matt. 22:36–40). This pivotal section of the book begins with Moses' explicit claim that God has charged him not simply to give Israel the law but "to teach" the descendants of Israel so that their days may be long and that it may go well with them in this new land (6:2–3). To live under the covenantal promise forged between God and the ancestors means that Israel is called to be a responsible partner in this covenantal relationship (6:10).

Close readers of the text will see that 6:4–5 actually re-present the First Commandment given in 5:6–7. In chapter 5, Moses carries God's words to the people, beginning in 5:6 with God's now-familiar

> "Teacher, which commandment in the law is the greatest?" He said to him, "'You shall love the Lord your God with all your heart, and with all your soul, and with all your mind.' This is the greatest and first commandment. And a second is like it: 'You shall love your neighbor as yourself.' On these two commandments hang all the law and the prophets."
>
> (Matt. 22:36–40)

> All the commandments are explications of the one commandment, to love God and to cleave to him (Deut. 6:5), and this one commandment is but the reverse side of the promise. It commands (*gebietet*) what the promise offers (*bietet*).
>
> Jürgen Moltmann, *The Theology of Hope: On the Ground and the Implications of a Christian Eschatology* (New York: Harper & Row, 1967), 121.

self-description: "I am the LORD your God, who brought you out of Egypt, out of the house of slavery." The confession with which 6:4 begins—the claim that the Lord is one—is intimately connected to God's self-description in 5:6. God's oneness is inseparable from God's identity as liberator. Thus the Great Commandment begins with the affirmation that this God who gives Israel commands to follow is the God who freed Israel from bondage. The same God who gave them life beyond slavery also gives them life through the commands. This God is undivided in identity.

Martin Buber's image of the flowing stream of Israel's history is once again apt: there is but one location for the stream that flows from this God who freed Israel. The ambiguity of the Hebrew word used to describe God as one, we must note, has created significant debate over the centuries. The word *'ehad* can be translated as "one" or "alone." Many emphasize God's undivided nature; at the same time, others argue that this claim stands as a confession of mono-theism. Whichever translation we may choose, we are left with a call for Israel's undivided allegiance to this one God. In chapter 5, God's self-description as the one who led Israel out of slavery is followed by the First Commandment as we most commonly hear it: "You shall have no other gods before me" (5:7). What follows from Moses' description of God's identity in 6:4—that God is "our God" and is one—is the positive recasting of the same commandment. To have no other gods before God means, then, "You shall love the LORD your God with all your heart, and with all your soul, and with all your might" (6:5).

> For the great command follows on a prior impulse named grace. We are commanded to love the One who has first loved us—more, who has lighted in us the flame of divine life. Thus the command signals a kind of recognition scene. Like knows Like, and is known; Like embraces Like, and is embraced. It is the holy in us who knows the Holy. It is the love of God in us that enables love. Like heliotropes, we turn to the Light, toward the God who first named us: "Mine."
>
> Daniel Berrigan, *Deuteronomy: No Gods but One* (Grand Rapids: Wm. B. Eerdmans Publishing Co., 2009), 45.

The word *Shema* itself means "listen," and the recital of the Shema is a supreme act of faith-as-listening: to the voice that brought the universe into being, created us in love and guides us through our lives.

Rabbi Jonathan Sacks, *The Koren Sacks Siddur: A Hebrew/English Prayerbook.* (Jerusalem: Koren, 2009), 96, as cited in Lois Tverberg, *Walking in the Dust of Rabbi Jesus* (Grand Rapids : Zondervan, 2011), 31.

This powerful Deuteronomic passage is well known to Christians. To say it is well known to Jews, however, is a great understatement. In Jewish circles, 6:4–9 is called the *Shema* (the Hebrew word for "hear" or "listen," which is the first word of the passage). The entire Shema recited by Jews also includes Deuteronomy 11:13–21 and Numbers 15:37–41. The Shema is the first prayer a Jewish child learns, and it is recited each morning and evening by Jews throughout the world.

FURTHER REFLECTIONS
The Greatest Commandment

That the Shema is vital for Jews is good to know, but what importance does the confession and command of the Shema have for Christians? As mentioned above, it is clear from the New Testament writings about Jesus that he, too, understood it as the Greatest Commandment. Asked by a lawyer in Matthew's Gospel (22:34–40), "'Teacher, which commandment in the law is the greatest?'" Jesus responds by reciting the words of the Shema, proclaiming that "'This is the greatest and first commandment.'" Then he also adds,

I began to understand that idolatry was more than the literal worshiping of graven images when I was able to see it in the context of the great commandment that Jesus gives in the gospels, to love God with all your heart and soul, and to love your neighbor as yourself. And all of these loves are interrelated: self-love is nothing if it doesn't include the love of our neighbor, and of the God who created us all in the divine image. A measure of balance in these objects of our devotion is a safeguard against idolatry, which can give any of the three too much weight.

Kathleen Norris, *Amazing Grace: A Vocabulary of Faith.* (New York: Riverhead Books, 1998), 88.

> *Thou SHALT love thy neighbor.* . . . In this *Thou shalt* every divine *Thou shalt not—not commit adultery; not kill; not steal; not covet* (Exod. xx:13–17, Deut. v. 17)—is summed up! In it the man who has been compelled to that 'not-doing' which in his turning back to God is once again impelled by God to action. . . . In this *Thou shalt!* there is manifested the flaming sword of death and of eternity. Therefore love is in itself perfect: it is the NEW doing, THE new doing, which is the meaning and fulfillment of all 'not-doing'.
>
> Karl Barth, *Romans*, trans. Edwyn C. Hoskyns (London: Oxford University Press, 1968), 496.

"'You shall love your neighbor as yourself'" (cf. Lev. 19:18). Jesus concludes by saying, "'On these two commandments hang the law and the prophets'" (see also Mark 12:28–34 and Luke 10:25–28 for invocation of the Shema and the Lev. 19 passage).

While Christians often envision Jesus as one who defied Jewish law and broke with his religious past, we see that with respect to the Shema, Jesus remains true to the Jewish conviction that this is the central command of faith. That Jesus links the Shema to the Leviticus 19 passage about loving one's neighbor also conveys a message that lies at the heart of Deuteronomy as well: to know God is to live out God's will in the world.

As we saw earlier in Deuteronomy, God's love for Israel, evidenced in and through God's covenant with Israel, calls for Israel to respond in kind. As God's people, then, following the commands is bound up with loving this God who issues such commands. In his interpretation of this passage, Martin Luther weds tightly the call for allegiance to God alone to the call to love God and all of God's creation. Luther writes,

> This means, not that we should love nothing else—since everything God has made is very good and should be loved—but that in love nothing should be made equal to or put ahead of God and the things that are of God, and that the love of all things is to be pressed toward fulfilling the love of God.[25]

25. Martin Luther, *Luther's Works*, vol. 9 (St. Louis: Concordia Publishing House, 1960), *LW* 9:68.

If God is loved as fully as Moses proposes, then human allegiance to all else will fall into place. As biblical scholar Patrick Miller suggests, the Shema is more than a demand; it is what makes life possible.[26]

The depth at which God's people are called to listen to, follow, and love God is powerfully illustrated in 6:6–9. Moses calls on the Israelites to keep these words in their hearts (v. 6). It is in this section where Christians can find significant challenge to our tendency to view the Old Testament, the Pentateuch, and the book of Deuteronomy as primarily narratives about external laws, rules, and commands. What the Shema in 6:4–9 gives us is a very different view of these commands. It demonstrates that God's commands are anchored in God's love; following the commands, then, means first and foremost that God's people are called to love God, and from such love obedience to God's ways will inevitably follow.

Moses' catechetical teaching about the Great Commandment moves in verse 7 to the command that Israel pass down these teachings, reciting them "when [they] are at home and when [they] are away, when [they] lie down and when [they] rise." If living rightly is primarily about relationship, as biblical scholar Marcus Borg suggests,[27] it is incumbent on the people of God to pass on the faith.

Jews and Christians alike build on this call of Moses for passing down the knowledge of the faith. But as verses 8–9 demonstrate, Moses calls on the Israelites to be connected to the word of God in physical, embodied ways. Since ancient times, many forms of Jewish practice have taken the call to bind these words to one's body literally. While Christian theologians like John Calvin have expressed concern that the phylacteries (another name for tefillin, which refers to black boxes containing scrolls of parchment that include verses from the Torah) encourage

> No, the word is very near to you; it is in your mouth and in your heart for you to observe.
>
> (Deut. 30:14)

---

26. Miller, *Ten Commandments*, 103.
27. Marcus Borg, as cited in Rev. W. Matthew Broadbent's sermon "Perfecting Faith," Feb. 2011, http://www.foothills-church.org/sermon-2-13-11.pdf.

viewing holiness as an external mark,[28] let us take note of the power of the physical connection to God's word. Like the words of Deuteronomy 30:14, the actions prescribed in chapter 6 emphasize in physical terms how near the word is to God's people.

6:10–25
Israel's Very Life as Gift

In these verses Moses turns to Israel's imminent entrance into the land God promised them. His description in verses 10–12 of the land awaiting the Israelites is heavy with claims that the land comes as sheer gift from God. It is full of cities they did not build, goods they did not buy, and food they did not plant. Lest they miss the point, Moses is direct: "Take care that you do not forget" (v. 12) that it is the God who led you out of Egypt who is giving you these things.

> Now, tardily, we have an admission: a "Canaanite people" exists. Such being the case, embarrassment arises. How explain the decree of their extinction? What necessity governs it?
>
> Daniel Berrigan, *No Gods but One* (Grand Rapids: Wm. B. Eerdmans Publishing Co., 2009), 72.

FURTHER REFLECTIONS
The Promised Land as Occupied Land

While it is clear that the hearers of Deuteronomy should get the point that Israel's imminent entrance into the land of Canaan is due solely to action on God's part and not at all because of any righteousness on Israel's part, we cannot ignore the fact that these cities that Israel did not build and the vineyards they did not plant were indeed built and planted by other people, people who, as we will see shortly, are reportedly destroyed by Israel at God's command. What can we say about this disconcerting reality?

---

28. John Calvin, *Harmony of the Law,* vol. 1, (Grand Rapids: Christian Classics Ethereal Library, 1998), 351, http://www.ccel.org/ccel/calvin/calcom03.v. viii.html.

Even though scholars agree that the actual historical narrative about the Israelites' move into Canaan is much messier than the biblical narrative suggests, we nevertheless must deal with the theological implications of a biblical narrative where God gives over to Israel land that is already inhabited by others. It is important to remember that, as indicated in chapter 2, the Deuteronomist hints that Israel is not the only nation to be given land by God (cf. 2:5–23). Indeed, Deuteronomy 2:22–23 suggests that God intervened on behalf of other nations in order that they have access to occupied land as well. While God's work on behalf of other nations receives only fleeting attention in Deuteronomy, there is nevertheless the suggestion that other nations are not merely stage props in the Israelite drama of journeying into the occupied land of Canaan; those other nations are also recipients of God's ongoing care, concern, and protection.

That said, a jarring tension remains between those views of God as protector of other nations and God's endorsement of Israel's occupation of the land of Canaan.

Many contemporary Jews contend that the land of Israel should be a state for Jews as well as a Jewish state, a nation suffused with core Jewish values of compassion and righteousness. But the challenge of how to treat non-Jews residing in the land is an ever-present issue, one that is still far from resolution today.

While Christians may acknowledge and lift up their discomfort over Jewish claims to land that other people have inhabited, it seems that we should also consider theologian Kendall Soulen's observation that the theme of God's giving land to God's chosen people has long made Christians uncomfortable. While Soulen agrees that concern for the well-being of all inhabitants of Israel today, whether Jew, Arab, or other, is certainly justified, he also wonders if Christian discomfort with the idea of God's giving Israel this land "also reflects a predisposition to overlook that dimension of the biblical testimony that is chiefly concerned with God's blessing in contrast to God's redemption. For God's gift of land is above all a life-giving embodiment of God's promised blessing on Israel."[29] It

---

29. R. Kendall Soulen, *The God of Israel and Christian Theology* (Minneapolis: Fortress Press, 1996), 124.

is vital to acknowledge that the role of the land in Deuteronomy—and in the wider story of Israel's history—does not merely serve as a backdrop for God's acts of deliverance and salvation. Canaan is a particular place where Israel's life is to be lived in covenantal relationship with its God, a place where particular attention is paid to the most vulnerable, and a place that supports the idea of the good life not just for Israel but for all nations (cf. Gen. 17). God's election of Israel is scandalously concrete and, we hear repeatedly, has positive ramifications for other nations beyond Israel. Still, the disturbing reality that Israel's move into the land of Canaan will displace others who are scandalously concrete remains, and we must continue to wrestle with this abiding tension.

Verses 13–19 emphasize yet again several themes frequently sounded throughout Deuteronomy: worship God alone, for God is a jealous and angry God; adhere to the commandments, statutes, and ordinances given to you by Moses; and do these things so that all may go well for you in the land promised to your ancestors.

Verses 20–25 review the foundational event of Israel's past. Those familiar with the Jewish seder know that just as in these verses in Deuteronomy, a child at the seder asks the questions that lead to the recounting of the Israelites' former identity—Pharaoh's slaves in Egypt—and how they were freed by the Lord, who brought them out of Egypt with a mighty hand. In 6:23 the NRSV translation says that God promised to give "on oath" the land promised to the ancestors. Biblical scholar Walter Brueggemann, however, points out that the English translation of the Hebrew word *sb'* in verse 23 is more accurately "to swear" and encourages interpreting the passage with this wording instead. Brueggemann writes, "God speaks an obligation

> The word "jealousy" has its root in "zealous," denoting extreme enthusiasm and devotion, and God's jealousy retains the word's more positive aspects. It helps us to trust. Who, after all, would trust a God, a parent, a spouse, or love, who said to us, "I really love you, but I don't care at all what you do or who you become?"
>
> Kathleen Norris, *Amazing Grace: A Vocabulary of Faith* (New York: Riverhead Books, 1998), 87.

to Godself about the future of Israel: this is not to be flattened into 'word of God,' this is out-loud speech: swear, give, bless."[30] Understanding this passage in terms of God's sworn obligation to Israel highlights again that the covenant between God and Israel is two-sided and that Israel's life depends on God's sworn commitment to be Israel's God and to give them the land God has promised.

7:1–26

Holy War and Its Limits: Saying "No" to the God of Militarism

After setting forth a positive explanation of the First Commandment—that allegiance to God entails love of God—chapters 7–10 set forth and reflect on other gods that Israel will be tempted to worship in Canaan. Biblical scholar Dennis Olson suggests that the first of three false gods to be named in chapters 7–10 is militarism.[31] This section calls Israel to holy war, and while we cannot ignore the brutality of the war imagery, we also must pay attention to Moses' cautions about how Israel should interpret its impending victory over the Canaanite peoples.

Moses' instructions to Israel about how they should enter Canaan and destroy the peoples living there is yet another episode of retelling in Deuteronomy of the well-known stories of Israel's past. This story of entrance and occupation of the land appears twice in Exodus (23:20–33 and 34:11–16) as well as in Numbers (33:50–56), and once again, the distinctive way it is told here helps illumine the Deuteronomistic theology at work in the text.

In the Deuteronomy version, the angel who leads Israel safely into the land in Exodus 23 has vanished, leaving it to God alone. The absence of any type of mediator between God and God's people serves to emphasize the Deuteronomist's focus on the allegiance to God alone, a theme prevalent in the previous chapter as well. The

---

30. Walter Brueggemann, *Theology of the Old Testament: Testimony, Dispute, Advocacy* (Minneapolis: Fortress Press, 2005), 165.
31. Dennis Olson, *Deuteronomy and the Death of Moses: A Theological Reading* (Minneapolis: Augsburg Fortress, 1994), chap. 4.

other difference between the Deuteronomy version and the earlier ones is significant: in the Exodus and Numbers accounts, the Israelites are told to drive out the various tribes who inhabit Canaan, while in Deuteronomy, Israel is told by God to "utterly destroy them" and "show them no mercy" (7:2). What do we make of this disturbing difference?

This is one of only a few passages within the biblical narrative that advocate total annihilation of a group of people. And as biblical scholar Johanna van Wijk-Bos insists, "The Bible itself in its entire witness makes a problem of the violence encouraged in Deuteronomy 7."[32] Indeed, this call for slaughter of the occupants of Canaan stands in direct tension to the Deuteronomic preoccupation with the welfare of the stranger, the widow, and the orphan. Still, it is part of the text: God commands annihilation of human and nonhuman life. What are we to say in response?

FURTHER REFLECTIONS
Slaughter of the Innocent

Centuries of Jewish and Christian commentators on this chapter have expressed skepticism that wholesale destruction of the Canaanites actually occurred. In fact, most contemporary biblical scholars and archaeologists suggest that Israel's movement into Canaan was much more gradual than is depicted in the text and that Israel and the various tribes of Canaan likely comingled. Many contemporary scholars believe that the rhetoric in this passage— and the other sections of Deuteronomy that call for destruction of groups of people (cf. 20:16–18)—is likely more revealing of the mood of a later prophetic movement than it is a reflection of actual historical events. Biblical scholar Lucien Legrand argues that the rhetoric became more radical because the prophets had little sense that their vision "could be translated into real policy."[33] Knowing

---

32. Johanna W. H. van Wijk-Bos, *Making Wise the Simple: The Torah in Christian Faith and Practice* (Grand Rapids: Wm. B. Eerdmans Publishing Co., 2005), 267.
33. Lucien Legrand, *The Bible on Culture: Belonging or Dissenting?* trans. Robert J. Schreiter, (Maryknoll, NY: Orbis Books, 2000), 7.

that these words were likely written and heard in a context of exile, where Israel had no ability to wage war of any kind, might lessen the immediate offense of the Deuteronomistic calls for destruction of others.

We who claim that the Bible is God's Word might breathe a bit easier after hearing those words—that God's calls for destruction of human life can be chalked up to zealous prophetic speech that was more flourish than fact. Still, does the claim that Canaanite destruction likely didn't happen do much to mitigate the fact that God's Word calls for the destruction of human life?

To answer this question, we must address the question of *why* God would call for such destruction in the first place. One justification given for the impending conquest of Canaan is God's judgment on the Canaanites for defiling the land, and Israel is warned it will suffer the same fate if it does not keep the commandments (cf. Lev. 18:24–30; 20:22–23). That said, it is important to note—even though it does not diminish the harshness—that the reason for the destruction is not based on ethnicity or some kind of nationalistic pride. In verse 4 we are reminded of why Israel cannot live with the Canaanites: if they live together—especially if they intermarry—the belief is that Israelites will defile the land by turning away from God and toward the gods of the others. Thus, at least in the narrative flow of Deuteronomy, the primary issue at stake in chapter 7 is Israel's obedience to the First Commandment to have no other gods before God. In order to faithfully fulfill this command, Moses insists that Israel not only needs to destroy the people of Canaan but also all of their altars, pillars, sacred poles, and idols (v. 5). Contrary to the common ancient practice of keeping the spoils of war, Israel is commanded to destroy it all. While we can observe that the aim of such wholesale destruction is to get rid of any and all temptations to idolatry by Israelites, rather than aiming to destroy the Canaanite people for the sake of destroying human life, the horror of such a request remains.

As we discussed in the introduction, the God of Deuteronomy—indeed, the God of the biblical narrative—is at once wrathful and merciful, violent and compassionate, angry and loving. This is an irresolvable tension. Jewish scholar David Blumenthal addresses such tensions directly in his controversial work *Facing the Abusive God: A Theology of Protest.*[34] In it Blumenthal argues that people who believe in the biblical God must acknowledge that God as *both* loving *and* abusive. Understandably Blumenthal's thesis has been met with much critique. In response, Blumenthal references the subtitle of his book, saying, "To protest, however, is to engage. To protest is to remain connected. To protest is to love, but to assert the rights inherent in the covenant.... That is religious monotheism at its best."[35] From the perspective of Deuteronomy 7, it is difficult to mount a defense against Blumenthal's claim that God is abusive. The brutality of the portrayal of God in Deuteronomy 7 must be acknowledged. At the same time, this commentary will side with van Wijk-Bos and argue that the more prevalent images of Israel's God in Deuteronomy and in the Bible as a whole depict God as more compassionate and loving than violent. Still the tension persists without clear resolution.

Finally, we also remember that it is a brutal vision, heard by a people despairing in exile, banished from the land and the life promised them by God. A central recurring theme of the book of Deuteronomy is that Israel will stray from worshiping God and following the commands they've been given. This story, we know, is told to those who struggle in the aftermath of Israel's wandering away from allegiance to their God.

As soon as Moses finishes telling Israel they will succeed in destroying the Canaanites and their foreign forms of worship, his speech moves to talk of Israel's special status as God's covenant people. Here Moses elaborates on the rationale for Israel's chosenness that he presented in 4:37. Just as in chapter 4, Moses recounts that Israel's chosenness is due purely to God's action. In his description of Israel's special status, Moses uses powerful words: God "set his heart" on Israel. Commenting on Moses' language in this passage, Johanna

---

34. David R. Blumenthal, *Facing the Abusive God: A Theology of Protest* (Louisville, KY: Westminster John Knox Press, 2002).

35. David Blumenthal, *Protesting the Abusive God,* letter to the editor, *The Chronicle of Higher Education,* Jan. 30, 2011, http://chronicle.com/article/Protesting-an-Abusive-God/126065/.

A little further on, therefore, [Moses] will say that those who then survived were dear to God, because He had already loved their fathers. But now he still further commends the goodness of God, because He had handed down His covenant from the fathers to the children, to shew that He is faithful and true to His promises. At the end of the verse, he teaches that the deliverance of the people was both an effect and a testimony of that grace.

John Calvin, *Commentaries on the Last Four Books of Moses, arranged in the form of a Harmony*, vol. 1, trans. Charles William Bingham (Grand Rapids: Wm. B. Eerdmans Publishing Co., 1950), 356-57.

van Wijk-Bos observes, "Lest we miss the point, to love and choice is here [in Deut. 7:7–8] added 'desire,' a word used elsewhere in the Bible of sexual love."[36] Not because of any inherent quality within Israel, not because they were mighty or great—indeed, Moses insists they were "the fewest of all people"—but simply because God has wed Godself to Israel. God is intimately bound to Israel, desires to be with Israel, and cannot bear the thought of life without Israel (Hos. 11:8–9).

How can I give up on you, Ephraim? How can I hand you over, O Israel? How can I make you like Admah? How can I treat you like Zoboiim? My heart recoils within me; my compassion grows warm and tender. I will not execute my fierce anger; I will not again destroy Ephraim; for I am God and no mortal, the Holy One in your midst, and I will not come in wrath.

(Hos. 11:8–9)

These affirmations of God's desire and love for Israel undergird Moses' charge to trust in God as they go to fight rather than putting their faith in the god of militarism. He assures the people that obedience to God's statutes and ordinances (v. 11) will translate into victory in battle against the Canaanites. Amid the discomforting claims of God's securing military victory for Israel, we note that the rhetorical thrust of the chapter is to be found in these verses about Israel's chosen status. The point here hearkens back to claims made by Moses in earlier chapters (e.g., 2:33; 3:3): that any and all military victory Israel enjoys is because

36. Van Wijk-Bos, *Making Wise the Simple*, 256.

of God alone. From God's foundational act of freeing Israel from bondage in Egypt, Israel's very existence is due to God's liberating and loving care. The exodus story is invoked yet again (especially in vv. 15, 18–19) to exhort the people to confront the astonishing narrative of their own past: that this liberator God enabled this enslaved band of people to triumph over Egypt's imperial might. God's self-identity is re-presented. Israel's response is replayed: God is one; love God and keep God's commands. Israel on its own is not mighty. The Israelites cannot put their trust in their own military prowess; their trust must be in God alone.

FURTHER REFLECTIONS
Chosenness

Jewish scholars and practitioners have long wrestled with what it means for the Jews to be chosen by God. Given the long and disturbing history of Jewish persecution, many Jews have clung to the affirmation of chosenness as support for their continued existence. More recently, however, some Jews have called for abandoning the designation because of the way it separates Jews from others, often in a hierarchical manner. Feminist Jewish scholar Judith Plaskow has proposed that Jews shift from chosenness to distinctiveness, emphasizing Jews' distinctive history as people of the one

---

The love of God is here referred back from the children to the fathers; for [Moses] addressed the men of his own generation, when he said that they were therefore God's treasure, because He loved them; now he adds that God had not just begun to love them for the first time, but that He had originally loved their fathers, when He chose to adopt Abraham, Isaac, and Jacob.

But although he more clearly proves that the descendants of Abraham had deserved nothing of the kind, because they are God's peculiar people only by right of inheritance, still it must be remarked that God was induced to be kind to Abraham by no other cause than mere generosity.

John Calvin, *Commentaries on the Last Four Books of Moses*, 353.

In Judaism election is not a gift, but rather a task; no contract with God, but rather his holy mission; no honor, but rather a heavy burden which is necessary to bear and to realize. Whoever has doubts about its continuing validity should reflect upon the passion of Israel, a two-thousand-year road of suffering, and should remember keenly the servant of God who is docile "like a lamb that is led to the slaughter" (Isa. 53:7).

Karl Rahner and Pinchas Lapide, *Encountering Jesus—Encountering Judaism: A Dialogue* (New York: Crossroad, 1987), 17.

God without, Plaskow suggests, any claims to superiority.[37] Rabbi Adam Spilker, the rabbi at Mount Zion Temple in St. Paul, Minnesota, where I have attended torah study, speaks of Jews as "God's treasured people" rather than God's chosen ones. Building on Deuteronomy's claim of Israel as God's "treasured possession" (7:6; 14:2; 26:18; see also Exod. 19:6), Rabbi Spilker suggests that the term *treasured* connotes God's deep love for God's people, but he argues that it also suggests a special responsibility to live in the world as people of compassion and righteousness.

While it was mentioned in the introduction that Christian theologians have often usurped the "chosenness" nomenclature in a supersessionist manner, there is also the theological tradition of emphasizing—as we shall do here—the unmerited character of the chosenness designation, be it for Israel or for Christians who see themselves as spiritual descendants of God's original covenant partner. As challenging as it may be to do so, we want to hold in tension this profoundly discomforting rhetoric of Israel's call to slaughter others with the powerful imagery of Israel's chosenness based solely on God's love.

Immediately following Moses' insistence that God's love for Israel is sheer gift, we hear a conditional claim in 7:12–13 that stands in tension to what we just heard: *if* Israel obeys all the commands, *then* God will "love [them], bless [them], and multiply [them]." This tension between God's sovereign control of Israel's destiny and the

---

37. Judith Plaskow, *Standing Again at Sinai: Judaism from a Feminist Perspective* (San Francisco: HarperOne, 1991), 101–4.

command that Israel faithfully follow God-given statutes and ordinances does not neatly resolve itself throughout the Deuteronomic writings. Indeed, this tension between God's rewarding Israel's obedience and God's punishing Israel's disobedience continues up to the present day for Jews and for Christians, especially in light of events like the Holocaust. If we follow the theological claim that God's chosen people suffer at God's hand due to their own disobedience, we can end up with the revolting conclusion that God used Hitler to punish Jews for something they did (or did not do). While there are Jews and Christians who believe that is the only logical conclusion for those who desire to uphold belief in God's sovereignty, many other Jews and Christians reject such an interpretation and instead emphasize that there is more than one scriptural logic in effect in Deuteronomy and other OT books. In his influential text titled *After Auschwitz*, Jewish rabbi and scholar Richard Rubenstein is articulate in his rejection of any theology that even hints at Jewish responsibility for the Holocaust. At the same time, Rubenstein communicates with piercing honesty the challenge of remaining a person of faith who believes in the God who chose the Jews to be God's treasured people in light of horrific suffering and pain:

> For those of us who lived through the terrible years, whether in safety or as victims, the *Shoah* conditions the way we encounter all things sacred and profane. Nothing in our experience is untouched by that absolutely decisive event. Because of the *Shoah*, some of us enter the synagogue to partake of our sacred times and seasons with those to whom we are bound in shared memory, pain, fate, and hope; yet, once inside, we are struck dumb by words we can no longer honestly utter. All that we can offer is our reverent and attentive silence before the Divine.[38]

As we discussed in the commentary introduction, Christians tend to want to resolve such biblical and theological tensions. Perhaps we have more to learn from our Jewish sisters and brothers about how

---

38. Richard L. Rubenstein, *After Auschwitz: History, Theology, and Contemporary Judaism,* 2nd ed. (Baltimore: Johns Hopkins University Press, 1992), 200.

to live with and in the midst of tensions about the nature of God and God's relationship to God's people that will not go away.

Continuing his focus on Israel's impending military battles with other groups, Moses also discourages Israel from trusting too little in God's ability to grant them victory in war in 7:17–26. To ward off doubts or fears on the part of the Israelites that their enemies may have mightier militaries than their own, Moses reminds them again that the God to whom they belong is the "great and awesome God" (v. 21) who led them out of Egypt. God's identity and God's fidelity are consistent, and God will provide what Israel needs.

The chapter concludes with more troubling words: the Lord will hand the kings of the Canaanites over to Israel and Israel "shall blot out their name from under heaven" (v. 24). Even worse for Israel, if they attempt to take any of the spoils of war for themselves instead of destroying them as instructed, those Israelites—just like their ene-mies—"will be set apart for destruction" too (v. 26). Scholars have noted the similarities between these verses and the language and format of ancient suzerain treaties that contain lists of blessings that will come from following the conditions of the treaties along with lists of curses that will follow if the terms of the treaty are ignored. The brief list of curses here is but a small foretaste of the expansive lists of curses in chapters 27–28, where again we will have to wrestle with the image of God as bringer of curses, death, and destruction.

8:1–20

Do Not Forget: Warnings against the God of Materialism

Chapter 8 begins with Moses telling Israel that its forty years in the wilderness was, in fact, a test or a trial brought on by God. The NRSV states that God did this to "humble" Israel, but biblical scholar Rob-ert Alter observes that the word "afflict" is a more suitable English form of the Hebrew word *'inah*. This verb appears in 6:16, when Moses warns Israel against "afflicting" or testing God through dis-obedience. This verb is also used in the story of Abraham and Isaac to describe what it is that God does to Abraham by demanding the sacrifice.[39] Such affliction leads again, Moses seems to be insisting, to the recognition that God is in charge. One more time Moses reminds the Israelites that keeping God's commands is not merely a matter of external conformity to particular laws. Instead Moses emphasizes that it is a matter of the heart (v. 2), of internal conformity to God's commands.

This section helps illumine why Christian references to Deuteronomy and the other books of the Pentateuch as "books of the law" can be misleading, for Moses' impartation of torah in Deuteronomy is much more expansive than simply a giving of laws. Moses suggests that life in covenantal relationship to God orients one's heart as well as one's mind and spirit. And when the community fails to embody faithfulness to that covenantal relationship, one's heart—indeed, one's very life—is in a state of affliction.

Verse 3 ends with words Christians also hear in the New Testament: "One does not live by bread alone, but by every word that comes from the mouth of the LORD." Jesus quotes this passage when confronted with Satan's demand to turn stones to bread as a demonstration of his divine power (Matt. 4:4; Luke 4:4). Both Moses' and Jesus' use of these words indicates again that the physical, external compliance to a set of rules is not all that matters. Rather, fidelity to God is also an internal, spiritual matter as Jesus demonstrates in his refusal to be tempted by the physical displays of power with which Satan attempts to bait him.

But when we juxtapose the claim to living by God's word in 8:3 to Moses' recounting of how God fed Israel while they wandered the wilderness in 8:16, it becomes clear that while one's spiritual, internal state matters greatly, physical bread is important too. In his own interpretation of these passages, Martin Luther notes that God gives Israel bread in the wilderness "[so] that the immeasurable care of God for us might be praised. He is a God to us and dispenses everything bountifully also when everything is most hopeless." For Luther, then, this section that begins with the assertion that we do not live by bread alone and moves to its conclusion by reemphasizing

39. Robert Alter, *The Five Books of Moses: A Translation with Commentary* (New York: W. W. Norton & Co., 2004), 921.

God's role as provider of food that keeps Israel alive once again points us back to the First Commandment. Luther writes, "[So] where abundance prevails, do not be puffed up or carelessly forget God. Whether everything is on hand or everything is lacking, cling to your God always with the same heart."[40] In Luther's theology, just as in the Deuteronomistic theology, our internal and external lives are intimately interrelated.

FURTHER REFLECTIONS
Parent God

In Deuteronomy 8:5 Moses uses parental imagery to make his point about God's disciplining Israel when it disobeys. Again heart language is used: "know in your heart" that God treats you as a parent treats his or her children. It is not the first time in Deuteronomy that God is imaged as a parent. Recall that in 1:31 Moses tells Israel that God has carried them from Egypt to safety "as one carries a child." While the parental imagery of Deuteronomy is decidedly less pronounced than the image of God as divine warrior, it nevertheless deserves attention. There has been a theological tradition that stretches from Augustine to Julian of Norwich and even to Pope John Paul II of exploring and lifting up parental images for God and suggesting that such images evoke the view not only of God as Divine Father but also as Divine Mother.

> God is our father; even more God is our mother. God does not want to hurt us, but only to do good for us, all of us. If children are ill, they have additional claim to be loved by their mother. And we too, if by chance we are sick with badness and are on the wrong track, have yet another claim to be loved by the Lord.
>
> Pope John Paul II, *Osservatore Romano*, Engl. ed., September 21, 1978, 2.

While Deut. 1:31 suggests an image of God as intimate, caring, and protective, characteristics often associated with mothering, feminist theologian Elizabeth Johnson also makes the point that

---

40. Luther, *LW* 9:96.

Christianity—even in its feminist hue—can ill afford to abandon the notion of God's wrath, an aspect of God's character present in the parental imagery of discipline in Deuteronomy 8:5. Johnson writes, "The wrath of God is a symbol of holy mystery we can ill afford to lose....True, God's anger lasts but a moment; true, it is always instrumental, aimed at change and conversion. But it stands as an antidote to sentimentality in our view of God's holy mystery as love."[41] The discipline of which Moses speaks comes to a people who have done exactly what Moses bade them not to do: they have forgotten God, their parent, and God's vision for a blessed, fulfilled life. And in Deuteronomy 8, God's parentlike discipline is related to God's wrath over Israel's straying from God's commands.

Verses 7–10 paint a compelling portrait of the land Israel is poised to inhabit. Some scholars have described this section as "hymnic" as it begins with almost-intoxicating descriptions of a parched people receiving a land flush with water and ends with the claim that the promises of the new land will not simply provide Israel with the necessities but will also be a place where Israel will "lack nothing" (8:9).

Into the midst of this visioning a future of abundance, however, Moses interjects more words of caution: in this place of plenty, do not forget. Do not forget who you are—the people of God—and how you came to occupy the land—by God's hand alone. Do not forget that you were slaves and that the prosperity you will soon enjoy is sheer gift.

With the call not to forget, Moses rhetorically takes the people back, once again, to the First Commandment: hear and remember, O Israel, that your God is one and that you are to love this God with everything you've got. But Moses' call not to forget also includes a warning to Israel to heed the seductive nature of the material life. Moses predicts that when the Israelites come to the point where they lack nothing, they will be tempted to forget their God and begin to neglect the First Commandment.

41. Elizabeth Johnson, *She Who Is: The Mystery of God in Feminist Theological Discourse* (New York: Crossroad, 1991), 258.

From our vantage point as hearers of God's Word in the twenty-first century, it is clear that just as with the god of militarism, the god of materialism continues to tempt us, as it tempted ancient Israel, to idolatry. Theologians from the biblical period onward have attempted to name the particular forms these gods have taken. With the recent emergence of global capitalism, theologians today speak about how consumerism has become a religion that worships the god of accumulation.

Moses warns the people of Israel against becoming caught up in the intoxicating allure of economic prosperity. His mantra of "Do not forget" is accompanied by the call to "remember the LORD your God," remembering, too, that God is the one from whom the prosperity flows. A religion of consumption, as theologian Sallie McFague suggests,[42] is yet another way the people of God will be tempted away from worship of and allegiance to their God. Moses concludes this chapter with these ominous words: "If you do forget the LORD your God and follow other gods . . . you will surely perish" (v. 19). Today we see the deadly effects of global capitalism's worship of consumer culture, not only in the form of depletion of natural resources but also in the modern industrialized complexes that neglect basic worker rights to enable the production of products those of us in affluent contexts consume. Indeed, we have countless contemporary examples of how people of faith have forgotten the call to love the Lord our God and all of God's creation. These

---

If religion, most basically, is that which makes us understand the world and our place in it, then market capitalism and its worldview as epitomized in consumerism, is not only *a* religion but surely one of the most successful. It *is* so successful in part because it has few alternative views of the good life with which to contend. As a result, it can become "invisible," the most desired condition for any ideology. That is, the contemporary economic worldview, resulting in our consumer culture, is generally not considered to be *one* way to live, but the *only* way.

Sallie McFague, *Life Abundant: Rethinking Theology and Economy for a Planet in Peril* (Minneapolis: Fortress Press, 2001), 84.

---

42. Sallie McFague, *Life Abundant: Rethinking Theology and Economy for a Planet in Peril* (Minneapolis: Fortress Press, 2001), 84.

words of Deuteronomy can serve as a wake-up call for contemporary Christians today.

9:1–10:11
Remember: The God of Moralism Is Not Your God

Deuteronomy 9:1 echoes 6:4 as Moses tells Israel once again to "hear" the command of the Lord. In the past Israel has refused to listen but now Moses commands them as they "are about to cross the Jordan" to hear and obey what God is calling them to do. In chapter 9 Moses then reminds Israel that God will lead Israel in to occupy Canaan, a land full of people mightier than Israel. As Moses has said before, Israel's military success is not due to its own military might. In 9:3 Moses again invokes the image of God as a "devouring fire" (cf. 4:11) who will go before Israel and destroy their enemies—in this case the Anakim, the Canaanite tribe feared as gigantic (e.g., see Num. 13:22, 28, 33; Deut. 1:28; 9:2)—quickly and decisively.

The force of this chapter, though, comes when Moses once again makes the point that God will lead Israel to military victory in war not because of any merit or any "uprightness of . . . heart" on the part of Israel (9:5). Moses focuses here on what Martin Luther calls "spiritual pride," the trusting in one's own works of which no "opponent of faith or trust in the mercy of God is more destructive."[43] Misplaced confidence in our own ability to behave righteously, as many know, was at the heart of many Reformation theologians' critiques of late medieval Christianity. Luther uses Moses' discussion of Israel's temptation to bow before the god of moral righteousness to make one of his favorite points—that we humans are constantly tempted to make our own perceived righteousness our own personal god to worship: "Not on account of our righteousness is any good thing given to us, but in order that God may fulfill the Word which He willed from eternity, lest we be puffed up and make an idol out of our righteousness."[44]

43. Luther, *LW* 9:102.
44. Luther, *LW*. 9:102.

In his series of final speeches to the Israelites, Moses tries to get this point to sink in. As we have heard repeatedly throughout the opening chapters of Deuteronomy, Moses reminds the Israelites that they will not inherit the land due to any righteousness on their part. Rather, it is due to the wickedness of the other nations that they will be dispossessed of their land (v. 5). Since the time of Abraham, there has been reference to the sin of the Amorites, one of the nations inhabiting Canaan (cf. Deut. 1:7; Gen. 15:16). References to the Amorites invoke images of idolatry and iniquity (e.g., Josh. 24:15; Judg. 6:10) and thus signal a threat to Israel. At the same time, this chapter stresses that Israel itself is no stranger to sin and wickedness.

> Now if you are unwilling to serve the Lord, choose this day whom you will serve, whether the gods your ancestors served in the region beyond the River or the gods of the Amorites in whose land you are living; but as for me and my household, we will serve the Lord.
>
> (Josh. 24:15)

In order to make piercingly clear that Israel's imminent military victories over the groups inhabiting Canaan should be viewed as having nothing to do with exemplary moral behavior on Israel's part, Moses' speech remains consistently within the Deuteronomic framework of commanding Israel to remember: this time he invokes a litany of examples of Israel's repeated disobedience to God's commands. Beginning with their wanderings in the wilderness, Moses testifies that the Israelites have been "a stubborn people" (v. 7). Moses retells one more time the story of receiving the Ten Commandments at Horeb, stressing that while God was giving him the foundational commands of the covenant, Israel was already deep into disobedience. As we compare Deuteronomy's versions of the Ten Commandments and the golden calf stories to the Exodus versions, we see once again an abbreviated version in Deuteronomy as well as one that highlights Moses' faithful obedience and role as suffering servant and intercessor on the one hand and Israel's brazen disobedience on the other.

Unlike the extended story of the golden calf in Exodus 34 that is told by an omniscient narrator, the abridged version in Deuteronomy

9 is told by Moses in the first person. While both versions report that God orders Moses to attend to the ones that Moses—not God—brought out of Egypt, the way Moses deals with the situation differs in each version. In the Exodus version, God's telling of Israel's disobedience prompts Moses to plead with God then and there for Israel's life. But in Deuteronomy, Moses' retelling depicts Moses as leaving God on the mountain after he hears of Israel's waywardness. Moses then witnesses firsthand the golden calf and proceeds to lay prostrate before the Lord for forty days and forty nights, neither eating nor drinking, all done as intercession on Israel's behalf.

> After the golden calf [in the Deuteronomy version of the story] there is no declaration that Yahweh is slow to anger and abounding in love, forgiving wickedness, rebellion and sin (in contrast to Ex. 34:6–7). . . . There is nothing but the prayer of Moses, the silence of Yahweh and the replacement of the tablets.
>
> J. Gary Millar, *Now Choose Life: Theology and Ethics in Deuteronomy* (Grand Rapids: Wm. B. Eerdmans Publishing Co., 1998), 170.

Theologians have often noted the significance of the number forty and the way it was used throughout the biblical text to signify a time set apart. Augustine, for example, suggested that

> this is why Moses fasted for forty days, and Elijah, and the Mediator himself, the Lord Jesus Christ: because in this time-bound state of ours restraint from bodily attractions and allurements is very necessary. The people also spent forty years wandering in the desert, and forty days of rain produced the flood. The Lord spent forty days after his resurrection with his disciples, to convince them of the reality of his risen body.[45]

What is noteworthy in Deuteronomy 9 is that this is the second time in the Deuteronomic retelling of Israel's history that Moses goes without food and drink for forty days and nights. The first time Moses is on the mountain with God, receiving the commandments. This incident finds a parallel in Exodus 34:28, where in his second

45. Augustine, *Sermon* 51.32, as quoted in *Exodus, Leviticus, Numbers, Deuteronomy*, Ancient Christian Commentary on Scripture, Old Testament 3, ed. Joseph T. Lienhard (Downers Grove, IL: InterVarsity Press, 2001), 253.

reception of the tablets, Moses neither eats nor drinks during the forty days he's with God. But Deuteronomy's reporting of the second fasting in verse 18 has no parallel in the Exodus story. This second prostration is done, we hear, "because of all the sin [Israel] had committed" (v. 18). This act of prostration—which itself resembles the posture of death—reinforces the later theme of Moses' denial and impending death that culminates in chapter 34.

In Exodus, Moses questions why God would want to destroy those whom God had freed from bondage. In Deuteronomy, however, Moses asks no questions of God. The accent is on Moses' extraordinary faithfulness to God and to the people of Israel, as well as on God's heeding of Moses' intercession and God's granting Israel continued existence. The chapter ends with a final, bold intercessory prayer by Moses that uses the same framework of appeal that he uses when speaking to Israel directly: "Remember," he says to God, that these are "the people of your very own possession, whom you brought out by your great power and your outstretched arm" (9:27–29). Just as Moses calls Israel to remember and not forget, so too he calls on God to remember the covenant and the promises God made to this beloved people. And God heeds Moses' call.

The "forty days and forty nights" refrain is repeated no fewer than five times in chapter 9, presenting a stark contrast between Israel's stubborn refusal to hear, listen, and obey and Moses' costly obedience on behalf of the wayward people.

FURTHER REFLECTIONS
Moses as Intercessor

Yet another role of Moses is presented in this portion of Deuteronomy: this time, he is cast in the role of intercessor. In 9:18, Moses "lay prostrate before the Lord" for forty days and forty nights, an act designed to convince God not to destroy the disobedient Israelites. This role is a costly one for Moses—he neither eats nor drinks for those forty days—and this act of intercession is closely tied to Moses' role of suffering servant (e.g., 3:12–29). The Deuteronomic Moses stands in a long line of servants who intercede on behalf of those who sin against God (cf. Isa. 53:13; Amos 7:1–6).

It is extraordinary that, just as with Amos, Moses' plea results in God's changing God's mind. After being reminded of the covenantal relationship, of how God has loved Israel into its present existence, God is persuaded and listens to Moses.

This change of mind occurs also in the New Testament when Jesus is confronted by a Canaanite woman who pleads for healing for her daughter (Matt. 15:21–28). Jesus tries to dismiss her, but she challenges his claim that his ministry is only to Israel, and he reconsiders, telling the woman that her faith is great and that he will heal her daughter (v. 28).

> This is what the Lord GOD showed me: the Lord GOD was calling for a shower of fire, and it devoured the great deep and was eating up the land. Then I said,
>
> > "O Lord GOD, cease, I beg you!
> >
> > > How can Jacob stand?
> > >
> > > He is so small!"
>
> The LORD relented concerning this;
>
> > "This also shall not be," said the Lord GOD.
>
> (Amos 7:4–6)

Contrary to the view that a faithful response to events in life involves passively accepting one's situation, we see in Moses and later in the Canaanite woman that challenging divine decrees can indeed be a faithful act. Both are powerful examples of a theology where protest has its place.

In the protestations of Moses, we do not hear a call for God to act in a manner that is inconsistent with God's will; rather, we see Moses

---

The church taught me how to pray and, more subtly, how not to pray. One was to praise God, but not protest; to petition God, but not interrogate; and in all things to accept and submit to the sometimes incomprehensible will of God, never challenge or rebel. Yet when life's circumstances would not permit either such passivity or such piety, this advocacy of a rather monotonic relation to God seemed destined to silence if not exclude me and, I suspected, other struggling questioners from the ranks of the truly committed, the genuinely faithful. . . . If one cannot question God, then to whom does one direct the questions?

Samuel E. Balentine, *Prayer in the Hebrew Bible: The Drama of Divine-Human Dialogue* (Minneapolis: Fortress Press, 1993), 4–5.

pleading with God to be faithful to God's own will and promises of the past (cf. 9:19). If Christians can begin to really appreciate the intimate relationship that exists between the gospel message and the OT narratives, we will be able to see more clearly that there is gospel in the Old Testament as well as law.

The golden calf story functions as representative of Israel's waywardness. In the Deuteronomic narrative, Moses also alludes to other examples of disobedience in verses 22–23, but the golden calf story brings to the surface the most salient point: that Israel forsook the commandment against idolatry before it was even given and remains unable to fulfill it.

Chapter 10 moves to conclude the story of the golden calf and the Ten Commandments with Moses' explanation of the creation of a second set of tablets. That God would replace the first set of tablets, which Moses broke after witnessing the golden calf (cf. 9:17), suggests that God not only heeds Moses' intercessory prayer and spares Israel but that God will also honor the covenantal relationship governed by the tablets. An American figure many called the new Moses, Abraham Lincoln is famous for his invocation of God's help during the Civil War. After the Confederate victory at the Second Battle of Bull Run, Lincoln said, "I have been driven many times upon my knees by the overwhelming conviction that I had nowhere else to go."[46]

> You shall put the mercy seat on the top of the ark; and in the ark you shall put the covenant that I shall give you. There I will meet with you, and from above the mercy seat, from between the two cherubim that are on the ark of the covenant, I will deliver to you all my commands for the Israelites.
>
> (Exod. 25:21–22)

In the opening verses of chapter 10 we have an abbreviated story of the fashioning of the ark of the covenant (cf. Exod. 25:10–22), a chest created to house the Ten Commandments and to move with the Israelites in their years in the wilderness. Compared with the elaborate story given in Exodus

---

46. James A. Reed, "The Later Life and Religious Sentiments of Abraham Lincoln," *Scribner's Monthly*, July 1873, 340, citing Noah Brooks's article in *Harper's Monthly*, July 1865.

about how the ark should be built, in Deuteronomy 10 the Deuteronomist offers only scant information on the ark. Here Moses claims to have made the ark (v. 5), whereas Exodus 37 describes the ark being built by Bezalel. Some scholars suggest that this discrepancy may mean that there were two arks, or it may be that the Deuteronomist wanted to keep the narrative focused on Moses, accentuating whenever possible his essential role. Additionally, scholars suggest that Deuteronomy's relative disinterest in the ark may have to do with the writers' attempts to downplay the anthropomorphic conceptions of God that accompany the ark. For the ark was viewed as God's footstool, and placing the tablets inside the ark suggested that they were placed at God's feet.[47] Deuteronomy's depiction of God accentuates God's transcendence rather than God's particular locatedness in the ark or the tabernacle.

> The holiness and utter transcendence of God present throughout all creation have always been central affirmations of the Jewish tradition and its grafted branch, Christian faith. God as God, ground, support, and goal of all, is illimitable mystery who, while immanently present, cannot be measured, manipulated, or controlled. The doctrine of divine incomprehensibility or hiddenness is corollary of this divine transcendence. In essence, God's unlikeness to the corporal and spiritual finite world is total.
>
> Elizabeth A. Johnson, *She Who Is: The Mystery of God in Feminist Theological Discourse* (New York: Crossroad, 1991), 104–5.

In Christian circles, with the common practice of focusing on God's immanence in the person of Jesus Christ, there is sometimes a neglect of the biblical affirmation of God's utter transcendence. Deuteronomy's emphasis on God's otherness helps us reconsider the relationship between God's transcendence and God's immanence. Contemporary theologian Mayra Rivera has recently taken up Christian neglect of God's otherness. She writes, "In practice, we have too often failed to respect otherness and live peacefully and responsibly with our differences. The limitations of our models of

47. Jeffrey Tigay, *The JPS Torah Commentary: Deuteronomy* (Philadelphia: Jewish Publication Society, 1996), 104–5.

interhuman difference stem from our difficulties envisioning divine otherness."[48] Attending more closely to the Deuteronomic view of divine otherness—particularly as it relates to God's care for the stranger, the widow, and the orphan, who are "others" within Israel—could prove fruitful in setting forth theologies of divine otherness like the one Rivera proposes.

Deuteronomy 10:6–9 contains a brief digression from Moses' speech. In these verses, the Deuteronomist recalls the death of Aaron, which prompts us to discuss another contrast between Deuteronomy's retelling of the golden calf story and its corollary version in Exodus. In the Exodus version, even though Moses' brother, Aaron, plays a central role in facilitating the formation of the calf image, he is not singled out for punishment (cf. Exod. 32:2–5, 21–35). In Deuteronomy, by contrast, Moses reports that God was so angry with Aaron that God was prepared to kill him (9:20–21), but Aaron is spared because of Moses' intercession. Once again, Moses in the role of intercessor successfully prevents God from destroying God's covenant people—in this case, his brother, Aaron.

While Aaron avoids death as punishment for the golden calf incident, the Deuteronomist tells of Aaron's death, which actually takes place long before Moses' final speeches and long before Israel's entry into the land promised by God (cf. Num. 33:37–39 for the first telling of Aaron's death). Again Moses' retelling of this portion of Israel's history serves a theological point: God's anger at Aaron and at Israel stems from the covenantal fidelity that has been breached. In addition, Moses' critical role as intercessor is laying the groundwork for the Deuteronomist's final words of this book: "Never since has there arisen a prophet in Israel like Moses, whom the LORD knew face to face" (34:10).

Verse 8 transitions from the death of Aaron, who himself had functioned as Israel's High Priest, to the tribe of Levi whom God "sets apart" to carry the ark of the covenant. The Levites, however, do not assume the role of priest after Aaron dies but rather at the time of the golden calf (cf. Exod. 32:26–29) because it was they who carried out

---

48. Mayra Rivera, *A Touch of Transcendence: A Postcolonial Theology of God* (Louisville, KY: Westminster John Knox Press, 2007), ix.

Moses' call to punish the worshipers of the calf. In response to their protest against the worship of a false god, the Levites are rewarded with the roles of priests. Their special roles include ministering to the Lord and blessing God's name. So that they could devote themselves fully to their priestly duties, the Levites were not given any tribal territory (10:9); instead, they were to be supported by the income given to the sanctuaries.

In 10:10–12, Moses' speech resumes, and he returns yet again to the role of intercessor (cf. 9:25–29).

> The Lord said to Aaron: . . .
> So bring with you also your brothers of the tribe of Levi, your ancestral tribe, in order that they may be joined to you, and serve you while you and your sons with you are in front of the tent of the covenant. They shall perform duties for you and for the whole tent. . . . It is I who now take your brother Levites from among the Israelites; they are now yours as a gift, dedicated to the Lord.
>
> (Num. 18:1–3, 6)

He reiterates that God has pledged to listen to Moses and has promised not to destroy Israel. God commissions Moses, saying "'Get up, go on your journey at the head of the people, that they may go in and occupy the land I swore to their ancestors.'" (v. 11). These instructions from God in Deuteronomy differ once again from the Exodus version of the story. In Exodus, God first tells Moses an angel will lead the people to the promised land, but then in response to Moses' protests, God agrees to lead the people personally (cf. Exod. 33:1–3). Once again the Deuteronomic writer presents Moses as one who is trusted and charged by God to lead the people on.

10:12–22

Back to the Heart of the Law

Here Moses' pivotal speech that began in chapters 5 and 6 with the commandments and the Shema begins to draw to a close. "So now, O Israel," Moses asks in 10:12, "what does the Lord your God require of you?" The question is reminiscent of Micah 6:8 and is a succinct restatement of the main points of Moses' sermon. Having

> It is one and the same reality which underlies the internal turning to God and
> the external serving of the world. There is one conversion: the . . . "conversion
> to the world" has little to do with the fashionable notion that God is to
> be found in the world or in the service of others rather than in prayer and
> interiority. If conversion does not begin in each person's private hell, in the
> meeting with God the crucifier and the crucified in the depths of the heart,
> there is no ground for the second level of conversion. . . . But once the self has
> been dethroned . . . there is only one possible "translation" of this into bodily
> life, and that is the service of the neighbor. . . . It is "active holiness."
>
> Rowan Williams, *Christian Spirituality: A Theological History from the New Testament to Luther and St. John of the Cross* (Atlanta: John Knox Press, 1980), 154.

just reviewed Israel's persistent disobedience, Moses poses this
question: What is it that God's people are to do? Moses answers his
own question by boiling it down to the basics: fear and love God;
follow the commands and serve God (v. 12). At the same time, he
reemphasizes God's mysterious and gracious love for this tiny band
of people (v. 15). To drive the point home as he approaches the
end of this speech, Moses calls on Israel to "circumcise, then, the
foreskin of [their] heart" (v. 16). We know that circumcision is the
physical mark of belonging to the Israelite covenant community and
has served since the earliest days of Israel as a visible "sign of the
covenant" (cf. Gen. 17:11; Josh. 5:1–9). But 10:16 offers again the
wider view of torah seen throughout Deuteronomy as the people
are called to make their covenantal circumcision not just a physical
mark but also a "mark" of the heart. The interior lives of the people
of God shall bear the mark of covenantal relationship and fidelity.

At the point where Moses is boiling down what it means to be a
faithful covenant partner with God, he talks not of the central, visible
sign of covenantal relationship—male circumcision—but rather he
invokes circumcision in a metaphorical way, suggesting that Israelites
are called to remove the "foreskin" of the heart—that which blocks
the heart and renders it inaccessible to God's teachings.[49] The call to
circumcise the heart appears here for the first time in Deuteronomy;

49. Tigay, *JPS Torah Commentary,* 107.

it also appears in other places in the Old Testament (Lev. 26:41; Jer. 4:4; 9:26; Ezek. 44:9). Being a faithful covenant partner is not simply fulfilling the law; it is more encompassing than that. Faithful following of God is, at its most basic, about the transformation of the heart.

> Circumcise yourselves to
>   the LORD,
>
>   remove the foreskin of
>   your hearts,
>
>   O people of Judah and
>   inhabitants of Jerusalem,
>
> or else my wrath will go forth
> like fire,
>
>   and burn with no one to
>   quench it,
>
>   because of the evil of your
>   doings.
>
> (Jer. 4:4)

FURTHER REFLECTIONS
Thinking in New Ways about the Law

From a Christian perspective, the passage in Deuteronomy 10:16 encourages us to revisit the common Christian distinction between the law and the gospel. As we discussed in the introduction, Christian theologians who speak of the law/gospel distinction do not typically refer to the Old Testament as law and the New Testament as gospel although that has become a common on-the-ground way in which Christians approach Scripture. What Deuteronomy 10:16 helps us see, however, is what theologians like Martin Luther claimed long ago: that law and gospel are intertwined throughout both testaments. Further, this passage suggests that we return to the word *torah* rather than *law* to describe what it is that Moses is passing down to his hearers.

The torah—the guidance or instruction—given here by Moses is far beyond any simplistic notion of external adherence to a particular command. In fact, the use of a term that typically refers to a physical condition—*circumcision*—serves to cause a reevaluation of conventional notions of what it means for Israel—and in turn, for Christians—to be faithful followers of God. And to live in covenantal relationship with God, the Deuteronomist shows us again in 10:18, is inseparably linked to care for the widow, the alien, and the orphan.

In the New Testament, the apostle Paul picks up on this "circumcision of the heart" imagery in Romans 2:25–29 where he wrestles

> Compassion is placed in its widest context. It is a stigma, an "indelible mark" much resembling the "circumcision of the heart" Moses urges. It changes attitudes; it is visible and tactile, alert toward others, notably toward the despised and excluded.
>
> Daniel Berrigan, *No Gods but One* (Grand Rapids: Wm. B. Eerdmans Publishing Co., 2010), 80.

with what exactly makes one a Jew. He concludes with the claim that "a person is not a Jew who is one outwardly, nor is true circumcision something external and physical. Rather, a person is a Jew who is one inwardly, and real circumcision is a matter of the heart—it is spiritual and not literal." Here Paul suggests, similar to Deuteronomy 10:16, that "true circumcision" is fulfilling the spirit—and not simply the letter—of the law; that is, living out the love and compassion required of God's people.

To a wayward people Moses implores the circumcision of hearts in order to be faithful to the one God. Chapter 10 then concludes with a reiteration of God's execution of justice for the least among Israel—the orphan, the widow, and the stranger (v. 18). In response to the question of who cares for the widows and the orphans, Martin Luther responds, "No one, no one at all. But here they shall see with

> Promise in the form of gospel, or promise in the form of law—that is the question. And it could well be that "promise in the form of gospel" brings to light once more the original meaning of the law as being the injunctions that are bound up with the promise.
>
> Jürgen Moltmann, *The Theology of Hope: On the Ground and the Implications of a Christian Eschatology* (New York: Harper & Row, 1967), 124.

a sure heart, where it is said for their joy: 'God of gods, Lord of lords, the great, powerful, and dreadful God—He executes judgment for the widow and the orphan.'"[50] In a similar vein, Daniel Berrigan calls this God the original "Good Samaritan."[51] This fundamental Deuteronomistic view of God is also at the heart of Psalm 68:5, where the psalmist calls God "the Father of orphans and of widows."[52]

---

50. Luther, *LW* 9:110.
51. Berrigan, Daniel, *No Gods But One* (Grand Rapids: Wm. B. Eerdmans Publishing Co,, 2009), 78.
52. Luther, *LW* 9:112.

And because you are God's people, Moses continues, because you were once a stranger in the land of Egypt, you shall also love the stranger (v. 19).

To understand God as the original Good Samaritan, and for Israel to be called to love God and to love the stranger, are both suggestive of Jesus' later iteration of the Great Commandment: that we are to love the Lord our God with all our heart, mind, and soul and to love our neighbor as we do ourselves.

11:1–32

Remembering the Past and Trusting in the Future:
Israel's Choice of Blessing or Curse

This final chapter of Moses' second address reiterates the call to love "the LORD your God." Central to loving God is the act of remembering what it is that God has done for God's people. Again we hear Moses stressing to his audience that it is neither their ancestors nor their children but the Israelites themselves who must acknowledge God's greatness. Moses refers here to God's destructive acts in Egypt to Pharaoh, his army, and all in his land (vv. 2–4). Moses also references God's mighty acts of punishment to Israel in the wilderness. Even though the present generation was not physically present in Egypt or in the wilderness wandering, Moses insists, "It is your own eyes that have seen every great deed that the LORD did" (v. 7). This generation is also well aware of what will happen to those who thwart God (cf. Num. 14:34).

After the call for Israel to remember its past and God's mighty signs as well as God's deeds of punishment, Moses turns in verses 8–12 to the future, to Israel's upcoming entrance into the land God has promised them. Just as God spoke to Israel and gave them the commands for the first time at Horeb, here God can be heard speaking again to Israel at Moab, giving them the commands once again; this time they are given for the purposes of flourishing in the land "the LORD [their] God looks after" (v. 12). Moses repeatedly emphasizes in this section that obedience to the commands are key to living well in this land. So much is at stake in the call for Israel's loyalty and obedience to God.

Several passages in verses 13–21 link back to the focal point of this second speech of Moses, the Shema in 6:4–9. The instruction given in 6:7 and repeated again in 11:18–19, to "speak of . . . these words . . . when you lie down and when you get up," has been interpreted by Jewish scholars as a call to recite these words when lying down at the end of the day and rising at the dawn of the day. This practice of recitation, traced back to the late Second Temple period, is still practiced. The entire Shema that Jews recite today includes the words from Deuteronomy 6:4–9; 11:13–21; and Numbers 15:37–41.

The instructions Moses delivers in 11:18–21 are almost identical to those given in Deut. 6:6–9. Once again, the Israelites are reminded to keep the words in their heart, to physically bind the words to themselves, pass them down to their children, and display them on their property. Do all this, Moses instructs, "so that your days and the days of your children may be multiplied in the land that the LORD swore to your ancestors" (v. 21).

Binding God's word and command to the body suggests a kind of intimacy with the commands that goes far beyond hearing and obeying particular laws. It is not enough to hear the commands proclaimed and do what is expected. Rather, God's commands are to be seen and felt in all moments of life. To embody the commands takes more than being able to recite the commandments or a creed by heart. To help Christians understand the internal connections between the command to love God and obey God's commands, biblical scholar and theologian Marcus Borg proposes that we replace the word *commandment* with the word *relationship*. When we recite

---

So far [Moses] has been discussing and urging this First Commandment, and therefore He is so concerned about it that He commands it be taken to heart, to be bound as a sign on hands and eyes, and to be taught to the children, just as He did above; for it contains the whole sum and fulfillment of all the commandments that follow. So we see that Moses omits nothing that pertains to the understanding of the First Commandment, just as he has amply discussed everything that promotes faith and everything that impedes it.

Martin Luther, *Lectures on Deuteronomy*, LW 9:118.

the Shema, then, we hear that our greatest relationship is to love God with all our heart, soul, mind, and strength. Borg goes on to say, "You can keep the commandments and still be a jerk. But you can't be in relationship with the loving God without being continually transformed."[53] Keeping the words in our hearts means that our lives will reflect them in what we say and do.

The catechetical teachings of Moses, then, aim not just at forming a people who are adept at following rules. Rather his teachings aim to inculcate wisdom in God's people, wisdom and understanding that transform them into faithful covenantal partners with God, partners who live and breathe God's will and who in turn will receive God's blessing.

Chapter 11 builds to its climactic conclusion in verses 26–32, where Moses says to Israel, "See, I am setting before you today a blessing and a curse: the blessing, if you obey the commandments of the LORD your God that I am commanding you today; and the curse, if you do not obey the commandments of the LORD your God . . . to follow other gods that you have not known" (vv. 26–28). It is noteworthy that the blessing and the curse are each set forth in this chapter as live possibilities. Thus the people are called to make a choice. Both choices, according to the Deuteronomist, are directly related to how the Israelites will fare in the land that has been promised them. If they follow the commands, God will bring rain (v. 14) to the land; if Israel worships other gods, God "will shut up the heavens" (v. 17). Once again, Moses cautions Israel not to be seduced by other deities, such as the fertility gods of the Canaanites who supposedly bring rain to the land (cf. Hos. 2:4–20). Moses is clear: the Lord God is the one who gives and withholds the rain. And whether or not it will go well for Israel, the Deuteronomist suggests here, is dependent on whether the Israelites choose blessing or curse.

Once again, it is important to point to the ways in which a vision of God as one who rewards those who obey and punishes those who fail to fulfill the commands is called into question, both within the biblical text as well as by countless number of human beings who

---

53. Marcus Borg, as cited in Rev. W. Matthew Broadbent's sermon "Perfecting Faith," February 2011, http://www.foothills-church.org/sermon–2–13–11.pdf.

have suffered innocently throughout the ages. As we see in the book of Job, a tidy theology of retribution is simply not up to the task of explaining why humans suffer, especially with respect to those who, like Job, do nothing to deserve it. In his wrestling with the theology of retribution articulated by Job's friends, liberation theologian Gustavo Gutiérrez proposes that Job's relationship with God witnesses to a different theological approach to human suffering. Gutiérrez writes:

> God's speeches [cf. Job 38–41] are a forceful rejection of a purely anthropocentric view of creation. Not everything that exists was made to be directly useful to human beings; therefore, they may not judge everything from their point of view. The world of nature expresses the freedom and delight of God in creating. It refuses to be limited to the narrow confines of the cause-effect relationship.[54]

Gutiérrez articulates well a biblical counterexample from the book of Job challenging interpretations of Deuteronomy 11:13–17 that insist that the God of Israel follows a tidy theology of retribution. Once again, we must acknowledge an ongoing theological tension within the text, one that defies easy answers.

In the closing verses of the chapter, Moses directs the people that once they have entered the land they shall "set the blessing on Mount Gerizim and the curse on Mount Ebal" (v. 29). These two mountains—Mount Gerizim, lush and verdant, and Mount Ebal, barren and dry—that lie north of Jerusalem will serve as visible markers of Israel's impending choice. In chapters 27–28, the Deuteronomist returns to these mountains and to the subject of blessings and curses; the culmination of the story is found in Joshua 8:30–35. Once in the land, Joshua takes the Israelites to both mountains, where he first copies the law and then reads "all the words of the law, blessings and curses, according to all that is written in the book of the law" (Josh. 8:34).

Unlike other biblical narratives where blessings and curses are to

---

54. Gustavo Gutiérrez, *On Job: God-Talk and the Suffering of the Innocent* (Maryknoll, NY: Orbis Books, 1987), 74.

take effect as they are pronounced (see Noah's bestowal of blessing and curses on his sons in Gen. 9:25–27), Moses sets the blessings and curses *before* Israel. Israel has been under God's curse before, and now the Israelites must choose whether to obey God as they transition to the land God has promised them.

> The theology of Deuteronomy is beautifully concretized in the stark opposition of these two mountains, for the book repeatedly stresses the forking alternatives of prosperity and disaster, depending on Israel's faithfulness to God's laws.
>
> Robert Alter, *The Five Books of Moses* (New York: W. W. Norton & Co., 2004), 938.

We come now to chapters 12–26, the section that contains the presentation of the statutes and ordinances that follow from the Shema and the Ten Commandments that Israel is called to diligently observe (v. 32). Thus the call to choose blessing or curse serves to frame the chapters detailing the specific commands. As biblical scholar Patrick Miller observes, these chapters stand on the boundary between land and landlessness, between life and death.[55] In the commentary that follows, we will investigate ways in which law and gospel continue to intermingle within this legislation-heavy section.

---

55. Miller, *Ten Commandments*, 128.

12:1–26:19

A New Vision for a New Land: Comprehensive Covenant Living

12:1
Laws for a New Life

This section of Deuteronomy begins with the words "These are the statutes and ordinances that you must diligently observe in the land that the LORD, the God of your ancestors, has given you" (12:1), which reiterate Moses' closing words in his speech that concludes in 11:32. This section is also understood to be the oldest portion of the book of Deuteronomy, and it contains a number of similarities to ancient Near East treaties. Scholars place this legal core in the north shortly before the fall of the northern kingdom in mid-eighth century BCE, suggesting that it is edited and expanded, first in Judah during Josiah's reign (622 BCE) and later by the Priestly editors in postexilic Jerusalem. Church father Jerome (347–420 CE) was the first to suggest that Deuteronomy 12–26 was the scroll found in the Jerusalem temple during the reign of King Josiah as recounted in 2 Kings 22. Today this view has widespread support among biblical scholars.

Some have called chapters 12–26 an interruption of the narrative; in the first eleven chapters we have Moses' oftentimes-soaring rhetoric regarding the covenantal relationship between Israel and the God of its past, present, and future. At first glance, chapters 12–26 might look to the contemporary reader like a list of outdated laws, which is likely part of the reason the Christian lectionary ignores these chapters altogether.

But as we continue to rethink the place of the law in Christian

In the eighteenth year of King Josiah, the king sent Shaphan son of Azaliah, son of Meshullam, the secretary, to the house of the LORD. . . . The high priest Hilkiah said to Shaphan the secretary, "I have found the book of the law in the house of the LORD." . . . When the king heard the words of the book of the law, he tore his clothes. Then the king commanded the priest Hilkiah, Ahikam son of Shaphan, Achbor son of Micaiah, Shaphan the secretary, and the king's servant Asaiah, saying, "Go, inquire of the LORD for me, for the people, for all Judah, concerning the words of this book that has been found; for great is the wrath of the LORD that is kindled against us, because our ancestors did not obey the words of this book, to do according to all that is written concerning us."

(2 Kgs. 22:3, 8a, 11–13)

understandings of Scripture, we must pause and consider the role the laws of chapters 12–26 play in the larger narrative of Deuteronomy. Recall that in the first eleven chapters we are reminded repeatedly that the statutes and ordinances set forth in these chapters are God's gracious gift given for the sake of the life and well-being of Israel (cf. 5:33, 6:24). Chapters 12–26 seem to follow roughly the themes and the structure of the Decalogue even as they move beyond it to the statutes and ordinances given by Moses. These chapters spell out what the guiding principles of chapters 5–6 look like when they are enfleshed in the everyday life of the community. These laws concern practical matters of worship, politics, economics, business and judicial practices, sexuality and marriage, family life, and relationships with other communities. Thus, in contrast to the Ten Commandments and the Shema—which as they reappear throughout the Pentateuch do not change in substantive ways—the laws in chapters

I understand by the word "law" not only the Ten Commandments, which set forth a godly and righteous rule of living, but the form of religion handed down by God through Moses. And Moses was not made a lawgiver to wipe out the blessing promised to the race of Abraham. Rather, we see him here repeatedly reminding the Jews of that freely given covenant made with their fathers of which they were the heirs. It was as if he were sent to renew it. This fact was very clearly revealed in the ceremonies.

John Calvin, *Institutes*, 2.7.1 in *Theological Guide to Calvin's Institutes: Essays and Analysis (Calvin 500)*, ed. David W. Hall (Phillipsburg, NJ: P&R Publishing, 2008), 186.

12–26 are not meant to be understood as timeless and immutable.[1] The laws set forth in this section constitute a concretizing of the vision for ancient Israel's new life in the new land.

As the Deuteronomist reports in numerous places throughout the text, these laws are given so that Israel's life in the land may be a blessing for everyone within the Israelite community. The laws cannot be understood apart from the land; in the words of Moses, obeying them will lead to the blessings—rather than the curses— set forth in 11:26–28 and later in chapters 27–28.

In the commentary that follows, we will attend to the way in which law and narrative are interwoven. We will also note the ways that the Decalogue serves as a framework for understanding particular laws. It is noteworthy that in the explication and concretization of the commandments we see that the people's relationship to God, to one another—particularly to the least among them, and to the rest of the created order—are consistently attended to.

12:2–13:18

Observing the First Commandment in the New Land

References to the First Commandment, that Israel should love God alone and follow no other god, appear continually throughout chapters 12–26, undergirding many of the specific statutes and ordinances and reinforcing Deuteronomy's fundamental claim of total allegiance to God alone.

FURTHER REFLECTIONS:
Divine Exclusivity in a Land of Many Gods

Deuteronomy's repeated emphasis—taken to a heightened pitch in chapters 12–13—on Israel's commanded loyalty to God alone is punctuated in these chapters by calls to obliterate all evidence of worship of other gods. Endorsement of such violence against

---

1. Terrence Fretheim, "Law in Service of Life," in *A God So Near: Essays in Honor of Patrick Miller,* ed. Brent A. Strahn and Nancy R. Bowen (Winona Lake, IN: Eisenbrauns, 2003), 183–99.

people of other religions begs the question for twenty-first-century readers: How do we approach the Deuteronomist's claim of militant divine exclusivity in a land of other gods? While we can appreciate and applaud the Deuteronomist's steadfast opposition to abhorrent practices such as child sacrifice within other traditions (cf. Deut. 12:31), it is the call to obliterate Canaanite peoples and their places of worship that remains persistently troubling as we move through the text. As discussed earlier in the commentary on Deuteronomy 7, we know that the logic behind the call to destroy Canaanite objects of worship was understood as necessary to protect Israel from the temptation to worship Canaanite gods. And as we saw in Deuteronomy 6:18 and 7:1–11, the Deuteronomist makes it clear that temptation to idolatry must be resisted at any price. Still, chapter 12 confronts us with more images of brutal violence and religious intolerance. What are we to say in response?

It is important to highlight again the tension that exists in the text as a whole around this issue. In the Song of Moses in Deuteronomy 32, the text declares that God "apportioned the nations" and "divided humankind," fixing "the boundaries of the people according to the number of the gods" (v. 8). According to the Song of Moses, it seems not only that God permits other people's worship of other gods but also that the God of Israel structured the world in such a way that other gods would be worshiped by other peoples. Deuteronomy 32:8 suggests once again a monolatrous, exclusive worship of one god without denying the existence of other gods rather than a strictly monotheistic view of the God of Israel.

We also know that a primary motivating factor for such recommended destruction of Canaanite worship sites had to do with the command for Israel to maintain its covenantal relationship with its

> Idolatry makes love impossible. Perhaps that is why it is the first of all the commandments that God gives to Israel . . . "you shall have no other gods before me." If we break any of the other commandments, the ones that (literally) get prime time, we have already broken the first one. We have already elevated ourselves and our perceived desires above all else.
>
> Kathleen Norris, *Amazing Grace: A Vocabulary of Faith* (New York: Riverhead Books, 1999), 88.

God. What's threatened in the temptation to worship other gods is, for the Deuteronomist, nothing less than Israel's love of God.

While we can appreciate the importance of Israel's attempts to fulfill its covenantal relationship with God, many readers of this section today will continue to recoil at the violence called for by the text. At the same time, it is important to set the counterclaims discussed at the beginning of this excursus alongside the calls for violence: that there is biblical warrant to support the divine right of other peoples to worship other gods at the same time as there are calls to wipe out those who do not worship Israel's God.

In chapters 12–13, Israel is again commanded to follow faithfully the First Commandment, but this time the command is coupled with a sustained polemic against the imminent threat posed to Israel by Canaanite religious practices. The command to destroy all the places where the Canaanites worship their gods as well as the objects with which they worshiped (commands similar to those rehearsed in Deut. 7) is set alongside the revolutionary command to worship God at a centralized place of God's choosing (12:5). Even though contemporary biblical scholars believe that taking over Canaanite worship sites is likely exactly what Israel actually did, chapter 12 expressly disallows this practice out of concern for the ways in which it would tempt Israel to stray from the First Commandment. Rather than worshiping at many sites—places ripe with temptation—the Israelites are instructed to worship their God in a centralized location. Much scholarly debate has ensued about whether the *centralized* location referred to in Deuteronomy 12 is also a *sole* location. Contemporary scholars tend to distinguish between the two, suggesting that the centralized location for worship could well have moved over time. Indeed, the Deuteronomist does not name the location that God chooses, and while many suspect it to be the city of Jerusalem, others suggest it also could be Shiloh, another ancient religious center for Israel just north of Bethel, as referenced in Jeremiah 7:12, the place where God says, "I made my name dwell at first." That the location was not specifically named seems to serve the larger theological point of the Deuteronomist in chapters 12–13:

what matters is that Israel obediently worship God alone only in the place of God's choosing and that it be a place free from any Canaanite association.

This limitation of sacrificial worship to a centralized location is perhaps the most distinctive and far-reaching law in Deuteronomy, for it affected not just the lives of individual Israelites but also the way that festivals were conducted, how the economic system was to be set up, and even how the judicial system was intended to operate. After repeated claims about the importance of the Israelites' journeying to a centralized place of worship, however, the Deuteronomist then lists a few exceptions to the rule. For example, since there will no longer be sacrifices at localized places of worship, Israelites are now permitted to eat the meat from their sacrifices even when they cannot get to the central place of worship. The simple reality would have been that distance was an obstacle for many in honoring God's command to worship at a central place, which is why scholars suspect that these activities actually took the place of regular sacrificial worship.

What we have in this section and in the sections to follow is the foundation of a new vision for life lived in a new land. In 12:8–12, for instance, we see that this anticipated future of good living in the land is fundamentally different from Israel's past of slavery, wilderness wandering, struggle, and scarcity. At the heart of the difference between their anticipated future and their past is the command for the Israelites to live differently: no longer shall they act according to their own desires; rather they will worship God and rejoice in this new land (12:8).

This passage also demonstrates that in the section devoted to giving the law, Moses spends as much time exhorting the people to follow the law as he does explaining the

> The commandment of God is something different from what we have so far referred to as the ethical. It embraces the whole of life. . . . It does not only forbid and command; it also permits. It does not only bind; it also sets free; and it does this by binding. . . . The commandment of God is the permission to live as [a human being] before God.
>
> Dietrich Bonhoeffer, *Ethics*, ed. Eberhard Bethge (New York: MacMillan Co., 1965), 277, 280.

details of the laws themselves. We see again that following the statutes and ordinances is more than simply following this or that rule; what is presented here requires a whole new way of being.

Of further significance in Deuteronomy is that this new way of being includes a definition of community that encompasses not just Israel's own sons and daughters but also their male and female slaves, as well as the Levites. Levites, the designated priests of Israel who live off of the parts of sacrificial meat as well as donations, would have struggled financially with the centralizing of sacrificial worship and the fewer sacrifices that would have been performed on site. They are thus often included in the lists of economically vulnerable groups to which Israel is called to pay attention. That the phrase "Take care that you . . ." in 12:19 is typically reserved for remembering God's revelation to Israel at Horeb (Deut. 4:9), God's identity as the one who led them out of Egypt (Deut. 6:12), or the command not to turn away from God (Deut. 11:16) suggests that Israel's commanded caretaking of the Levites is inseparable from their identity as covenantal partners with God.

As we move toward the end of chapter 12 and its deep concern over idolatry, verse 28 reiterates the call for Israel "to obey all these words" that Moses commands "today." This passage is suggestive of Deuteronomy 5:22, where Moses concludes his recitation of the Ten Commandments by saying, "These words the Lord spoke . . ." To be faithful followers of these foundational commands in the land, the Deuteronomist indicates, is intimately tied to Israel's ability to love and enjoy God while refraining from all temptations to idol making or worshiping.

Chapter 12 concludes with the passage in verses 29–32 that insists again that those who worship God are set apart from other groups of people, that worshiping God means God's people behave differently than other groups of people. Of particular mention here is the practice of child sacrifice in verse 31. Scholarship is inconclusive on whether or not such sacrifices actually took place in Canaan. But again, the Deuteronomist's

> **Therefore come out from them, and be separate from them, says the Lord.**
>
> (2 Cor. 6:17)

theological accent is on the way that Israel as God's covenant partner is set apart; the Israelites live, eat, sacrifice, and even worship differently than those around them.

Chapter 13 introduces a second major way in which Israel will be tempted to put other gods before God: by listening to the voices of those who can lead them astray. While chapter 12 focuses on the threat of idolatry, the main concern in chapter 13 is what follows from idolatry, that which is often referred to as apostasy, or the abandonment of one's faith. Moses' words in this chapter are again narrative in style (thus earning the term "preached law" by biblical scholars) where he not only lays down the law but also preaches about how apostasy functions as a potentially deadly threat to the Israelite community.

Moses begins by naming prophets or others who claim revelatory powers and whose words and actions might tempt Israel to follow their lead and worship other gods. In the face of such threats, Moses implores Israel to listen to God's words alone (v. 4). And the chapter is bracketed by the very familiar refrain that Israel shall follow God's commands (vv. 4, 18) and do "what is right in the sight of the LORD [their] God" (v. 18).

But the threat is not simply a threat of leadership. Moses suggests it might even be closer than those who preach and proclaim for a living. In verses 6–12 he informs them that such voices may even come from family members as close as a sibling or a child. Not only should false prophets be put to death, Moses instructs, but Israel is also called to show even close family members "no pity or compassion." We see in this section that harsh punishment is not just reserved for those outside the community; if they take on the role of apostate, even blood relations of

> There is a certain pride inherent in apostasy, which often manifests itself as magnificent faith in oneself, as in "I alone know what is right for me." Teachers, traditions, the family stories and the beliefs of the common herd are all suspect; suspicion rather than trust is what defines the apostate. And it defines our age. The individual stands alone, a church of one, convinced that he or she is free of the tyranny of any creed or dogma.
>
> Kathleen Norris, *Amazing Grace: A Vocabulary of Faith* (New York: Riverhead Books, 1999), 202–3.

Israelites shall be subject to death.

The last group to be singled out to be "purged from [Israel's] midst" is an entire pagan-worshiping community. If other communities tempt Israel away from their allegiance to Yahweh, the text instructs that after a "thorough investigation," Israel shall destroy everything in the town, all the way down to the livestock (v. 15).

FURTHER REFLECTIONS
Apostasy

What should be done about these voices that lead God's people away from the worship of "the LORD [their] God"? Twice in chapter 13 we hear the reminder that Israel has been led out of the deathly conditions of slavery to the life-giving land of promise (vv. 5, 10). When this new life in the land is threatened, Moses' response is blunt and merciless: any apostate poses a threat to this new life and should be put to death—stoned, killed with a sword, or put to death by the hands of the Israelites. In the case of the threat coming from a particular non-Israelite community, Moses instructs Israel that the entire town should be wiped out. We might be able to take some solace in the fact that in the section dealing with the non-Israelite communities (vv. 12–18) there is a call for an investigation before any violence is wrought against the accused. The section that deals with potential apostasy within Israelite families, however, contains no such instruction to investigate before bestowing punishment (cf. 13:8–10). There is no attention given to the need

> The specification of the enemy within Israel as a member of a person's own family, from among the closest personal relationships possible, is jarring. The prohibitions of Deut. 13:8 paradoxically draw attention to the attitudes that should be characteristic of such a close relationship: love, pity, mercy, and care. In place of these expected attitudes, the Israelite is called upon to cast the first stone at this close relative or friend, to initiate his or her execution for idolatry. It is not a pleasant picture.
>
> Caryn A. Reeder, *The Enemy in the Household: Family Violence in Deuteronomy and Beyond* (Grand Rapids: Baker Academic), 32.

to adjudicate accusations of potential apostasy; rather, there are only calls for immediate, violent action along with the instruction to "show them no pity or compassion" (v. 8).

Why are the commands so extreme? Based on the inner logic of the text, Israel must rid its community of such persons because they threaten the covenantal relationship between Israel and God. Once again, though, we are aware that there is little evidence Israel actually wiped out the pagan practices of the Canaanite cities they came to inhabit; what we might have here, then, is an example of a zealous anti-pagan polemic on the part of the Deuteronomic writer. In other words, these calls to "purge evil" from their midst could have been more rhetorical flourish than actual Israelite practice.

While we can neither deny nor bypass the harsh punishment that is advocated for those who abandon their Israelite faith and tempt others to do the same, we can also observe that for the Israelites, the self-understanding that flows from their covenantal relationship with God is that God, the people, and torah are irrevocably connected. And when an individual abandons the faith, he or she threatens the stability of the entire covenantal relationship.

14:1–21
The Nitty-Gritty Details of Faithful Covenant Living

This section begins with the affirmation that each individual is a child of God (see also Deut. 32:5, 19 for similar affirmations). What follows are the details of forbidden activities as well as a presentation of which animals Israelites are forbidden to eat; all of these practices are off-limits because they are done by those outside of Israel. Verse 1 deals with the cutting of body parts and the shaving of hair. Some scholars suggest that the Deuteronomist is referencing here the mourning rituals of other groups and emphasizing again that Israel should not follow other people's rituals. Such prohibitions could also be linked to the discussion of the prophets of Baal in 1 Kings 18 and what the prophets did when they sought Baal's response: "They cried aloud and, as was their custom, they cut themselves with swords and lances until the blood gushed out over them" (1

Kgs. 18:28). In the prohibition against self-cutting in Deuteronomy 14, we hear a clear reaffirmation of a central theological theme of Deuteronomy: the Israelites are forbidden to do such things because they are God's chosen possession. Indeed, this chosen or treasured status has many concrete implications; we hear in verse 21 how all Israelites must maintain a quasi-priestly level of holiness (cf. Lev. 19:2).

> Speak to all the congregation of the people of Israel and say to them: You shall be holy, for I the LORD your God am holy.
>
> (Lev. 19:2)

The Deuteronomic list of animals Israel is permitted or forbidden to eat is similar to but more concise than the list given in Leviticus 11. Deuteronomy 14:3 calls the forbidden foods "abhorrent," a term not used in the Leviticus account. By adding the term *abhorrent*, the Deuteronomist invokes images of idolatrous or immoral acts. It is here that we can see a connection between such purity laws and the Second Commandment prohibiting the taking of the Lord's name in vain. Both the Second Commandment and the purity laws are concerned with maintaining proper boundaries of holiness, cleanliness, and life.[2] Transgressing these boundaries, then, leads to unholiness, uncleanliness, and death.

Ancient and medieval Christian interpreters of these cleanliness laws often spoke of them in spiritual or allegorical terms. Many Christians then (as do many today) wanted to know why it is unholy or unclean to eat animals like a camel or a hare. While various possible explanations have been proposed by scholars—ranging from concerns about hygiene to suspecting that pagans ate such animals—the explanation given in this section of Deuteronomy is simple and to the point: these foods are unclean *for Israel* (vv. 7–8, 10, 19). Jewish writer Ruth Sohn interprets these restrictions for the people of Israel, saying,

> According to the Torah, God asks that we abstain from eating certain foods, not because they are unhealthy or intrinsically problematic, but simply as an expression of our devotion. . . .

---

2. Dennis Olson, *Deuteronomy and the Death of Moses: A Theological Reading* (Minneapolis: Augsburg Fortress, 1994), 72.

These prohibitions are like the requests of a beloved; we may not understand them, but we are, in essence, asked to follow them purely as an expression of our love. Daily, the observance of kashrut [Jewish dietary laws] calls us back to a personal relationship with God.[3]

Sohn's interpretation of Jewish dietary laws helps Christians see that even the law code section of chapters 12–26 can be understood with the help of a wider lens; indeed, such dietary restrictions do not simply restrict. As torah, they orient God's people to right relationship with God. As an expression of love, they bind the people to God multiple times a day. Eating becomes a religious act. Even the most basic daily acts have religious implications.

14:22–16:17
Sabbatical Living: the Heart of the Vision

Deuteronomy 14:22–29 is closely related both to the previous section on what to eat and to the upcoming section on Sabbath living. When Israelites harvest food in the land, they are to give a portion of their harvest back to God to remind them that the land is a gift. Given that there will be a centralized place of worship and that the distance to travel in order to sacrifice a portion of their harvest may be too great, a provision is made here for farmers to turn their tithed portion into money (v. 25). This money can then be used to purchase food or drink to consume "in the presence of the LORD" (v. 26) when they make the trip to the place where God dwells, which occurs during the festivals described later in chapter 16. Scholars have noted that this traveling to the sanctuary and eating the tithes in Deuteronomy also allows the tithes to function as a link between the Israelites and the sanctuary and to provide Israelites with a tangible religious experience there.[4]

---

3. Ruth Sohn, "Contemporary Reflection," in *The Torah: A Women's Commentary*, ed. Tamara Cohn Eskenazi and Andrea L. Weiss (New York: URJ Press, 2008), 1137.
4. Jeffrey Tigay, *The JPS Torah Commentary: Deuteronomy* (Philadelphia: Jewish Publication Society, 1996), 142.

Special provisions for the Levites are made again in 14:27–29, similar to the provision described in chapter 12. Once again we note that this focus on the vulnerable is a distinctive concern of Deuteronomy. Israelites are called on to share their sanctuary meals with the Levites, and every third year Israelites are asked to give over their entire tithe to those most at risk in the community. The Levites, along with the stranger, the orphan, and the widow, become the barometer of Israel's faithfulness to its new vision for a new land. As biblical scholar J. Gary Millar suggests, "Yahweh gives to Israel, and Israel gives to the excluded, in the stead of Yahweh. In a very real sense, the Levites, widows, and orphans represent Yahweh to Israel."[5]

That God is represented to the people in the form of the most marginalized persons in society is a claim that carries through Deuteronomy and the Old Testament all the way to the New Testament. In Matthew 25, Jesus tells his followers that whenever they have provided for the needs of the hungry, the thirsty, or the naked, they have provided these things to Jesus himself. When liberation theologian Gustavo Gutiérrez deals directly with this passage from Matthew, he also notes the intimate connection between the divine and society's most marginalized. He connects this story to the Good Samaritan story, arguing that the answer to Jesus' question about which of the men was a neighbor to the man in the ditch is that "the neighbor was the Samaritan who *approached* the wounded man and *made him his neighbor*. The neighbor, as has been said, is not the one whom I find in my path, but rather the one in whose path I place myself, the one whom I approach and actively seek."[6] Connecting Gutiérrez's insight back to Deuteronomy's linkage of the divine and those on the margins of society, we see that the Shema's command to love God with everything one has translates into active, neighborly love toward the widow, the stranger, and the orphan, the ones claimed by nobody.

That such sharing with the least among them is an economic sacrifice of the Israelites is not ignored in Deuteronomy 14:29; just as those who do not have adequate means are allowed to eat their fill,

5. J. Gary Millar, *Now Choose Life: Theology and Ethics in Deuteronomy* (Grand Rapids: Wm. B. Eerdmans Publishing Co., 1998), 120.
6. Gustavo Gutiérrez, *A Theology of Liberation: History, Politics, and Salvation* (Maryknoll, NY: Orbis Books, 1988), 113.

the Israelites will also be blessed: "The LORD your God [will] bless you in all the work that you undertake." This dynamic of sharing and blessing lies at the heart of the sabbatical principle, the subject of the next chapter.

The sabbatical principle presented in chapter 15 is an expansion of the Third Commandment's call to honor the Sabbath and keep it holy. In Exodus 23 and Leviticus 25, we hear that the land, like Israel, deserves a rest every seventh year. In Deuteronomy, however, the call to rest extends from the agricultural to the economic sphere.[7] Once again, the distinctive vision of the sabbatical principle in Deuteronomy is rooted in the writers' theological commitment to a new way of living that integrates the least among them into the fabric of communal living. In the Exodus version, for instance, Israel is also instructed in a sabbatical year every seventh year, where the ground shall lie fallow and the poor may eat (23:11). Deuteronomy's more extensive treatment of the sabbatical principle in 15:1–23 carries the sabbatical principle of Exodus and Leviticus beyond its primarily agricultural roots into an even wider sphere of concern.

This radical vision for sabbatical living begins with the remission of debts every seven years (vv. 1–2). Any member of the community shall be granted such remission. A foreigner is the one exception to the rule, for foreigners, it is assumed, merely pass through rather than become an integral part of the community. Such a radical vision likely brought with it anxiety about how such remission would be possible. But Moses' preaching on this point

> For six years you shall sow your land and gather in its yield; but the seventh year you shall let it rest and lie fallow, so that the poor of your people may eat; and what they leave the wild animals may eat. You shall do the same with your vineyard, and with your olive orchard.
>
> (Exod. 23:10–11)

once more takes on a reassuring tone: "There will, however, be no one in need among you, because the LORD is sure to bless you in the land" (v. 4).

---

7. Miller, *Deuteronomy*, Interpretation: A Bible Commentary for Teaching and Preaching (Louisville, KY: Westminster John Knox Press, 1990), 135.

In his commentary on this vision of a sabbatical release of debts, Martin Luther's reflections on how life would be different if such practices were the case strike a particularly modern tone:

> Would that today the rulers of the world might imitate it! Then they would have fewer questions and commotions; for people would know that suits, disputes, debts, dealings, agreements, judgments, seals, and letters would all be removed at one time and canceled in the seventh year, whether that be close or far away, and not be postponed and continued forever into endless litigation.[8]

Luther's perspective on the passage helps twenty-first-century Christians see the applicability of Deuteronomy's sabbatical principle for our current context. Just as Moses suggests that living in this way would translate into a radically different way of being in the world, a way that would bring blessing to the community, so too should Christians be challenged by this Deuteronomic vision of a society that operates according to standards that challenge current economic practices in the United States and elsewhere.

> For the love of money is a root of all kinds of evil, and in their eagerness to be rich some have wandered away from the faith and pierced themselves with many pains.
>
> (1 Tim. 6:10)

The lending principle at the heart of sabbatical living is at its most powerful when it turns its attention to the actions of individual members of the community toward one another. "Open your hand" is the heart of the command (15:11). If anyone in the community is in need, the call is to respond with an open hand. There's no room in this vision for "hard-hearted" or "tight-fisted" approaches to the needs of neighbors (15:8). No indeed. In this section Moses returns to the powerful and familiar Deuteronomic claim that following the law is a matter of the heart (cf. Deut. 10:16; 11:18). "You should . . . open your hand, willingly," Moses tells Israel, and give those in need enough to meet their need, "whatever it may be" (v.

8. Luther, *LW* 9:144.

8). There's no place for mean-spirit-edness or a stingy attitude; no place for thinking that eventually, in the next year or the year after, during the sabbatical year, they will get what they need. If the need exists now, the time to give is now. And do it "ungrudgingly" (v. 10).

This command to help liberally the most vulnerable within Israel echoes the way God gave liber-ally to the Israelites during their enslavement in Egypt. Israel knows that God crushed pharaoh (Exod. 3:23–25) because he failed to help the poorest and most vulnerable in his own midst. Thus loving the poor means that God will bless those who live according to this new vision. Deuteronomy's typical categorization of the needy—the widow, the orphan, the stranger, and the Levite—is broken open to a new beyond: give to anyone in need, for any reason.

> It is certain that possessions by themselves do not impede us from following God, but, due to the perversity of the human mind, it is almost impossible that those who have great abundance not be intoxicated by it.
>
> John Calvin, commentary on Matthew 19:23, *Harmony of the Evangelists* (Grand Rapids: Wm. B, Eerdmans Publishing Co., 1949), 2:395-96.

FURTHER REFLECTIONS
"Open Your Hand": New Testament Connections

For Christians, Jesus not only stands in the tradition of torah and its interpretation, but Christians also believe that Jesus goes beyond interpretation to actual *embodiment* of torah, of God's Word. This is what Jesus proclaims in Luke 4:18–19 when he reads the words of Isaiah (61:1–2) in the synagogue:

> "The Spirit of the Lord is upon me,
>   because he has anointed me
>   to bring good news to the poor.
> He has sent me to proclaim release to the captives
>   and recovery of sight to the blind,
>   to let the oppressed go free,
>   to proclaim the year of the Lord's favor."

> [The Lord] has brought down
> the powerful from their thrones,
>   and lifted up the lowly;
> he has filled the hungry with
> good things,
>   and sent the rich away empty.
> He has helped his servant Israel,
>   in remembrance of his mercy,
> according to the promises he
> made to our ancestors,
>   to Abraham and to his
>   descendants forever.
>
> (Luke 1:52–55)

Jesus informs those around him, "Today this scripture has been fulfilled in your hearing." Embodying the Word of God is not simply an abstract claim; the end of the Isaiah passage Jesus reads talks about the year of the Lord's favor—sabbatical year, the year of jubilee—where the principle is enacted. For Christians, then, Jesus becomes the embodiment of the sabbatical principle itself. We see in his life a radical opening of the hand to anyone in need.

It is in the call to "open your hand" to anyone in need that the sabbatical principle can be understood as much more than a once-every-seven-year event, as significant as that is on its own terms. Rather, it calls for a radical restructuring of how the people of God are to live in community. Once again, love of God and service of neighbors in need go hand in hand.

Deuteronomy 15:11 states that "there will never cease to be some in need," a statement similar to a statement made by Jesus in the Gospel of John (12:8). Indeed, many interpreters of Scripture have used such passages to justify the persistent presence of poverty in our midst. But it seems more likely that this Deuteronomic reference to the poor always being with us is a starkly realistic rather than a prescriptive claim: given the reality of human nature and the imperfect societies we set up, there will always be someone in need.

Living and true faith enables us to hear the eschatological Judge in the cry of the oppressed: "I was hungry. . ." (Matt. 25:35). This same faith bids us give heed to that voice, resounding through an act of liberation: "and you gave me to eat." Without this liberating practice that appeases hunger, faith barely plants a seed, let alone produces fruit: not only would we be failing to love our sisters and brothers but we would be failing to love God too.

Leonardo Boff and Clodovis Boff, *Introducing Liberation Theology* (Maryknoll, NY: Orbis Books, 1986), 50.

Martin Luther sees this passage in a realistic light as well, proclaiming in response, "But constant care should be taken that, since these evils are always in evidence, they are always opposed."[9] In light of the human reality of vulnerability, the text is insistent: open your hand and give to those in need.

The sabbatical principle of release and rest in every seventh year applies also to Israelite men and women who have become slaves within Israel, likely in order to survive. In verses 12–15, Moses

> [Jesus said,] "You always have the poor with you, but you do not always have me."
>
> (John 12:8)

instructs Israelites on the release of such persons, elaborating once again on the Exodus instructions regarding male slaves (Exod. 21:2–6). We note that within a context of slavery, a practice we today find abhorrent, we can nevertheless glimpse a vision of a different life, a life where women as well as men could be freed from bondage, where the cycle of vulnerability and impoverishment could be interrupted. Once again Moses invokes the powerful exodus narrative as justification for such a revolutionary way of living: Remember, Israel, that you were a slave in Egypt, and the Lord redeemed you. Therefore, you are called to play a redeeming

> **The Sabbatical Year of liberation of slaves breathes the theology of the exodus.**
>
> Haroldo Reimer, "A Time of Grace in Order to Begin Anew: The Sabbatical Year in Exodus 21:2–11 and Deuteronomy 15:1–18," in *God's Economy: Biblical Studies from Latin America*, ed. Ross Kinsler and Gloria Kinsler (Maryknoll, NY: Orbis Books, 2005), 72.

role vis-à-vis your own slaves who help you prosper in the new land.

This divine act of liberation lies at the heart of God's covenantal relationship with Israel, and we see once again how the Israelites' identity as freed slaves shapes the vision of how their community ought to be structured. Embedded in these commands is a vision where those at the bottom of society are not sentenced to remain there indefinitely. Divine blessing depends on Israel's communal practice of solidarity. This section of Deuteronomy's legal corpus allows Christians to see the interconnection between law and gospel.

9. Ibid., 147.

Solidarity as a practice of mutuality is indeed an intrinsic element of the process of liberation and salvation. It is through solidarity with the "least" of our sisters and brothers (Matt. 25) that the gospel command to love our neighbors as ourselves finds expression in our world today. By examining the process through which solidarity is established and the politically effective praxis through which it is expressed, we come to understand what our ethical behavior is to be today, if we are to call ourselves Christian.

Ada Maria Isasi-Diaz, "Solidarity: Love of Neighbor in the 1980s," in *Lift Every Voice: Constructing Christian Theologies from the Underside*, ed. Susan Brooks Thistlethwaite and Mary Potter Engel (San Francisco: Harper, 1990), 39.

The sabbatical principle, embodied also in Jesus' life and ministry, is life-saving torah practice for Jews, and it beckons to Christians to meditate on how this injunction in Deuteronomy reveals a gospel message within the law. For in both Deuteronomy 15 as well as Gospel texts like Matthew 25, it is clear that salvation and liberation are socially and corporately understood. Our participation in God's promised future is bound up with our participation in life with others—in particular, with the most vulnerable—in the here and now.

The sabbatical principle of chapter 15 is also connected with the practice of gleaning in Deuteronomy 24:19–21. We see yet again that care for "the alien, the orphan, and the widow" is integral to the agricultural and economic as well as social practices of Israel. Amid all this talk of a radically different way of living that the sabbatical principle engenders, the Deuteronomist knows that such commands will prove difficult to follow; indeed, other voices within the biblical narrative, like Jeremiah's, talk of how Israel veers away from this practice:

> Thus says the LORD: You have not obeyed me by granting a release to your neighbors and friends; I am going to grant a release to you, says the LORD—a release to the sword, to pestilence, and to famine. I will make you a horror to all the kingdoms of the earth. (Jer. 34:17)

In response to this knowledge that Israel will falter in its faithfulness, Moses' speech includes yet another round of assertions: Follow these commands and "the LORD your God will bless you in all that you do" (15:18). Biblical scholar Haroldo Reimer suggests that the sabbatical principle "intervenes directly in the social and economic relations of the people of ancient Israel," and by extension, Reimer concludes, it should shape our contemporary imaginations in the establishment of such "times of grace" where the impoverished and indebted can begin life anew. Such interventions, Deuteronomy 15 shows us, reflect the will of God.[10] Once again, the Deuteronomist presents a stark challenge to contemporary Christians regarding how we embody—or fail to embody—anything remotely similar to the sabbatical principle in our individual and collective lives.

Chapter 15 concludes with a section on reserving the firstborn of livestock to give as offering to God. It is noteworthy that guidelines for honoring and worshiping God are set alongside the commands to distribute a generous justice to community members who need it most. Worship, we note, is not to be understood as secondary to the practice of justice. Rather, worship of God and justice for neighbor go hand in hand.

Reflections by Christian ethicists and theologians on the function of worship in a Christian context can be seen as having resonance with the understanding of worship set forth in Deuteronomy 16. For instance, ethicist Stanley Hauerwas emphasizes how the practice of worship forms the character of those who worship. Hauerwas writes, "Ethics is a way of seeing before it is a matter of doing. The ethical task is not to tell you what is right or wrong, but rather to train you to see. That explains why, in the Church, a great deal of time and energy is spent in the act of worship. In worship, we are busy looking in the right direction."[11] According to the Deuteronomist,

> **Worship turns out to be the dangerous act of waking up to God and to the purposes of God in the world, and then living lives that actually show it.**
>
> Mark Labberton, *The Dangerous Act of Worship: Living God's Call to Justice* (Downers Grove, IL: InterVarsity Press, 2007), 13.

---

10. Haroldo Reimer, "A Time of Grace in Order to Begin Anew: The Sabbatical Year in Exodus 21:2–11 and Deuteronomy 15:1–18," in *God's Economy: Biblical Studies from Latin America*, ed. Ross Kinsler and Gloria Kinsler (Maryknoll, NY: Orbis Books, 2005), 72.

11. Stanley Hauerwas and William Willimon, *Resident Aliens: A Provocative Christian Assessment of Culture and Ministry for People Who Know Something Is Wrong* (Nashville: Abingdon Press, 1989), 95.

looking in the right direction is looking at God, who in turn is looking at those who are overlooked in Israel's midst.

Finally, the sabbatical principle of chapter 15 extends to Israel's marking of time. Not only is Israel called to rest on the seventh day, but Israel is also instructed to mark the years in increments of seven. This marking of time is further punctuated in chapter 16 by the three main agricultural festivals that Israel is called to observe at its central sanctuary. The first is Passover (vv. 1–8), where the instructions in Deuteronomy represent an expansion and punctuation of the way in which the Passover festival should remind Israel of being led by God out of Egypt from bondage to freedom. The text suggests that observing Passover is more than just a ritual of remembrance; indeed, the descendants of those who were liberated from Egypt are called on to observe it as if they themselves were the ones who were liberated. The past, for Israel, is a living past.

> [In] Deuteronomy, God advises the Israelites to celebrate Passover as if each celebrant had personally come out of Egypt. God's lesson here is clear: only by entering the story ourselves can we truly understand its meaning.
>
> Bruce Feiler, *Walking the Bible: A Journey by Land through the Five Books of Moses* (New York: HarperCollins, 2001), 420.

Passover is oriented around rituals that recall the exodus: from the Passover sacrifice that is offered (v. 6) to the unleavened bread that is eaten, Israelites are brought back to their hasty, dramatic departure from Egypt (v. 3). These instructions are similar to Exodus 23:14 with one important difference: Israelites must perform the Passover sacrifice in the central location rather than locally (vv. 5–6). This festival also tracks time with a Sabbath rhythm: on the seventh day, there shall be no work (v. 8). Once again we see within the Passover that eating is understood as a sacred act, and sacred eating is integrally related to sacred time, which in turn orients Israel not just to the past and the present but also to a future when the promises of God have been fulfilled. As discussed in the commentary for chapter 1, we see repeatedly in Deuteronomy that the memory of Israel's past grounds them in a historical identity as a people freed from slavery by a liberating God, a God who now commands continued obedience in the new land.

While Christians do not typically celebrate Passover and the other rituals detailed here, the link between ritual worship, Israel's God, and the identity of Israel articulated by the Deuteronomist is nevertheless still worth pondering by Christians today. If the God of the New Testament and the God of the Old Testament are one and the same, then Christian identity is also shaped by understanding the identity of the God of Israel as portrayed in Deuteronomy 16. Contemporary American public theologian Brian McLaren's insight into the link between worship and Christian identity relates well to the Deuteronomic vision of how worship of the liberating God shapes worshipers in becoming more like God:

> Worship, ultimately, is about honoring God for who God is. Too often, though, we assume an answer to the question of who God is by projecting a larger image of ourselves with all our prejudices, ideologies, and presumptions. If the God we worship is a projection of who we are now, our worship will form in us a hardened version of our current identity. But if our vision of God is ahead of us—better, more compassionate,

---

Up does become down—Pharaoh and his entire army are vanquished. Down becomes up—When the waters of the Sea of Reeds close, Moses stands tall with our ancestors in freedom. In other words, we have a comic ending! All's well that ends well. Or as the Haggadah [a Jewish text that sets forth the order of the Passover Seder] puts it . . . we have traveled from slavery to freedom, from degradation to celebration, from the rule of evil to the rule of God! This is, my friends, a comic vision of history! It's not Jack Benny; it's not the Marx Brothers; it's not Jerry Seinfeld or The Daily Show with Jon Stewart. You don't laugh when you encounter Passover's comedy because this is comedy in the broadest sense of the word. It's a telling of the human story where there is hope in the end. Moses isn't Hamlet, Othello, or Oedipus. Our Jewish story isn't a tragedy that implodes in on itself. Our story is instead a vision that promises something better can always happen. . . . True, there is much sadness in our Jewish experience and the overall human experience. That is why you can't have a Seder without salt water and maror. But you also can't have a Seder without sweet charoset and freedom bread matza, without four cups of wine, and without the ultimate punch line—L'shana ha-ba-a b'Yerushalayim [next year in Jerusalem].

Rabbi Mark Dov Shapiro, "Passover as a Comedy," http://www.sinai-temple.org/passover/passover_comedy.php.

more wise—our experience of worship will change our identity as it brings the radiance of God's identity more fully into
view.[12]

The Festival of Weeks is the next ritual to be considered, a sum-
mertime festival that marks the beginning of the harvest and calls
on Israel to celebrate God's identity as provider. The instructions
for this festival connect to several recurring themes in this legal section of Deuteronomy. The people are instructed to offer a portion
of their harvest, proportionate "to the blessing [they] have received
from the LORD [their] God" (16:11). A key word, "rejoice," directs
Israel in their attitude during worship, just as Israel is instructed to
do in 12:12.

And rejoicing is not simply an individual act; it is done with family, slaves, the Levites, the orphans, the widows, and the strangers
(16:12; see also 12:12; 14:28–29).
If the vision of God is, as McLaren
says, ahead of God's people rather
than limited to the people's own
projections of what they want God
to be, we see that inclusion of the
most vulnerable in society in worship is fundamental to worshiping
the One who protects the most
vulnerable.

> Rejoice in the LORD, O you
> righteous.
>   Praise befits the upright.
> Praise the LORD with the lyre;
>   make melody to him with
>   the harp of ten strings.
> Sing to him a new song;
>   play skillfully on the strings,
>   with loud shouts.
>
> (Ps. 33:1–3)

The call for the entire community to rejoice comes one more
time in the description of the third festival, the Festival of Booths,
in verses 13–17. Israel is instructed to observe the festival for seven
days. This festival and the two preceding it not only follow the agricultural cycle, but they also wed the gifts of the land to the people's
covenantal relationship to the God who blesses them with the land
and the fruit it brings forth. In addition, this third festival focuses
attention not just on the gifts from the land but on the "produce

12. Brian McLaren, "After the Worship Wars: Christian Identity and Worship," Patheos.com,
    January 9, 2012, http://www.patheos.com/Resources/Additional-Resources/After-the-
    Worship-Wars-Christian-Identity-and-Worship-Brian-McLaren-01-09-2012.html.

from [the] threshing floor and wine press" (v. 13). The people are called to rejoice in the gifts of the land, most certainly, but also in the human ability to take those gifts and make something new. As they open their hands to the needy in their midst, they open their hands to God in thanksgiving for the gifts God has bestowed on them.

16:18–18:22
Sharing the Power

A crucial issue that has yet to be addressed in the legal structure of the new vision for a new land is who is in charge of what. As Moses prepares for his own death, his speech at this point envisions the shift for Israel from a nomadic people loosely regulated (note the references to the twelve tribal leaders in Num. 34:16–29 and the seventy elders in Num. 11:16) to a society in which the judges, king, priests, and prophets all share the power. The laws in this section concerning communal leadership share with the Fifth Commandment (cf. Deut. 5:16) on honoring one's parents a similar stance toward the role and purpose of authority. Recall that from its very first chapter, the Deuteronomistic text is preparing Israel to transition from Moses' leadership to a full-fledged civic structure with numerous levels of leadership. Noteworthy here is how each type of authority is placed not under other earthly authorities but instead under the authority of torah—the instruction of God.[13] In addition, we see that justice is the operative governing principle; even future kings come under its rule. Finally, every member of the community is entitled to the same justice in civil and religious matters.

Deuteronomy 16:18–20 focuses on judges, and again we hear strong echoes of Deuteronomy 1:9–18, particularly in the call to appoint lay people as judges, in the need for impartiality, and in the overarching emphasis on wisdom needed for

> You must not be partial in judging; hear out the small and the great alike; you shall not be intimidated by anyone, for the judgment is God's.
>
> (Deut. 1:17)

---

13. Miller, *Ten Commandments*, 141.

proper adjudicating of disputes. In his *Life of Moses*, fourth-century theologian Gregory of Nyssa defines wisdom as that which "holds to the mean between shrewdness and simplicity. Neither the wisdom of the serpent nor the simplicity of the dove is to be praised, if one should choose either of these with respect to itself alone. Rather it is a disposition which closely unites these two by the mean that is virtue."[14] Just as God is one who takes no bribes (Deut. 1:17), so shall the judges resist the inclination to accept bribes, a common practice in the ancient Near East. The Deuteronomist once again emphasizes the distinctiveness of the vision for Israel's social configuration in the new land.

> The temptation for judges and government officials to accept bribes is found in every time and place. In the ancient Near East taking bribes became almost institutionally accepted in bureaucratic situations as competing parties attempted to outmaneuver each other.
>
> John H. Walton, et al., *The IVP Bible Background Commentary: Old Testament* (Downers Grove, IL: InterVarsity Press), 573.

But what about God's partiality toward the most vulnerable in Israelite society? Returning to Deuteronomy 10:17–19, we see that for the Deuteronomist, fair and impartial adjudication in judicial matters is thoroughly compatible with respect to God's character as the One who executes justice "for the orphan and the widow" and shows love for the stranger. As theologian Miroslav Volf explains, God's justice is qualitatively different from the disinterested notion of justice that theorists like John Rawls have described. Volf's articulation of divine justice, especially vis-à-vis ancient Israel, is worth quoting at some length, for it sheds light on the dynamic tension within Deuteronomy between God's impartiality and God's gratuitous commitment to Israel as well as to the stranger, the widow, and the orphan:

> There is a pattern in Israel's history which goes something like this: the Israelites suffer, they cry out to the Lord, God hears them, and God delivers—and this is called justice (Judges 5:11). . . . God is interested in the good of the Israelites, and

---

14. Gregory of Nyssa, *The Life of Moses*, trans. Abraham Malherbe and Everett Ferguson (Mahwah, NJ: Paulist Press, 1978), 128.

this interest is part of God's justice. God never treats Israel as though she were not God's covenant people, never steps outside the relationship to gain a detached objectivity, never suppresses interest in their salvation. If God did that, God would, so to speak, step outside Godself and no longer be God. Hence, God's justice and God's kindness (Psalm 145:17), God's righteousness and God's salvation (Isaiah 45:21), are intertwined. When God saves, God does justice; when God does justice, God saves.[15]

Even as the judges are called to strive for impartiality in adjudication of the cases that come before them, Israel's judicial practices are at the same time shaped by the character of God, the divine judge.

Much has been made by biblical interpreters of the repetition of the word *tzedek*—"justice"—in verse 20: "Justice, and only justice you shall pursue so that you may live and occupy the land. (16:20). Justice lies at the heart of this new vision for a new land. Just rulers are paramount to the well-being of Israel in its life in the new land. To understand more concretely the role of justice in Israel's new life, Deuteronomy 17:2–7 offers a

> Let justice roll down like waters, and righteousness like an ever-flowing stream.
>
> (Amos 5:24)

case study on what *tzedek* within Israel should look like. This section returns to the issue of apostasy (cf. Deut. 13) as it addresses what should be done with an Israelite who violates the First Commandment and worships another god. As we saw most explicitly in chapter 13 but also implicitly in many other chapters, the Deuteronomist consistently warns against this forbidden practice, arguing that turning from the people's covenantal relationship with God leads nowhere other than to death. In contrast to the absence of guidelines for adjudication in parts of chapter 13, here in chapter 17 Moses instructs the judges that if they hear of "such an abhorrent thing," they should first "make a thorough inquiry" (v. 4) before taking any action. Administering justice within the community, we

---

15. Miroslav Volf, *Exclusion and Embrace: A Theological Exploration of Identity, Otherness, and Reconciliation* (Nashville: Abingdon Press, 1996), 221.

see here, is not simply a mechanical or legalistic issue; that is why wisdom is required.

Additionally, it is also imperative that more than one witness testify to the transgression (v. 6). If there is evidence of this crime, "the hands of the witnesses shall be the first raised against the person to execute the death penalty" (v. 7). While a zealot may be tempted to make false claims in order to bring down an enemy, the requirement for more than one witness works against such temptations. This section ends with the phrase "You shall purge the evil from your midst" (v. 7), the phrase also used in chapter 13 and repeatedly throughout the following chapters.

While there is much to applaud in the sophisticated process of adjudication laid out in Deuteronomy 17, this case study also contains elements that leave a sour taste in the mouths of contemporary readers. The harshness of the death sentence, for instance, is difficult to ignore. And yet we note that amid the harsh climate of the ancient Near East, provisions for a thorough inquiry and more than one witness offer a glimpse into a startlingly different way of living within this harsh, ancient context. Just as we discussed in the commentary on chapters 12–13, we know that central to the vision of a good life in this good land is Israel's faithful allegiance to their God. Following other gods, following other practices, the Deuteronomist insists, brings death. Another message here is also clear: that good life in a good land is possible *only* if there's justice. And justice requires punishing those who turn from the covenantal way of life.

In his writings about justice, theologian Paul Tillich talks about the ability of justice to "preserve what is to be united." Even in the midst of the sour taste regarding the harsh punishment commanded in Deuteronomy 17, we can link Tillich's understanding of the preserving power of justice with the Deuteronomist's strong

---

Love does not do more than justice demands, but love is the ultimate principle of justice. Love reunites; justice preserves what is to be united. It is the form in which and through which love performs its work. Justice in its ultimate meaning is creative justice, and creative justice is the form of reuniting love.

Paul Tillich, *Love, Power, and Justice: Ontological Analyses and Ethical Applications* (London: Oxford University Press, 1954), 71.

connection between justice and the preservation of the covenantal community. Even in the midst of calls for harsh punishment within Deuteronomy, at the same time we glimpse that loving God and loving neighbor is at the heart of Israel's vision of a just society.

In the midst of strong speech about the essential role justice must play in life in the new land, the Deuteronomist also acknowledges the potential limitations of any human judge. In verse 8 Moses says to the judges, "If a judicial decision is too difficult for you to make," bring the matter to the Levitical priests and "the judge who is in office in those days" (17:8–9). We see here that the judicial system is understood as a system with limitations and that other leaders— namely here the priests—may need to become involved in the juridical process as well.

In 17:14–20, Moses acknowledges that establishing a kingship for Israel in the new land may be the next step in structuring society; indeed, such leadership was promised to Abraham and Sarah long before (Gen. 17:5–6). But we know that early in its national life, there were conflicting views within Israel about whether or not it should be

> No longer shall your name be Abram, but your name shall be Abraham; for I have made you the ancestor of a multitude of nations. I will make you exceedingly fruitful; and I will make nations of you, and kings shall come from you.
>
> (Gen. 17:5–6)

ruled by a king (cf. 1 Sam. 8). One of the biggest concerns reflected in 1 Samuel—and a concern that persists throughout the history of kingship in Israel—is how Israel will understand its relationship to God, whom for Israel is the ultimate authority, when a king is also present.

> Then all the elders of Israel gathered together and came to Samuel at Ramah, and said to him, "You are old and your sons do not follow in your ways; appoint for us, then, a king to govern us, like other nations." . . Samuel prayed to the Lord, and the Lord said to Samuel, "Listen to the voice of the people in all that they say to you; for they have not rejected you, but they have rejected me from being king over them. . . . Now, then, listen to their voice; only—you shall solemnly warn them, and show them the ways of the king who shall reign over them."
>
> (1 Sam. 8:4–9)

The Deuteronomist knows that Israelite history following entrance into the promised land involved kings, and he casts Moses in Deut. 17 as offering Israel permission for a king if it desires one. Moses' acknowledgment of future kings, however, is accompanied by a set of surprising limitations on royal authority, reflecting again a sense of ambivalence regarding the concept of kingship. In Deuteronomy, it is clear that a king is not to take the place of God but rather to be a leader chosen by God (17:15) who has limited authority over the people. Just as God requires a faithful people, so God requires a faithful king. Selecting a king "whom the LORD your God will choose" echoes the reference to a centralized location for judicial proceedings, to a centralized place of worship of God's choosing, and to the claim made throughout Deuteronomy that God's sovereign control reaches all corners of Israel's life.

In establishing a profile for the ideal, faithful Israelite king, the Deuteronomist sets forth some important parameters. First, even though the office of king is borrowed from other nations, Israel must elect someone from within its own community. Second, verse 16 puts forward a limitation on how many horses the king acquires for himself in a context where numbers of horses serve as barometer of a king's military strength (e.g., passages such as 1 Kgs. 10–11 point out Solomon's excesses as king). In a book that devotes significant attention to preparing for and going to war, such limitations on the king's power are striking. Beyond the stated military limitations, verse 17 also limits the number of wives the king may have (again Solomon is guilty of such excesses, reportedly having more than a thousand wives; cf. 1 Kgs. 11:1–5), as well as issues a warning that the king should avoid the pomp and extravagance commonly associated with kingdoms (cf. 1 Sam. 8:10–18). If he doesn't avoid these excesses, "his heart will turn away." Within this legal section of the book, we once again see in Moses' speech a concern for obedience to God that goes beyond the letter of the law. Yet again obedience is understood as ultimately a matter of the heart.

> Solomon gathered chariots and horses; he had fourteen hundred chariots and twelve thousand horses, which he stationed in the chariot cities with the king in Jerusalem.
>
> (1 Kgs. 10:26)

What Deuteronomy gives us is a vision of kingship that compliments and supports the Mosaic instructions given throughout the book. Indeed, we see here in 17:18 an explicit reference to "a copy of this law" that will be "written for" the king. As discussed in the introduction to this commentary, this verse's reference to *mishneh torah,* or "a copy of the law," is one of the Hebrew names given to the book of Deuteronomy (the other is taken from the first line of the book: "These are the words"), and this second name was translated into the Greek *Deuteronomion,* meaning "second law," which eventually became the Latin and later the English name for the book. Ironically, the name "Deuteronomy" stems from a mistranslation of 17:18, which talks of a "copy" rather than "second law," which it has come to be known.[16] Further, this verse sets the stage for Moses' command to Israel in Deuteronomy 27:3 to write down "all the words of this law." When Moses dies, it takes more than Joshua and the elders to take his place. To remember all the words of the law, the people need a written copy. And this written copy, we hear in chapter 17, should be followed faithfully by any king of Israel.

And if the copy of the law referenced in 17:18 is talking about the entire text of Deuteronomy, then the king would have not only a covenantal vision of history but also a substantive set of laws binding on him. Indeed, the king is called to "diligently observe" the laws and statutes just as every other Israelite is called to do (17:19). In the context of the kingdoms of the ancient Near East, that Israel's king was instructed to abide by preestablished laws and statutes rather than create them is again an important mark of limited authority.

The ancient hearers of the words of Deuteronomy would have heard these stipulations as part of the larger Deuteronomic History of Israelite kings who abused their office and power (e.g., Saul, David, and Solomon). Anticipating the checkered future of kingship in Israel, Moses establishes guidelines for a faithful king, one who adheres

> So the king took counsel, and made two calves of gold. He said to the people, "You have gone up to Jerusalem long enough. Here are your gods, O Israel, who brought you up out of the land of Egypt."
>
> (1 Kgs. 12:28)

---

16. Tigay, *JPS Torah Commentary,* xi.

to the commandment to worship God alone. But in hearing the words of Deuteronomy, an exiled Israel would also know that the dominant story line in Deuteronomic history was not the faithful but the unfaithful king. Thus Deuteronomy's vision for an ideal king remains largely just that: an ideal vision.

Christian readers know that Jesus is also referred to as a king in the line of Israelite kings. For instance, the angel Gabriel says to Mary in Luke 1, "And now, you will conceive in your womb and bear a son, and you will name him Jesus. He will be great, and will be called the Son of the Most High, and the Lord God will give to him the throne of his ancestor David" (Luke 1:31–32). How, then, might the kingship of Jesus relate to the Deuteronomic vision of kingship? Even with prophetic pronouncements like the one from Gabriel, Jesus refuses to claim such a title before Pilate (Luke 23:3). A central aspect of the Gospel stories of Jesus is that his words and actions seem at odds with conventional conceptions of kingship. In response to this tension between Jesus' life and actions and ancient views of kingship, biblical scholar Patrick Miller offers the following insight:

> Much has been written about the way the messianic passages of the royal psalms and Isaiah point us to and find their actuality in Jesus of Nazareth. It is possible we have overlooked the text that may resonate most with the kingship he manifested [Deut. 17]; he was the one who sought and received none of the perquisites of kingship, who gave his full and undivided allegiance to God, and who lived his whole life by the instruction, the torah, of the Lord.[17]

Could it be, then, that Christian understandings of Jesus' kingship would be enhanced by turning to Deuteronomy's presentation of what it means to be a faithful, obedient, Israelite king? Miller, for one, would answer in the affirmative. In addition, hymns such as "What Child Is This?" cast Jesus in a decidedly Deuteronomic light when it comes to the tradition of kingship he comes to fulfill. To be

---

17. Patrick Miller, *Deuteronomy*, Interpretation: A Bible Commentary for Teaching and Preaching (Louisville, KY: Westminster John Knox Press, 1990), 149.

What child is this, who, laid to rest, on Mary's lap is sleeping?
Whom angels greet with anthems sweet while shepherds watch are keeping?
This, this is Christ the king, whom shepherds guard and angels sing;
haste, haste to bring him laud, the babe, the son of Mary!

Why lies he in such mean estate where ox and ass are feeding?
Good Christian, fear; for sinners here the silent Word is pleading.
Nails, spear, shall pierce him through; the cross be borne for me, for you.
Hail, hail, the Word made flesh, the babe, the son of Mary!

So bring him incense, gold, and myrrh; come, one and all, to own him.
The King of kings salvation brings; let loving hearts enthrone him.
Raise, raise the song of high. The virgin sings her lullaby.
Joy, joy, for Christ is born, the babe, the son of Mary!

"What Child Is This?" *Glory to God* (Louisville, KY: Westminster John Knox Press, 2013), 145.

the type of king the book of Deuteronomy envisions, then, is to rule in a way that keeps the focus on the ultimate authority of God.

Separate from the sphere of kingly rule is the office of priest. In 18:1–8 we hear again of the Levites' special priestly role within the community. The Levites as the only Israelites without land inheritance were also a constant and tangible reminder of Israel's dependence on God. Just like the king would be, Levites were "chosen by God" to minister to God on Israel's behalf. And just like the image of the king, the portrait of the Levitical priest here is the ideal or model Israelite. When viewed through the lens of the Levites, Israel's prosperity will be realized only in and through its dependence on God. What the Levites did was regulate sacrificial worship so that Israel might avoid turning to "the abhorrent practices" of other nations (18:9). Verses 10–14 enumerate

> Of necessity, empire engages in works of magic. These promise the powerful a sure and prosperous passage, through wily turns and twists of polity, pacts and betrayal of pacts. And when sweet talk fails, try incursion and seizures. In sum, condemn the word of God in favor of a demonology of death. As in the time of Deuteronomy, so at the present writing.
>
> Daniel Berrigan, *No Gods but One* (Grand Rapids: Wm. B. Eerdmans Publishing Co., 2010), 104.

more of such practices, from putting one's children through the fire to consulting divination or soothsayers.

The list of prohibitions in verses 9–14 all involve human attempts to figure out, with the help of magic, what the future will bring. But magical ways are rejected in favor of another, divinely initiated way: in verse 15 we learn that God will raise up a prophet like Moses. The emphasis here and throughout Deuteronomy is on God's giving God's Word to be spoken by the prophet.

That magic is contrary to faithful following of God has resurfaced recently in Christian circles thanks to the immense popularity of J. K. Rowling's Harry Potter series. Many Christians have been highly critical of the series and the magical world it depicts. "Let me say something about Harry Potter. Warlocks are enemies of God," said Becky Fischer, a Pentecostal pastor. "And I don't care what kind of hero they are; they're an enemy of God." Fischer continued, "Had it been in the Old Testament Harry Potter would have been put to death. You don't make heroes out of warlocks."[18] Similar to the concerns expressed here in Deuteronomy, Christians like Fischer worry that people of faith will be seduced away from God's Word by the allure of Rowling's wizarding world. A major difference between the magic condemned in Deuteronomy and the magical world of Harry Potter, however, is that the latter is a work of fiction. And that fictitious world, many other Christians have noted, often addresses important religious themes—such as the reality of evil, hope for salvation, and belief that in the end love is stronger than death. Perhaps the enjoyment of Rowling's world by millions of people who also claim religion suggests that good literature can potentially enhance rather than threaten faithful adherence to God's Word.

Just as it is with the king, the prophet will come from the community and will be one of the people; yet the prophet will also be set apart in being chosen by God for this special role. In 18:16–18, the story of Moses as mediator at Horeb (Deut. 5:22–27) is retold. The prophet will be able to persist in the face of the divine fire on behalf

18. Danielle Elizabeth Tumminio, "My Take: Why We're Drawn to Harry Potter's Theology," CNN.com Belief Blog, July 13, 2011, http://religion.blogs.cnn.com/2011/07/13/my-take-why-were-drawn-to-harry-potters-theology/.

of the people and not perish. At the same time Moses' humanity—indeed the humanity of all the prophets who follow him—is also highlighted (and it hearkens back to Deut. 1:9–18 and Moses' inability to adjudicate properly all the conflicts in Israel). Deuteronomy 18 reassures the people that after Moses is gone, God will raise up another prophet who will continue to mediate God's word to the people.

While Moses reassures Israel that God will continue to speak to the people through other prophets like him, he also raises the thorny issue of false prophecy (vv. 20–22), an issue repeatedly addressed throughout in OT writings (e.g., 1 Kgs. 22; Jer. 5:10–15; 14:13–16). Moses poses a critical question in 18:21: How is Israel to distinguish true prophets from false ones? Moses responds by identifying two kinds of false prophets: the one who speaks illegitimately in the name of the Lord and the one who speaks in the name of other

> Then I said: "Ah, Lord God! Here are the prophets saying to them, 'You shall not see the sword, nor shall you have famine, but I will give you true peace in this place.'" And the Lord said to me: The prophets are prophesying lies in my name; I did not send them, nor did I command them or speak to them. They are prophesying to you a lying vision, worthless divination, and the deceit of their own minds.
>
> (Jer. 14:13–14)

gods. One indication that a prophecy is the word of the Lord is that it comes to pass (v. 22). But this is not an airtight approach, as is seen in Jer. 28, where Jeremiah and Hannaniah speak contradictory prophecies in the name of the Lord. Eventually Jeremiah's prophecy comes to pass, but in Jer. 28:5–9 we hear that sometimes even Jeremiah himself is unsure who is speaking the word of the Lord.

Further still, the Deuteronomist also acknowledges in chapter 18 that sometimes prophesies of false prophets do take place (cf. Deut. 13:1–5). Nevertheless, in 18:20, Moses' claim is clear: true prophecy never draws God's people away from God. Only when it comes from the one true God is the prophet worthy of Israel's trust.

FURTHER REFLECTIONS
A Prophet Like Moses

Deuteronomy's Moses is a prophet extraordinaire (cf. 34:10–12), not just because of the signs and wonders he performs (13:1) but also because of his speaking the divine Word to the people of God. And while chapter 18 claims that God will raise up a prophet like Moses, those words stand in tension with the closing words of Deuteronomy: "Never since has there arisen a prophet in Israel like Moses" (34:10). Further, two later streams of religious tradition, Christianity and Islam, both claim to have arisen out of the tradition of Moses but also to have gone beyond it. Christians understand Jesus as the successor to Moses (cf. John 6:14; Acts 3:22–26; 7:37). In John 6, Jesus' feeding bread to five thousand is compared to Moses' role as giver of manna to the wandering Israelites. In addition, Christians have long talked about the work of Jesus Christ in terms of the offices he holds, hearkening back again to Deuteronomy 16–18 and the discussion of prophet, priest, and king.

> But we must not think here of the pattern of the great prophets of judgment, but of the way in which Moses himself discharged the duties of his office in accordance with the Deuteronomic conception: interceding, suffering as the representative, actually dying (Deut. 4:21f.; 9:18ff., 25ff.).
>
> Gerhard von Rad, *Deuteronomy: A Commentary* (Philadelphia: Westminster Press, 1966), 124.

Focusing specifically on the role of prophet here, Christians understand Jesus as embodying the same roles that Moses takes on in Deuteronomy. As biblical scholar Morna Hooker claims, "Jesus was regarded as a prophet, not simply because he *spoke* like a prophet, but because he *acted* like a prophet."[19] Jesus, like Moses, is a servant who suffers vicariously for a sinful people; he, like Moses, intercedes on behalf of those people; and finally, like Moses, Jesus is understood as the embodiment of God's Word. Jesus refers to himself as a prophet in response to those who challenge him as he teaches in Nazareth, his hometown: "But

19. Morna Hooker, *The Signs of a Prophet: The Prophetic Actions of Jesus* (Harrisburg, PA: Trinity Press International, 1997), 16.

[he] said to them, 'Prophets are not without honor except in their own country and in their own house'" (Matt. 13:57). Others also refer to Jesus as a prophet (cf. John 4:19; 9:17). But the NT narrative also goes beyond claims that Jesus embodies God's Word in a prophetic way through claims that Jesus is also divine (cf. John 1:14).

> **Virtually every major element in Muhammad's prophetic vocation finds its counterpart in the life of Moses.**
>
> Jane Dammen McAuliffe, "Connecting Moses and Muhammad," *The Old Testament in Byzantium*, ed. Pau Magdalino and Robert Nelson (Washington, DC: Dumbarton Oaks Research Library and Collection, 2010), 288.

In addition to Christians laying claim on Jesus as the one foretold in Deuteronomy 18:18, Muslims also interpret God's words to Moses in this verse as referring to Muhammad, who, according to Islam, is the last in the line of prophets that dates back to Moses: "I will raise up for them a prophet like [Moses] from among their own people; I will put my words in the mouth of the prophet, who shall speak to them everything that I command."

What is suggested in Deuteronomy 18:15–18 is that God's use of human beings as mediators of God's Word will continue beyond Moses. And for Christians, the other writings of the Old and New Testaments lay claim to this continuing tradition. Even though crafting a theology of religious pluralism is beyond the scope of our task in this commentary, it is important for Christians to pause at this pregnant section of Deuteronomy and acknowledge that Muslims have

> **We believe in God and that which is revealed unto us and that which was revealed unto Abraham, and Ishmael, and Isaac, and Jacob, and the tribes, and that which Moses and Jesus received, and that which the prophets received from their Lord.**
>
> Al-Baqarah, 2:136, *The Holy Qur'an*, trans. Abdullah Yusuf Ali, 11th ed. (Elmhurst, NY: Tahrike Tarsile Qur'an, 2003).

also practiced a form of *midrash*—ongoing interpretation of God's Word—that has a family resemblance to Christian interpretations of this passage. Indeed, Moses is mentioned in over five hundred verses in the Qur'an,[20] and Muhammad is understood as receiving

---

20. Ziad Elmarsafy, *The Enlightenment Qur'an: The Politics of Translation and the Construction of Islam* (Oxford: Oneworld Publications, 2009), 217.

the revelation of God's Word in the tradition of Moses and Jesus. Claims to Moses by Christians and Muslims as a central figure in a common heritage represent important opportunities for interfaith conversation and interreligious learning.

19:1–22:12
Glimpses of Justice in the Midst of Murder and War

Chapter 18's concluding passages on the role of the prophet are some of the most significant parts of what is often called "the preached law" of Moses in chapters 12–26. In chapters 19–26, we see that the narrative flow of the previous chapters becomes more muted as the text moves more toward lists of laws. The passage in 19:1–13 returns to an issue raised earlier in Deuteronomy (cf. 4:41–43), the issue of Israel's establishment of cities of refuge in order to offer sanctuary to those who have killed another person unintentionally.

> **If it was not premeditated, but came about by an act of God, then I will appoint for you a place to which the killer may flee.**
>
> (Exod. 21:13)

We see that this issue is also related to the Sixth Commandment's injunction not to kill. What is being addressed with the designation of cities is the ancient practice of family revenge: when a member of the family was killed, other members of that family in the ancient world were expected to exact blood revenge for the killing. In Israel, however, there had long been a distinction between premeditated killing and unintentional killing (cf. Exod. 21:13). Chapter 19, then, proposes what to do with someone who kills another person unintentionally (vv. 4–7).

There is certainly a humanitarian dimension to the practice of sending those who did not mean to kill to a city set aside as a sanctuary for protection. The Deuteronomist is advocating throughout the text a system of justice in Israel that differs in some significant ways from the systems of justice surrounding it in the ancient world. At the same time, the practice of familial revenge is not done away with; instead it is simply restrained. In addition, Moses requires Israel to follow these practices not just out of concern for the safety of the persons seeking refuge but also because Israel must do everything in their power to keep the land God is giving them in an undefiled state (v. 10). God's covenantal relationship with Israel is repeatedly affirmed here, along with repeated reminders to Israel that God has given them this land as a gift and their response is to keep God's commandments (vv. 1, 3, 8–10).

In 19:14–15, there is brief attention paid to prohibiting the movement of property boundary markers. The action of moving such markers then reappears in Deut. 27:17 as a curse. The Deuteronomic concern for justice continues with verses 15–21, where the focus is on witnesses and their role in the punishment of those who commit crimes. First we hear that one witness is not enough to convict someone of a crime (v. 15). Rather there must be two or more witnesses so that their stories can be corroborated. But the real focus in this section is on a witness who commits perjury and lies about another person's criminal activity (vv. 16–21). Such behavior defiles the land and goes against the judicial processes set forth in chapter 16. Thus, the Deuteronomist returns to a now-familiar refrain when discussing what to do with the one who perjures: "You shall purge the evil from your midst" (v. 19), for such actions threaten the viability of a community wedded to God in covenantal relationship.

The section concludes with an infamous refrain: "Show no pity; life for life, eye for eye, tooth for tooth, hand for hand, foot for foot" (v. 21). Referenced in Deuteronomy and in two other places in the Old Testament (Exod. 21:23–25; Lev. 24:19–22), the *lex taliones*, or "law of retaliation" is often referred to by Christians as the prime example of the way in which Jewish morality differs from (and is inferior to) Christian morality. Certainly Matthew 5 can be read as adding weight to such a claim. In Matthew 5:38–39, Jesus says, "'You have heard that it was said, "An eye for an eye and a tooth for a tooth." But I say to you, Do not resist an evildoer. But if anyone strikes you on the right cheek, turn the other also." Christian interpretation, even up to the present day, views this juxtaposition of Moses' call for an "eye for an eye" and Jesus' call to "turn the other cheek" as evidence that second-century bishop Marcion was right when he claimed that the Christian God is superior to the OT God of law and judgment. In response to this passage in Matthew, Augustine takes issue with the scriptural claim, also in Matthew, that Jesus came not to abolish but to fulfill the law (Matt. 5:17–18). Augustine writes, "This [Matt. 5:38–9] is not fulfillment but destruction."[21] Take also this query by Daniel Berrigan in his commentary on Deuteronomy: "Dare we conclude that Jesus offers a more exigent God than the deity of Moses, a more consistent God, a superior ethic?" Berrigan answers his own question by concluding that with Jesus "something new is in the air, a new spirit for the old. Forgiveness and reconciliation become . . . possible. Possible even to ourselves, who, left to our own resources, might well fall under an ancient curse, the progeny of Cain."[22] While we do not want to deny that Christians see in Jesus the "new spirit" that Berrigan refers to, we also must take care not to distance Jesus from his role as a torah-abiding Jew (see the commentary's earlier discussion of Jesus and the Greatest Commandment) who stands in a long tradition of affirmation and dissention with respect to the interpretation of torah. In order to see Jesus' claim in Matthew 5 as not simply condemning some broader OT ethic, let us return to Deuteronomy 19:21 for a deeper understanding of the *lex taliones* in the context of Deuteronomy.

> **Often this legal principle [the *lex talionis*] has been seen as the essence of Old Testament law, but that is clearly not the case, whatever may be the force of the principle.**
>
> Patrick Miller, *Deuteronomy,* Interpretation: A Bible Commentary for Teaching and Preaching (Louisville, KY: Westminster John Knox Press, 1990), 146.

That the rule of exacting an eye for an eye is mentioned only three times in the entire Old Testament suggests that it is not a defining principle for how justice is understood in ancient Israel. Scholars point out that it is virtually guaranteed that such a statement was never taken literally. Highlighting the fact that punishment in ancient Israel was meted out in the form of bodily mutilation only in one guideline for punishment (see Deut. 25:11–12), scholars claim that the "eye for an eye" injunction would not have been followed in a literal way. In fact, what scholars often claim instead is that the *lex*

21. Augustine, *Contra Faustum,* Book 19, www.newadvent.org/fathers/140619.htm.
22. Daniel Berrigan, *No Gods but One* (Grand Rapids: Wm. B. Eerdmans Publishing Co., 2009), 111.

taliones favors proportional justice over vengeance, which is why it makes sense that the *lex taliones* comes at the end of a section that begins with talk of cities of refuge to prevent acts of vengeance.

Within these last chapters of the law section of Deuteronomy, attention is given to statutes dealing with proper conduct during war. The Deuteronomist provides criteria for what war looks like for Israel, chief among them being loyalty to God alone. Again we want to note the attention given in this section to some instances of humane and compassionate treatment of Israel's enemies in the midst of the destruction of war.

Rather than discussing specific tactics and strategies necessary for war, Deuteronomy 20:1–9 contains something more akin to a war sermon that reviews the ideology of a divinely endorsed war. In fact, Deuteronomy contains the only ancient Near Eastern legal code that extensively deals with the question of correct wartime behavior.[23] In this sermon Moses begins with the claim that the same God who brought them out of Egypt is the one who leads them in battle (v. 1). The message that God is in charge hearkens back to Deuteronomy 2:1–3:11, and God's sovereign control continues to be a prominent message throughout Deuteronomy. Every victory listed in chapter 20 is attributed to God (vv. 4, 13–14, 16). The theological point is clear: these military victories cannot be counted as human victories. Israel is victorious only because God led the battle charge.

In the midst of the unsettling ideological rhetoric of God-ordained war, we should not lose sight of a

> Partially hidden [within the conquest narratives of the Old Testament] was the basic fact that tribal groups were in need of land, [that Israel] had been both slowly and quickly moving in on territory occupied by others, coming into hostile contact with the prior occupants and seeking to move them out. There were political and sociological factors (not all of them discoverable) which caused the formation of an ideology.
>
> Patrick Miller, "Faith and Ideology in the Old Testament," in *Magnalia Dei, The Mighty Acts of God: Essays on the Bible and Archaeology in Memory of G. Ernest Wright*, ed. Frank Moore Cross, Werner E. Lemke, and Patrick D. Miller Jr. (New York: Doubleday & Co., 1976), 471.

23. Tamara Cohn Eskenazi and Andrea L. Weiss, eds., *The Torah: A Women's Commentary* (New York: URJ Press, 2008), 1158.

key point being made here by the Deuteronomist: whether Israel is victorious or defeated in war, whether it flourishes in the land or not, all is under the providence of God, for God carries Israel "just as one carries a child" (1:31).

The rules of warfare in chapter 20 begin with repeated calls to those who are fighting not to be afraid, lose heart, panic, or be in dread (cf. 20:1, 3, 8). Biblical scholar Gerhard von Rad explains that being discouraged in those ways was regarded in Israel as a lack of faith; therefore, von Rad suggests, discouragement should not be understood "only [as] a personal affair for the man who has been assailed by it; [rather it should be seen as threatening] the whole army."[24] Verses 3–4 contain a refrain that reappears throughout the biblical story of God's chosen people: be not afraid, for God is the one who goes with you. "Fear not" is given as a command (v. 1), and Israel is called once again to trust in God even as they go to war. This call to trust is integral to the ideological presentation of rules of war.

In verses 10–18 distinctions are made between battles against peoples outside the promised land (v. 15) and battles waged against those inside the land (vv. 16–17). With respect to tribes living outside the land, Israel is directed first to attempt to make peace (vv. 10–11); if peace is not possible, then Israel is to follow standard war practices of the day, which involved killing the men and keeping the women, children, and provisions as spoils of war (cf. 21:10–14). With respect to military campaigns against those who inhabit

> Despite the friendships made, [World War II Veteran Burnell Wollar] makes no bones about the terror of waging war. "When you're on the front lines and someone's shooting at you; I don't care what anybody says you're scared and you're scared every day. All you can think about is, when's this going to end or when is the bullet aimed at me that has my name on it."
>
> Jamie Greco, "Barrington World War II Veteran Remembers Being 'Scared Every Day,'" *Barrington Patch*, May 28, 2012, http://barrington-il.patch.com/articles/barrington-world-war-ii-veteran-remembers-being-scared-every-day.

24. Gerhard von Rad, *Old Testament Theology: Essays on Structure, Theme and Text*, vol. 1, ed. Patrick Miller (Minneapolis: Augsburg Fortress, 1992), 131.

the land, however, Israel is instructed to destroy them totally (vv. 16–18), which is again consistent with earlier instructions given in 2:34. The rationale for total destruction of those in the land is given in verse 18: that their presence would cause Israel to break the First Commandment of loyalty to and worship of God alone. In addition, the concerns regarding the pollution of Israel by the other tribes living in Israel also relates to the concern for keeping Israel's war camp pure (Deut. 23:9–14). Central to Israelite identity, we hear once again, is the requirement to reflect the holiness of God through all aspects of their lives, which meant that even the realities of going to war were no exception. Even in war, Moses' war sermon professes, the Lord is with them (23:14), and Israel is called on to respond to that reality through actions that keep them pure and set them apart.

As mentioned earlier, in the midst of this ideological presentation of war are glimpses of a humane and compassionate vision both for those who participate in battle as well as for elements of the natural world endangered by military action. In 20:5–7, Israel is instructed to allow special dispensation for anyone who has just built a house, planted a vineyard, or become engaged to be married.

Compassion is extended to those who have not yet been able fully to enjoy the material fruits of life, and the text instructs them to go and do so. Indeed, the vision for an Israel who flourishes in the land is not forgotten here. We even hear a painful echo of these blessings in the list of curses that will befall Israel in Deuteronomy 28:30 if they are disobedient: "You shall become engaged to a woman, but another man shall lie with

> The law in its humanity says that if a man has built a new house but has not yet enjoyed its fruit, or become betrothed to a girl but has not yet married her, he is to be excused military service.... It is also humane, in the calculation that the outcome of the war is uncertain and it is unjust for such a man not to benefit from his own labors or for someone else who has taken no trouble to possess the property of those who have put in the work.
>
> Clement of Alexandria, *Stromateis: Books One to Three*, 2.18.82.1–3.1, Fathers of the Church 85:213, as quoted in *Exodus, Leviticus, Numbers, Deuteronomy*, Ancient Christian Commentary on Scripture, Old Testament 3, ed. Joseph T. Lienhard (Downers Grove, IL: InterVarsity Press, 2001), 307.

her. You shall build a house, but not live in it. You shall plant a vineyard, but not enjoy its fruit." God intends for Israel to have a life of
blessing, full of enjoyment of the fruits of the land. But obedience
and blessings—and alternately disobedience and punishment—are
tightly linked throughout the Deuteronomic text.

These glimpses of compassionate behavior during war, however,
are set against the jarring instructions to Israel in 20:16 regarding
those who occupy the land God has promised Israel: the Israelites
"must not let anything that breathes remain alive." The text continues its verbal onslaught in verse 17 with the proclamation "You
shall annihilate them" and with the names of those who "deserve"
destruction: the Hittites, the Amorites, the Canaanites, the Perizz-
ites, the Hivites, and the Jebusites.

Why utter destruction for these tribes? The list of tribes in 20:18
re-presents what scholars have come to call "the Deuteronomistic
name formula" first seen in Deuteronomy 7:1. According to biblical
tradition, these tribes must be eradicated "so that they may not teach
[Israel] to do all the abhorrent things that they do for their gods."
Yet again, the text advocates annihilation of entire towns—indeed
whole tribes—in order to prevent Israel from being tempted to stray
from the First Commandment and follow other gods.

Verses 19–21 continue to demonstrate concern for material
fruits of life through a command for restraint with respect to the

---

Throughout human history, the environment has been one of war's many
victims. Thucydides records the scorched earth tactics used by the Greeks
during the Peloponnesian Wars. The Romans salted the soils of Carthage
after winning the Punic Wars. The Dutch breached their dykes in 1792 to
prevent a French invasion. More recently, during the Vietnam War, the United
States destroyed 14 percent of Vietnam's forests, including 54 percent of its
mangrove forests, through chemical defoliants, bulldozers and bombings.
Near the end of the Gulf War, Iraq burned hundreds of oil wells and dumped
massive amounts of oil into the Persian Gulf. And the ongoing civil war in the
Congo has decimated the country's wildlife, killing thousands of elephants,
gorillas and okapis.

David Bodansky, "Protecting the Environment During Wartime" (Athens, GA: University of Georgia
School of Law, Digital Commons, 2005), http://digitalcommons.law.uga.edu/cgi/viewcontent.
cgi?article=1013&context=fac_pm&sei-redir=1#search=%22environmental%20harm%20during%20
war%22.

nonhuman spoils in war. It was a common ancient practice to despoil the land gained in war. But here the Deuteronomist asks a startling question: "Are trees in the field human beings that they should come under siege from you?" (v. 19), followed by the command to preserve the trees that bear fruit. This call to protect the trees seems to be an attempt to limit the destruction of the natural world during military action; at the same time, the question also unnerves in its presumption that trees receive more mercy than the tribal people occupying Canaan.

In chapter 20, then, some startling examples of compassion in the midst of war sit alongside unnerving calls of violence, death, and destruction. Amidst the instructions for waging war is also a call to resist the devolution of military action—so often a reality in this world—into wanton destruction with no restraints. In the midst of the threat of death, there's a quiet insistence that this life, the pleasures of growing food, tending house, being married, and good gifts of the land—like the fruit trees—matter. There's an unresolved tension here between God's leading the charge to annihilate whole groups of peoples living in the land to preserving the beauty and affirming the integrity of human and nonhuman life.

> [Deuteronomy] is thoroughly saturated from the first to the last chapter by an outspoken war ideology, the origins and theological content of which cannot help becoming a problem to us.
>
> Gerhard von Rad, *Holy War in Ancient Israel* (Grand Rapids: Wm. B. Eerdmans Publishing Co., 1991), 115.

FURTHER REFLECTIONS
Holy War

No commentary on Deuteronomy can avoid the sustained attention given by the Deuteronomist throughout the book to issues of war. There is also no getting around the fact that in Deuteronomy war is an expressly religious phenomenon. While it is common to refer to passages in Deuteronomy as "holy war" texts, the OT writers actually did not use this term. The term was first applied to Israel's involvement in and understanding of its own wars in the early twentieth century by biblical scholar Friedrich Schwally and has become commonplace in analysis of Deuteronomy and other OT war texts in the years since. What does appear in OT writings is the phrase "wars of Yahweh" (cf. 1 Sam. 18:17; 25:28; Num. 21:14). Whatever term we use, we are faced with the phenomenon of God's leading the Israelites to war and purportedly securing military victory for Israel. While we can trace the practice by religious people of engaging in holy war throughout the centuries, the act of claiming that God is on the side of certain people and not others in war has become a part of our contemporary North American vocabulary, particularly as debate has raged over whether the terrorist attacks on September 11, 2001, constituted a holy war of Muslims against Christians and whether current U.S.-led wars in Iraq and Afghanistan represent a holy war of Christianity against Islam.

A commentary on the Deuteronomy war texts, then, must attend not only to the textual support of God-ordained slaughter of groups of people but also to the ways in which this Jewish and Christian Scripture can be used in the debates about holy war today. The *herem*, commonly referred to as the ban, is the call in Deuteronomy and other OT books for total obliteration of the enemy (cf. 2:24; 3:6, 7:2; see also Num. 21:12; Josh. 6:17–19; 1 Sam. 15:8). This was seen as an act of devotion to God in the midst of war, a practice not unique to Israel but also not very common in the ancient period. Scholars suggest that calls for the ban became a significant part of

---

The Deuteronomic directive to destroy entirely (*herem*) the Canaanites (Deut. 20:15–18) is a thoroughly violent commandment—and in modern times would be characterized as genocide. . . . Later readers of the Bible dramatically transformed this divine directive through the hermeneutic alignment of the Canaanites with the current detested "other." Thus the Canaanites have been identified with the Irish Catholics (by Oliver Cromwell), Native Americans (by the New England Puritans), Palestinians (by militant Zionists), and scores of other "enemies" of "Israel." In doing so, the violence perpetrated against these groups is not only justified, but indeed, part and parcel of the original divine plan.

Ra'anan S. Boustan, Alex P. Jassen, and Calvin J. Roetzel, "Introduction," *Violence, Scripture, and Textual Practice in Early Judaism and Christianity* (Boston: Brill, 2009), 4–5.

the ideology of war more in retrospect than in actual practice of the time. Actions that were taken by human initiative later become reflective of divine command. The Deuteronomic history overflows with references to Israel constantly being threatened by the possibility of apostasy. Israel's story is a story of being engaged in war for religious purposes; it is a story of the struggle for the soul of Israel, and the text now reflects those high stakes. There is no higher stake than a war ordained by God.

While we are mindful of the history of God-ordained war and the reasons that the ban is part of the rhetoric of Deuteronomy's holy war, we also acknowledge that the kind of war described here in the text would be given the term *genocide* today: that is, the deliberate destruction of a whole nation or race of people. As Interfaith Youth Core founder Eboo Patel suggests, then, the issue for Christians today is not simply to offer commentary on what Israelite holy war and practices of the ban meant in ancient Israel; rather, we must wrestle with how these texts should be interpreted and understood *today*. In doing so, we must start by resisting the temptation to dismiss or ignore these holy war texts. Second, we want to point again to the tension that exists internal to the text regarding God's endorsement of violence and harm of whole groups of people. In addition to the tensions within chapter 20 discussed above, we also want to note that there are moments in OT writings when Canaanites are embraced by Israelites. Take, for instance, the story of Judah in Genesis 38, where both his wife and his daughter-in-law, Tamar, are Canaanites. Noteworthy is the fact that Tamar is included in the genealogy of David (cf. Ruth 4:18) as well as in Matthew's genealogy

---

There are indeed explicit statements about violence in the scriptures of most major religious traditions. But to think that the statements of a religious text suddenly morph into armed reality is to have a profound misunderstanding of religion. There are several layers of meaning to any religious text: the explicit, the contextual, and the symbolic, to name just a few. A religious text comes to life through its interpreters. Violence committed in the name of a religion is really violence emanating from the heart of a particular interpreter.

Eboo Patel, *Acts of Faith: The Story of an American Muslim and the Struggle for the Soul of a Generation* (Boston: Beacon Press, 2007), 142.

Interpreted critically, however, the Hebrew commandments . . . mean that God alone is God, that no human doctrine or action can claim divine legitimation, that nothing in heaven above or on earth below is to be made into an idol. They mean that we are liberated from slavery to earthly lords and are required to think critically and prophetically, wary of all human presumption, our own and that of others.

Peter Hodgson, "Christian Theology in an Age of Terror," http://www.witherspoonsociety.org/2005/theology_of_war_on_terror.htm.

of Jesus (Matt. 1:3). Further, the strong prophetic tradition of the Old Testament is often highly critical of Israel's use of violence, such as Jeremiah's message to the king of Judah in 22:3:"Thus says the LORD: Act with justice and righteousness, and deliver from the hand of the oppressor anyone who has been robbed. And do no wrong or violence to the alien, the orphan, and the widow, or shed innocent blood in this place." Such prophetic utterances stand alongside the Deuteronomic passages that portray God as endorsing particular wars and should give us pause when we want to claim God for one particular side of any contemporary military campaign.

In chapter 21, the Deuteronomist turns to issues of purity and holiness, which are closely related to the topic of Israel's faithfulness and obedience referenced in 20:18. Concern for holiness takes several forms in the following two chapters. In 21:1–9 we see that just as with sexual offenses, murder is understood as polluting the land (cf. Deut. 24:4; Jer. 3:2). Building on the judicial procedures discussed in 16:18–17:13 and 19:1–21, the passage in 21:1–9 deals with the issue of an unsolved murder, which for Israel must be dealt with directly because criminal guilt is understood as polluting the land as well as the entire community. As God's holy people, the Israelites are called to be pure and set apart from other ways of living (Deut. 7:6; 14:2, 21). To deal with the impurity of an unsolved murder, then, requires Israel to conduct a purification ritual with a heifer and declare, "'Our hands did not shed this blood, nor were we witnesses to it. Absolve, O LORD, your people whom you redeemed; do not let the guilt of innocent blood remain in the midst of your people Israel'" (21:7–8). As one commentary suggests, this perplexing ritual of a broken-necked heifer is intended "to force the living to acknowledge their responsibility to the dead."[25]

These regulations concerning purity relate to several other practices that appear in chapters 12–26, such as the injunctions against self-mutilation and against eating certain animals in chapter 14 as well as the command to worship the Lord in ways that do not involve tainted money in 23:17–18. The recurring rationale given throughout Deuteronomy for Israel's need for purity is this: the call for purity is rooted in understanding that the land is a gift from God and such a gift should not be polluted (21:23).

> If the past does not determine our actions, at least it is such that we can not take a new decision except in terms of it.
>
> Jean-Paul Sartre, *Being and Nothingness*, trans. Hazel Barnes (New York: Washington Square Press, 1966), 637.

The next section in chapter 21 (vv. 10–14) returns to the rules of warfare with its discussion of how Israel should deal with female prisoners of war. In analyses of this and subsequent passages involving the treatment of women, many scholars point again to what seem to be glimpses of restraint in the midst of the brutal realities of war. This particular passage addresses the soldier in war who is attracted to a woman on the other side of the battle lines. He may take her as a prisoner of war, but then he is to follow a set of guidelines on how to treat this prisoner. In order to be able to integrate war prisoners into Israelite society, we see that such a woman must not only be distanced physically from her previous life (by shaving her head and paring her nails, as is instructed in v. 12), but she also should be given time to mourn the loss of her old life (v. 13). After a brief period of mourning, we hear that an Israelite man may take her as his wife, or he may let her go free.

> What might be the feelings of the captive as to either fate is unknown.
>
> Daniel Berrigan, *Deuteronomy: No Gods but One* (Grand Rapids: Wm. B. Eerdmans Publishing Co., 2010), 128.

---

25. Eskenazi and Weiss, eds., *The Torah*, 1161.

The text gives no indication that the woman is to be consulted as to her future; it is possible that she would be forced into marriage against her will. At the same time, the husband is not simply allowed to do with her what he wills. The text reports that if he is "not satisfied with her," he must "let her go free and not sell her for money" (v. 14). Why? Because the husband has dishonored her. The word used here for dishonored is *'innah*, a word sometimes translated as "rape" as it means to treat abusively or without regard for proper behavior. It is used in reference to Shechem's treatment of Dinah in Genesis 34:2 as well as to Sarah's treatment of Hagar in Genesis 16:6. In the ancient world, it was common practice to bring a female prisoner of war into a household to be a slave. Here, however, some startling limits are placed on the patriarchal power of a man as head of his household.

> **When Shechem son of Hamor the Hivite, prince of the region, saw [Dinah], he seized her and lay with her by force.**
>
> (Gen. 34:2)

Following the passage that deals with female captives of war, chapter 21 goes on to address several other matters pertaining to family law. Verses 15–17 address the issue of the rights of the firstborn sons of a father who has two wives and prefers one over the other and wants to designate the son of the favored wife as his firstborn. That birth order did not always determine the firstborn and inheritor of the family wealth is seen in several Genesis narratives, such as Esau's selling his "firstborn right" to Jacob (Gen. 25:29–34).[26] The legal statute presented here in Deuteronomy denies the father the power to designate the son of his favorite wife to be his firstborn, which results once more in a limiting of a father's patriarchal power over his household.

Immediately following the law on inheritance comes one of the most disturbing passages in Deuteronomy: the call for the stoning to death of a disobedient son. The law given in 21:18–21 regarding disobedient children is clearly associated with Fifth Commandment of honoring one's father and mother. While it is highly disconcerting to hear about parents giving their child up to be tried and then stoned

---

26. Tikva Frymer-Kensky, "Deuteronomy," in *The Women's Bible Commentary*, ed. Carol A. Newsom and Sharon H. Ringe (Louisville, KY: Westminster John Knox Press, 1992), 55.

for his disobedience, we can also take comfort in claims by biblical scholars who suspect that the statute was intended for rhetorical and educational purposes only in order to deter children from disobeying their parents.

So how are we to interpret this instruction: as an expansion of the Fifth Commandment or as a law that helps support the well-being of the entire community? One thing this statute shows us is what a grave issue dishonoring one's parents was considered to be. Indeed, dishonoring one's parents receives the same sentence—death—as those who strike or curse their mother or father (Exod. 21:15, 17).

Such behavior was understood as undermining the ability of parents to pass on the covenant to the next generation (cf. Deut. 6:7; 11:19). In addition, Deuteronomy 27:16 states that anyone who dishonors

> **Whoever strikes father or mother shall be put to death.**
>
> (Exod. 21:15)

his or her mother or father is cursed, pointing to the vital role parental respect plays in the Israelite conception of community.

The second thing to note is that in 21:18–21, it is not just the father who must appear as a plaintiff in the case against his son. This is significant, for in the ancient world a father's authority over his children was understood to be absolute (see, for example, Judah's ordering of the execution of his daughter-in-law in Gen. 38:24 without any trial). In addition, as Jewish feminist biblical scholar Tikva Frymer-Kensky notes, "In many societies sons control the mother; but not in Deuteronomy."[27] At the same time, it is also important to highlight once again the limits placed on the father's authority with the insistence that the mother as well as the father must bring their son before the elders. The father does not have the power to decide whether or not his son lives or dies.

Furthermore, an Israelite son's rebellion against his parents is framed with language similar to that which is used to describe rebellious Israel before God, such as in Isaiah 1:2 where God is imaged as the parent and Israel as the rebellious child (see also Jer. 5:23; Ps. 78:8):

---

27. Frymer-Kensky, "Deuteronomy," 56.

> Hear, O heavens, and listen, O earth;
>> for the Lord has spoken;
> I reared children and brought them up,
>> but they have rebelled against me.
>>   (Isa. 1:2)

In addition, earlier in Deuteronomy we hear of Israel's rebellion against God (9:7). Moses' intercession helps save Israel from punishment. This statute regarding the disobedient son lifts up the necessity of Israel's obedience to live and enjoy God's blessings. But up through the end of Deuteronomy, we know that Israel's future disobedience remains a pressing issue for Moses and for the whole community (see Moses' harsh words of warning in Deut. 31:27–29). Biblical scholar Caryn Reeder suggests that the example of the rebellious son in 21:18–21, set within the larger story of Israel's repeated disobedience, is "an individual example of the potential national disaster, and his behavior must be met with absolute judgment to prevent the destruction of Israel."[28]

In Deuteronomy and in the Old Testament as a whole, where the treatment of the neighbor can be seen as the barometer of moral conduct, we see here that for Israel, the neighbor is to be recognized even as a member of one's own family. Families are not simply subject to their own private morality outside of communal law. Quite the contrary: the matter of a disobedient child was a public, communal matter that necessitated a system of checks and balances, requiring both parents to bring their son before the community elders to a hearing where the elders would determine the legitimacy of the parents' claims. Only then would the son be subjected to a stoning that would involve the entire community (rather than just the witnesses, which is commanded in Deut. 17:12), demonstrating that the decision to take a life rests with the whole community rather than with the parents alone.

Even after we explore the wider framework of interpretation for the treatment of the disobedient son, however, we must continue to

---

28. Caryn Reeder, *The Enemy in the Household: Family Violence in Deuteronomy and Beyond* (Grand Rapids: Baker Academic, 2012), 44.

acknowledge the shock and discomfort brought on by this unnerving approach to juvenile delinquency, especially in light of the ongoing challenge for religious practitioners worldwide who still believe
that to be faithful requires interpreting the Bible literally. As we continue to name our discomfort, however, it is also important not to
overlook the ongoing tension that remains between the example of
the call for the execution of a disobedient son and the glimpses of
grace in Deuteronomy 32:36–42 regarding God the parent's actions
toward God's wayward Israelite children.

In ancient societies it was common practice to allow the bodies of
those executed because of criminal
activity to remain in public to serve
as a deterrent to others in the community (21:22). While Israelites
were permitted to execute criminals
by hanging them on a tree, as other
tribes did (cf. 1 Sam. 31:10), this
injunction requires the removal of
the body the same day of the execution, because "anyone hung on a
tree is under God's curse" (v. 23).
While Christians hear this passage
filtered through Paul's theologizing

> Christ redeemed us from the
> curse of the law by becoming
> a curse for us—for it is
> written, "Cursed is everyone
> who hangs on a tree"—in
> order that in Christ Jesus the
> blessing of Abraham might
> come to the Gentiles, so that
> we might receive the promise
> of the Spirit through faith.
>
> (Gal. 3:13–14)

of Christ's own death on a tree, the Deuteronomy passage reflects
the Israelite concern that a dead body represents the primary source
of ritual impurity for the community, likely because if it were left to
decompose, it would eventually become scattered throughout the
land, thus spreading the impurity. Ezekiel reflects this same sentiment when he describes burying the dead from Gog's army as a
cleansing of the land (Ezek. 39:11–16).

The opening verses of chapter 22 that command returning to
one's neighbor what rightfully belongs to the neighbor is reminiscent of Exod. 23:4 and its call to
return your enemy's ox or donkey
if it wanders away. While Deuteronomy speaks about one's neighbor rather than one's enemy as

> When you come upon your
> enemy's ox or donkey going
> astray, you shall bring it back.
>
> (Exod. 23:4)

> This commandment is identical with Paul's teaching in Phil. 2:4: "Look to the interests of others." This is a special characteristic of love (I Cor. 13:5): "Love does not insist upon its own way."
>
> Martin Luther, *Lectures on Deuteronomy*, LW 9:219.

referenced in Exodus, the verses here represent an expansion of the scope of the Exodus injunction. In Deuteronomy it appears that *any* property belonging to the neighbor is supposed to be looked after. Further, the text lays bare a very real human instinct—that is, our frequent *dis*inclination to reach out and help others: "You shall not watch your neighbor's ox or sheep straying away and ignore them" (v. 1), says the text. Many Christian commentaries make the connection between Deuteronomy 22:1–4 and the Good Samaritan story in Luke 10:25–37, where Jesus actually redefines an enemy as a neighbor; at the same time, Jesus also relies on the sentiment expressed in Deuteronomy 22 as well as elsewhere in the Old Testament that God's people are always to be concerned for the well-being of the neighbor, even when one would prefer to look the other way and ignore the need.

There is not a strong narrative structure that relates the various laws to one another in the final section of the Deuteronomic law code. Deuteronomy 22:5 prohibits men and women from wearing clothing typically worn by the other sex. Scholars often relate this prohibition back to Genesis 1:27, where God claims to have made human beings as male and female. Further prohibitions in the chapter, such as the one in verse 12 about wearing multiple fabrics at the same time, suggest that God intended a particular structure of human social life for living purely before God. Living so far removed from such views of purity tempts us to disregard these prohibitions altogether. But biblical interpreters

> [These laws], taken literally, can be aimed at enforcing an upright life; but I think that this, too, is a proverbial and general maxim by which the Jews are taught to be of one heart and mind, simple, pure, without divisions and party spirit. . . . For God, who loves simplicity and purity . . . also wants His citizens to be simple and wholly of one mind in feeling and manners.
>
> Martin Luther, *Lectures on Deuteronomy*, LW 9:221.

such as Martin Luther have also seen in these injunctions guidance for faithful living beyond the literal interpretation.

The call in 22:6–7 to protect a mother bird from being eaten or sacrificed likely has to do with preserving her life so that she will be able to have more offspring that could be used for food for Israel in the future. The claim in verse 7 that Israelites should let the mother bird go "in order that it may go well with you and you may live long" is actually a repetition, in reverse order, of the blessing promised for honoring one's parents in the Decalogue (cf. Deut. 5:16). Thus there may well be an allusion here to respect the mother bird for her role as a parent, just as respecting human parents is a core command of God's covenantal relationship with God's people.

22:13–24:4
Sex, Lies, and Proper Proceedings

Deuteronomy 22:13–29 deals with several extreme cases of sexual misconduct, from accusations of premarital infidelity to instances of adultery and rape. The cases appear in decreasing order of gravity according to Israelite sexual norms, from the most egregious to the least egregious, beginning with the issue of female chastity. It is noteworthy that both men and women are bound by the laws set forth in this section. At the same time, it is also the case that the laws are concerned with female sexual activity in a way that they are not concerned with the sexual activity of men.

The bulk of the section devoted to female chastity focuses not on the woman but on the issue of a husband's false accusation. The typical practice of Israelite divorce involved the husband's paying the wife support money required by the marriage contract. But if a husband were to show that his wife was unchaste before the marriage he could get out of the marriage without any financial cost to himself. The legal procedures demand proof of the husband's accusation of his wife's prior lack of virginity. The standoff in this legal battle, though, is not between the husband and wife but rather between the husband and the wife's father (cf. 22:19), which, contrary to 21:20 where both parents were involved, represents common understanding that the daughter was the father's property until she became the husband's property.

While scholars disagree over the exact meaning of the cloth used as evidence of virginity (v. 17), it is clear that the requirement of proof is significantly more than just the husband's own testimony; there must be material evidence that the woman (and the father) misrepresented her status to her husband. It is also noteworthy that the punishment for falsely accusing one's wife is not cheap: one-hundred shekels of silver, double the betrothal gift (cf. v. 29) for slander, to be paid to the wife's father, the grieved party in this case. In addition, the punishment is more than just financial; the husband is not allowed to divorce his wife "as long as he lives" (v. 19). While this no doubt sounds to us like a punishment to the wife as well as to the husband, we acknowledge that in ancient Near Eastern societies, such a ruling would be understood as protecting women economically by disallowing the husband's divorce.

> We need women commentators to bring out the women's side of the book; we need the stereoscopic view of truth in general, which can only be had when woman's eye and man's eye together shall discern the perspective of the Bible's full-orbed revelation.
>
> Frances E. Willard, *Women in the Pulpit* (Chicago: Woman's Temperance Publishing Association, 1889), 21.

We also cannot neglect the issue that the wife's parents have a lot at stake here as well. If the wife is innocent of the charges, her parents stand to benefit economically; if she is guilty, her guilt could put in jeopardy the marrying prospects of her parents' other children. And just as with the situation of the rebellious son in 21:18–21, the wife's parents must submit the case and the cloth to the elders and wait for their ruling.

Some scholars believe that verses 20–21—which address what happens if the husband's accusations are proven to be true—were added later to create a kind of symmetry within the text. If the wife was not a virgin at the time of her marriage, the father is held responsible and therefore publicly dishonored. The wife, however, must pay for this dishonesty with her life (v. 21). If we look ahead to verses 28–29 we see that premarital sex is not in itself a capital offense.

Rather it appears that the wife's misrepresentation is understood as the grievous offense. Here again we can see some interesting parallels between the case of the deceitful daughter in 22:21–22 and the case of the disobedient son in 21:18–21. In this case, the daughter has deceived her father as well as her husband. Additionally, this section concludes with a return to the phrase "So you shall purge the evil from your midst" (v. 21b), which the Deuteronomist reserves for the most serious of all violations of the commandments (cf. Deut. 13:5; 17:7; 19:19; 21:21). The gravity of this issue has to do with the daughter's disgracing her father's house (v. 21) by keeping her lack of chastity a secret. In doing so, she transgresses communal expectations of daughterly behavior as well as societal expectations regarding female sexuality.

Another issue of sexual misconduct, that of adultery, is addressed in 22: 23–27. While adultery is most often portrayed in the biblical text as an act of extramarital sex of or with a married woman, we see in this passage that the Deuteronomist also views a woman who is engaged to be married to have the same status as a married woman. To address the issue of adultery, the text offers two scenarios: one in which an engaged woman is a willing participant in sex with a man who is not her betrothed versus one in which she is forced to have sex. In both cases, the man is sentenced to die for his actions. If the woman's participation in the act is believed to be consensual, her sentence is death as well. However, if she is raped, the Deuteronomist instructs, "You shall do nothing to the young woman; the young woman has not committed an offense punishable by death, because this case is like that of someone who attacks and murders a neighbor" (v. 26). What is noteworthy is that the rape is clearly seen by the Deuteronomist as a crime of violence, and the woman bears no culpability for such an act. The word *'innah* or "violation" is also used in 21:24. Once again we see that the punishment of those who violate the status of an engaged woman is linked with the claim to "purge the evil from your midst" (v. 24), for it is a crime not only of rape but of adultery as well, both of which in this case threaten the institution of marriage in ancient Israel.

Moving to a less egregious issue than the above scenarios, verses 28–29 deal with a man having sex with a young woman who is not betrothed to anyone. Such an act is still improper, and the Deuteronomist uses the term *'innah* a third time in the chapter to describe the man's actions toward the woman. However, it is not a crime punishable by death. Additionally, the issue of whether the woman was raped appears to be inconsequential. Either way, the man is required to marry her and never divorce her. Even though this case is not understood as rape even if the woman was forced into sex, it is nevertheless understood as a transgression of the sexual norms of the society. That the couple must marry helps mitigate the transgression.

> This may seem shocking, but it has its positive aspects. On the one hand, the rapist is not a criminal, even if he forced her. On the other hand, the young woman is also not a criminal, even if she agreed.
>
> Tikva Frymer-Kensky, "Deuteronomy," in *The Women's Bible Commentary*, ed. Carol A. Newsom and Sharon H. Ringe (Louisville, KY: Westminster John Knox Press, 1992), 58.

The chapter ends with one final issue of sexual misconduct: that of a man who wishes to sleep with his father's wife (v. 30). Given the parameters of sexual activity within ancient Israelite society, we can safely say that the "father's wife" referred to in this passage would not be the man's mother, for that would be incest. In addition, the man's father would not still be married to this woman, for that would be adultery. Therefore, the context here is likely a polygynous marriage, and the reference must be to one of a man's father's cowives: either a widow or ex-wife. Even though she is technically eligible for marriage, she is off limits to her former husband's son.

FURTHER REFLECTIONS
Women, Limited Rights, and Glimpses of Justice

It is obvious that the Deuteronomic laws regarding women originated in an ancient patriarchal society where women had few rights. It is also the case that for centuries theologians held up patriarchal systems (and other oppressive systems—e.g., slavery) referenced in Scripture as tacit endorsement and reinforcement of harmful societal structures. For generations, women, African Americans, and many others harmed by such structures have had to negotiate their relationship to these scriptural texts. African American poet and theologian Howard Thurman tells of reading the Bible aloud to his grandmother, a former slave who could neither read nor write. She directed her grandson to passages from the Psalms or Isaiah but never to certain passages in Paul. Thurman writes,

> With a feeling of great temerity I asked her one day why it was that she would not let me read any of the Pauline letters. What she told me I shall never forget. "During the days of slavery," she said, "the master's minister would occasionally hold services for the slaves.... Always the white minister used as his text: 'Slaves, be obedient to them that are your master ..., as unto Christ.' Then he would go on to show how it was God's will that we were slaves and how, if we were good and happy slaves, God would bless us. I promised my Maker that if I ever learned to read and if freedom ever came, I would not read that part of the Bible." [29]

Thurman's grandmother's approach to certain scriptural passages represents the strong critique that women and other marginalized persons have brought to bear on passages that support oppressive structures. Indeed, early academic expressions of feminist theology and other liberationist theology focused heavily on the critique, the "No!" that needs to be voiced when encountering passages that do not problematize rape or slavery or other acts of harm against human beings.

In recent years, however, scores of contemporary theologians, such as feminists, womanists, and mujeristas, have tackled these texts head on and worked not just to critique but also to wrestle a life-giving blessing from them. These contemporary theologians acknowledge the biases of the text (e.g., the acceptance of slavery, the androcentric norms, the assumption of heterosexual orientation, etc.) while also uncovering the glimpses of the good news for women.

---

29. Howard Thurman, *Jesus and the Disinherited* (Nashville: Abingdon Press, 1949), 30–31.

Positively, what it *can* mean for feminists to acknowledge the authority of Scripture as a source for understanding human persons and human life is that (1) at least Scripture contains something more than a patriarchal view of human life, a support for sexism, and (2) the "more" that Scripture embodies rings at least in harmony with the truth of women's reality as understood in feminist consciousness. . . . For those for whom Scripture has this authority, the interpretive task becomes imperative.

Margaret Farley, "Feminist Conscious-ness and the Interpretation of Scripture," *Feminist Interpretation of the Bible,* ed. Letty Russell (Louisville, KY: Westmin-ster/John Knox Press, 1985), 49.

What, then, shall we say of the laws in Deuteronomy that govern women's lives as they inhabit a strongly patriarchal ancient con-text where the rights of women were severely limited? As we have noted in the commentaries of pas-sages like Deuteronomy 21:10–14 and 22:13–30, buried within the explanations of these laws we catch glimpses of views and treat-ment of women that run counter to what one expects in a society where the father lords over his household. For example, the call for a female prisoner of war to be set free rather than be sentenced to a life of slavery within an Israel-ite household (cf. Deut. 21:10–14) points to the way in which the text offers possible paths of resistance against the domination of men over women. Therefore, today's feminist, womanist, and mujerista theologians acknowledge that after the critique of biblical passages that portray women in a negative light, there's a need to retrieve aspects of the text that run counter to the dominant negative nar-rative, and then there's a need to reconstruct theology informed by these lesser-known parts of the stories. Deuteronomy is not simply "good news for women"; neither is it wholly bad news. Many con-temporary liberation theologians read stories like the ones in Deu-teronomy while they are also engaged in "justice and advocacy for the poor and oppressed, particularly for women."[30] The task of the church is to interpret Scripture for our current time and place, and

30. Sharon Ringe, "Reading from Context to Context: Contributions of a Feminist Hermeneutic to Theologies of Liberation," in *Lift Every Voice: Constructing Christian Theologies from the Underside,* ed. Susan Brooks Thistlethwaite and Mary Potter Engel (San Francisco: HarperSanFrancisco, 1990), 289.

the voices of theologians concerned with the on-the-ground realities of women and those on the margins of society offer the church
an important resource for interpreting the Bible critically and faithfully for today.

Chapter 23 moves from the legal challenges of sexual misconduct to
a discussion of those who are excluded from Israel's assembly. The
assembly was essentially a gathering of Israel's adult males that con-
vened to conduct public business, such as planning for war, hearing legal cases, distributing land, and performing worship. At first
glance, verses 1–2 seem to deliver an unnecessarily harsh prohibition against those who are emasculated or those who are considered
"illegitimate children" of parents not married to one another being
able to enter the assembly of the Lord. Scholars suspect, however,
that the sexual mutilation referred to in verse 1 was likely a practice associated with a Canaanite cult, and that those born of "illicit
unions" were likely children of mixed marriages between Israelites and non-Israelites (such as an Ammonite or Moabite, who are
denounced in vv. 3–6). Thus the exclusions from the assembly are
consistent with Israel's concern to remain pure and "unpolluted" by
Canaanites and their religious practices.

The exclusion of the Ammonites and the Moabites referenced
in verse 3 deserves further consideration. We must remember that
these tribes are Israel's kin and have also received God's blessings (cf.
Deut. 2:9, 19). The reason given for their exclusion in 23:4 suggests
that the prohibition follows from the fact that they did not provide
food and water for the Israelites as they journeyed out of Egypt;
scholars think this exclusion may
be more ideological than factual, as
this issue is not mentioned in either
the Exodus or Numbers account of
the wanderings. While the Ammonites and Moabites are excluded,
other groups like the Edomites,
also kin to Israel (cf. Deut. 2:1–8),
are allowed to participate in the assembly. Perhaps most startling of
all is the admonition in verse 7 that Israel should not "abhor" any of

> The Lord said to [Moses]: "Do
> not harass Moab or engage
> them in battle, for I will not
> give you any of its land as a
> possession.
>
> (Deut. 2:9)

the Egyptians, even though Israel was "an alien among them." Children of the third generation and beyond from Egypt are also allowed into the assembly. Therefore, we can see that there is no blanket exclusion of non-Israelites; indeed, offspring of their former oppressors can even be allowed in.

Verses 9–14 address matters of appropriate behavior within the assembly. Key to this section is verse 14, where the Deuteronomist gives the reason for such fastidiousness regarding practices of purity and cleanliness: it is because "the LORD [their] God travels along with [their] camp." It is more than just the ethnic purity referenced in the opening verses of the chapter. Indeed, we see in this section that concern for purity travels all the way down to matters of personal hygiene.

It is striking, especially in our current climate of concern over "illegal aliens" entering the United States, to see the injunction in verses 15–16 against returning runaway slaves to their owners immediately preceded by the mandate of holiness in Israel's camp "so that [God] may not see anything indecent among [them]" (v. 14). It appears that indecency includes prohibiting such former slaves from becoming part of Israelite society, which would put Israel at odds with practices of dealing with runaway slaves in the ancient Near East. Laws typically forbade the harboring of escaped slaves, and international treaties required nations to extradite them.[31] The Deuteronomic law, in stark contrast, treats the land of Israel as a sanctuary offering permanent asylum. Scholars continue to speculate on what this law meant for runaway Israelite slaves (acknowledging that Deut. 15:12–18 puts limitations on Israelite slaves as well). Even though the institution of slavery was

---

As You Go on Your Way

As you go on your way,
may God go with you.
May God go before you to
show you the way.
May God go behind you to
encourage you,
beside you to befriend you,
above you to watch over,
within you to give you peace.

(Common Lutheran Benediction)

---

31. Tigay, *JPS Torah Commentary,* 215.

woven into the fabric of ancient life, we notice recurring glimpses throughout Deuteronomy of challenges to the institution in how Israel is called to behave.

The absence in this section of a coherent larger narrative is evident as the text flits from one topic to the next, moving in verses 17–18 to an injunction against bringing into the temple any money garnered from illicit activities. While the NRSV speaks in these verses of "temple prostitute[s]," recent research suggests that this is most likely a mistranslation. Scholars today suggest that the reference here is more likely about male and female Canaanite priests. The fees referenced in verse 18 were likely garnered by the female priestess and viewed as representative of a woman outside the bounds of Israelite societal norms and thus threatening to the Israelite assembly and temple worship.

Verses 20–26 address the regulation of loans within Israel. The opening statement—that Israelites should not charge interest when money is lent to other Israelites—is typical of Deuteronomy's view of the communal relationships within Israel's simple agrarian economy of the time: "If you lend money to my people, to the poor among you, you shall not deal with them as a creditor; you shall not exact interest from them"(Exod. 22:25). It is likely then that lending money was done mostly in response to Israelites who were struggling financially (cf. Exod. 22:25; Lev. 25:36–37). Thus, charging interest in such cases was seen as morally problematic.

> If one has need of your assistance because he has not enough of his own wherewith to repay a debt, is it not a wicked thing to demand under the guise of kindly feeling a larger sum from him who has not the means to pay off a lesser amount?
>
> Ambrose, *Duties of the Clergy*, 3.3.20, NPNF[2] 10:70, as quoted in *Exodus, Leviticus, Numbers, Deuteronomy,* Ancient Christian Commentary on Scripture, Old Testament 3, ed. Joseph T. Lienhard (Downers Grove, IL: InterVarsity Press, 2001), 315.

Again scholars highlight that this command to charge no interest is distinct from typical practices of loaning money in the ancient Near East. That the same practice is not commanded when loaning to foreigners suggests that the foreigner likely was a businessman visiting the country in order to trade, who would then borrow money in order to make a profit. In this case, the moral imperative to refrain from charging interest is no longer applicable. The closing phrase of verse 20 references once again the blessings that will come with living in the land according to God's commands.

The "vows to the Lord" discussed in verses 21–23 might at first glance look like a version of bargaining with God: if God does x for you, you will do y for God. Vowing to praise or thank God is a frequent practice mentioned in the Psalms, such as in Psalm 22:20–23, where the psalmist petitions the Lord to "not be far away" and "come quickly" to his aid. In return, the psalmist pledges to "tell of your name" and to praise the Lord. The practice of vow making is also mentioned in other places in Deuteronomy (12:6; 23:19). We hear in verse 23 that making vows to God is a voluntary activity; therefore, those who make such vows need to follow through, otherwise they will "incur guilt" (v. 21).

While most contemporary Christians do not publicly make vows to God, Roman Catholic monastics still do. In her reflection on "Vows in the New Millennium," theologian and Catholic sister Mary Aquin O'Neill reflects on the changing practices of women religious heading into the twenty-first century. She lays out the challenges in this address to the Sisters of Mercy, saying, "The difficulty comes, it seems to me, when we try to explain to ourselves or to others the way we live out our vows. That is, what distinguishes our relationship to material possessions from that of our contemporaries who are not vowed?" In response to her own question, Aquin O'Neill calls her fellow women religious into conversation about how their vows of chastity, poverty, obedience, and service have been reinterpreted over time. In particular, Aquin O'Neill works to define obedience

> Deliver my soul from the sword,
>   my life from the power of the
>   dog!
> Save me from the mouth of
>   the lion!
>
> From the horns of the wild oxen
> you have rescued me.
> I will tell of your name to my
> brothers and sisters;
>   in the midst of the
>   congregation I will praise you;
> You who fear the LORD, praise
> him!
>   All you offspring of Jacob,
>   glorify him;
>   stand in awe of him, all you
>   offspring of Israel!
>
> (Ps. 22:20–23)

primarily in terms of "searching together for God's will in fidelity to mission" rather than the more narrow definition of obedience to legitimate ecclesiastical authority.[32] The practice of vow making between the Israelites and God opens space for reflection on how, for contemporary Christians like Roman Catholic women religious, vow making is a vital component of a life of faith.

Chapter 23 concludes with provisions for Israelites to help themselves to food grown in a neighbor's vineyard or field. Ultimately the land is God's, a gift bestowed on all of Israel through no merit of its own. At the same time, the Deuteronomist also places clear parameters around this enjoyment of the neighbor's crop: while you may eat grapes until you're sated, you may not bring a container and take more than you need. The final verse's permission to eat out of a neighbor's field forms the background for the story in Matthew 12:1–2 where Jesus' disciples pick heads of grain from a field and eat them. They are rebuked by the Pharisees not for plucking the grain but for doing so on the Sabbath. Similar to the story in Deuteronomy, in Matthew's version the allowance to eat from the neighbor's field is also balanced by the prohibition to bring any tools in to harvest more than what is absolutely necessary.

Chapter 24 continues this collection of miscellaneous laws begun in chapter 23. In verses 1–4, we return again to laws about marriage, this time through the case of a complicated "marriage-divorce-remarriage" scenario. The text presents the hypothetical case of a woman whose husband divorces her because he finds her

> At that time Jesus went through the grainfields on the sabbath; his disciples were hungry, and they began to pluck heads of grain and to eat. When the Pharisees saw it, they said to him, "Look, your disciples are doing what is not lawful to do on the sabbath." He said to them, "Have you not read what David did when he and his companions were hungry? . . . Or have you not read in the law that on the sabbath the priests in the temple break the sabbath and yet are guiltless?"
>
> (Matt. 12:1–3, 5)

---

32. Mary Aquin O'Neill, "Vows in the New Millenium," paper presented to the Sisters of Mercy, Omaha Regional Community, September, 1999, http://www.mountsaintagnes.org/uploadedFiles/Resources/Lectures/The%20Vows-%20Vows%20In%20The%20New%20Millennium.pdf, 15.

> But why does Moses mix up his laws in such a disordered way? ... The answer is that Moses writes as the situation demands, so that his book is a picture and illustration of governing and living.
>
> Martin Luther, "Preface to the Old Testament," in *Martin Luther's Basic Theological Writings*, ed. Timothy Lull (Minneapolis: Fortress Press, 1989), 124.

objectionable (v. 1). She then marries another man, who also dislikes her and divorces her (or he simply dies). The main point to this case seems to be that the husband is not permitted to marry his ex-wife a second time, "after she has been defiled," for "that would be abhorrent to the LORD" (v. 4).

From this strange case study we learn some important things about the Israelite view of marriage. First, marrying the same person twice is not acceptable. Second, while neither Exodus nor Leviticus mentions divorce, it is clear from this case study that divorce was indeed possible in Israelite society. Just how giving or receiving a "certificate of divorce" (v. 1) was viewed in Israel, however, remains unclear. Jeremiah's reliance on this imagery to talk about God's covenantal relationship with Israel in Jeremiah 3:1 suggests that like Israel, a divorced woman who married again would be viewed as a "whore with many lovers," for this is how Israel is cast in Jeremiah. Both Jeremiah 3:1 and Deuteronomy 24:1–4 also refer to the defilement of the land due to such behavior, which suggests once again that proper sexual relationships are viewed as fundamental to Israel's life of blessing in the land.

24:5–25:19

Miscellaneous Laws
(and a Provision for Genocide?)

The commandment in 24:5 for a newly married man to refrain from military service for a year so that he can "be happy with the wife whom he has married" hearkens back to the guidelines regarding who should serve as soldiers in times of war in 20:1–9 (most specifically, in v. 7). The NRSV uses the phrase "to be happy with the wife" while other translations talk of the man's giving happiness *to* his wife, leading commentators to suggest that the text reflects an unexpected concern for the sexual pleasure of the wife.[33]

Deuteronomy 24:6–9 contains several miscellaneous laws, beginning with the prohibition in 24:6 against taking a millstone for any pledge, as that would deprive a family of being able to provide for its basic needs. Ancient and medieval Christian interpretation of laws such as this one often offered allegorical interpretations of these specific laws, as we see in the following quotation from sixth-century Pope Gregory the Great:

> One who preaches to a sinner should compose his sermon with such balance that he does not take away fear by offering hope alone or leave the sinner only in fear by taking away hope. For the upper or lower millstone is taken away if the preacher's tongue separates either fear from hope or hope from fear in the sinner's heart.[34]

The law against kidnapping, enslaving, or selling a fellow Israelite for profit in verse 7 is significant in its strong denunciation of depriving any Israelite of freedom. It can be read as a recasting of the exodus narrative on an interpersonal level—that one Israelite has no right to enslave another—and we learn of the seriousness of the matter both by the punishment (death) as well as by the invocation once again of the phrase "So you shall purge the evil from your midst." The God of Israel freed the Israelites from their enslavement in Egypt so that they could inhabit the land God promised them and live a life rich in blessing; thus any infringement on the conditions created by God to enjoy the land is a crime against the covenant.

The reference to "leprous skin diseases" and the subsequent invocation of Moses' sister, Miriam, in verse 9, is an allusion to the story in Numbers 12:10–15 where Miriam is inflicted with a skin disease because she challenges Moses' authority. Moses' reference to her

---

33. Eskenazi and Weiss, eds., *The Torah*, 1179.
34. Paterius, quoting from Gregory the Great's *Moral Interpretation of Job* 33.12.24, "Exposition of the Old and New Testament, Deuteronomy 16," PL 79:780, in *Exodus, Leviticus, Numbers, Deuteronomy*, Ancient Christian Commentary on Scripture, Old Testament 3, ed. Joseph T. Lienhard (Downers Grove, IL: InterVarsity Press, 2001), 317.

> In the whole recapitulation, [Miriam] is forgotten . . . cast out of the camp and stricken with leprosy, in vengeance, she harbors no resentment, but comforts and cheers the women with songs and dances, all through their dreary march of forty years.
>
> Elizabeth Cady Stanton. *The Woman's Bible* (Boston: Northeastern University Press, 1993), 129.

in this Deuteronomic law code seems to illustrate the seriousness of skin diseases and simultaneously the importance of heeding God's commands.

Many of the remaining laws given in chapter 24 address economic issues, and through these laws we see that economics is understood as an important sphere of moral activity. Verses 10–13 deal again with loans. The prohibition against going into the neighbor's house to take the pledge (v. 10) reveals a fundamental respect for the dignity of the neighbor; even if he stands in need of money, his sphere of authority—his home—is left untouched. If the neighbor is poor and a garment is given in pledge, it must be returned to the neighbor before sunset so that he may have it to sleep in, again preserving his dignity. These instructions in verses 12–13 are a restatement of the commands given in Exodus 22:25–26.

Closely related to the commands in verses 12–13, the following two verses also insist that poor and needy laborers should be paid their wages promptly. Verse 15 states that such timely payment of wages is necessary, "otherwise they might cry to the LORD" and the employer "would incur guilt." It is interesting to note that a reference to crying out to the Lord also appears in Exodus 22 dealing with

> In the Lord's Prayer . . . we pray: "Thy Kingdom come, Thy will be done on earth as it is in heaven. . . . Give us this day our daily bread . . . and forgive us our debts as we forgive our debtors." It seems that the Kingdom whose arrival we seek to hasten is one wherein debtors are relieved of debt's onerous burden and the hungry receive daily bread—not because they have necessarily earned it, through hard work, etc., but because they are entitled as God's children to receive God's blessing.
>
> James Noel, "The Divine Economy and a Theology of Debt," *Unbound: An Interactive Journal of Christian Social Justice*, September 26, 2011, http://justiceunbound.org/journal/current-issue/the-divine-economy-a-theology-of-debt/5/.

issue of payment to the poor, but instead of guilt, the Exodus narrative references God's compassion.

The statute in 24:16 is also noteworthy. That children shall not be put to death for their parents' sins and vice versa is a rather revolutionary innovation in the administration of justice in the ancient world. Rather than vicarious punishment for the sins of others (we see examples of this in the Gen. 19 story of Sodom and Gomorrah, who are reportedly destroyed to atone for the sins of a few), each person is instead responsible for his or her own sin.

The remaining laws in chapter 24 deal specifically with the alien, widow, and orphan. Those granting loans to the poor are also prohibited from taking the garment from one who is poor or a widow (v. 12, 17). Amos 2:8 attests to this practice as well. The most vulnerable in society must be allowed the basic necessities of life. Theologian James Noel's "theology of debt" is applicable here: Noel claims that debt is our natural condition. We are all indebted to one another, which means that debt is relieved and bread is given to the hungry—not first and foremost because they earned it but rather because they, like the rest of us, are

> Our brother becomes our debtor when our neighbor is shown to have committed some sin against us. For we call sins debts. Thus the sinful servant is told, "I have forgiven you your whole debt." And each day in the Lord's Prayer we pray, "Forgive us our debts as we forgive our debtors." . . . It is no wonder that we are bidden to return the pledge before sunset. Before the sun of justice sets in us.
>
> Paterius, "Exposition of the Old and New Testament, Deut. 17," as quoted in *Exodus, Leviticus, Numbers, Deuteronomy,* Ancient Christian Commentary on Scripture, Old Testament 3, ed. Joseph T. Lienhard (Downers Grove, IL: InterVarsity Press, 2001), 317.

> Your punishments are for the sins which men commit against themselves, because although they sin against you, they do wrong to their own souls and their malice is self-betrayed. They corrupt and pervert their own nature, which you made and for which you shaped the rules, either by making wrong use of the things which you allow, or by becoming inflamed with passion to make unnatural use of things which you do not allow.
>
> Augustine, *Confessions* (New York: Penguin Books, 1961), 66.

entitled to God's blessing.[35] Noel's understanding of a theology of debt resonates strongly with the Deuteronomic laws of chapter 24. In addition, the chapter also deals with prompt payment of wages, using once again a poor worker as the prototype and rationale for why wages need to be paid promptly (vv. 14–15).

Finally, also addressed in the chapter is the relationship between those who grow the food and those in need of food. Those who are hungry are permitted to go into a field to get food to meet their basic needs (23:24–25). Additionally, farmers are instructed to leave some food behind in their fields and in their orchards "for the alien, the widow, and the orphan" (24:19–21). While there are clear commands to share food with those who need it, at the same time 23:24–25 prohibits those who go to others' fields to glean food from taking more than what they need for basic sustenance. Throughout the enumeration of these laws, the Deuteronomist reminds the Israelites that they are called on to practice such care for the most vulnerable among them because they themselves should remember they were once hungry, vulnerable, and in need of such help themselves.

> You shall not oppress a resident alien; you know the heart of an alien, for you were aliens in the land of Egypt.
>
> (Exod. 23:9)

FURTHER REFLECTIONS
Envisioning Economic Justice

One of Deuteronomy's most persistent concerns is the economic vulnerability of those on the margins of Israelite society. We are very aware by now that the stranger, the widow, and the orphan receive special attention; at the same time, prohibitions like the one in 23:19 against charging interest on loans are set forth to ensure that *all* members of the community are to be protected against practices that would jeopardize their access to the basic necessities of life.

It is also important to observe that while Israel's commandments

---

35. James Noel, "The Divine Economy and a Theology of Debt," *Unbound: An Interactive Journal of Christian Social Justice*, September 26, 2011, http://justiceunbound.org/journal/current-issue/the-divine-economy-a-theology-of-debt/5/.

> Why is God partial to widows and strangers? In a sense, because God is partial to *everyone*—including the powerful, whom God resists in order to protect the widow and the stranger. God sees each human being concretely, the powerful no less than the powerless. God notes not only their common humanity, but also their specific histories, their particular . . . embodied selves with their specific needs. When God executes justice, God does not abstract but judges and acts in accordance with the specific character of the person. . . . "Impartiality," writes Helen Oppenheimer . . . "is not a divine virtue, but a human expedient to make up for the limits of our concern on the one hand and the corruptibility of our affections on the other."
>
> Miroslav Volf, *Exclusion and Embrace: A Theological Exploration of Identity, Otherness, and Reconciliation* (Nashville: Abingdon Press, 1996), 221–22.

to care for the widow and the orphan were not unique in the ancient Near East, "in Israel such commandments were *narrativized* in a way that they were not, elsewhere; the exhortations carry motive clauses that appeal to the Israelites' own experience of hardship."[36] Biblical scholar Christopher Hays suggests that citizens of contemporary America could learn a few things from Deuteronomy's vision of a morally sustainable society. Indeed, Deuteronomy goes beyond platitudes of helping the poor; the text offers a vision for a society where all are fed, clothed, and protected through adherence to a particular set of laws. If we, like the Deuteronomist, were to "narrativize" our own collective history of hardship in the United States, we might think differently about our current treatment of the most vulnerable among us.

Even as the text issues disconcerting instructions for punishment of disobedient members of the community as well as ideological rationales for waging holy war on other peoples, at the same time

> If we can also remember, as we set national policy, that we were once religious refugees, hardscrabble pioneers, and many waves of tired, poor, huddled masses—that would be something to celebrate.
>
> Christopher B. Hays, "The Right-Wing Bible and the Politics of Impotence," *Religion Dispatches*, March 7, 2011.

36. Christopher Hays, "The Right Wing Bible and the Politics of Impotence," *Religion Dispatches*, March 7, 2011, http://www.religiondispatches.org/archive/atheologies/4325/the_right_wing_bible_and_the_politics_of_impotence.

Deuteronomy persists in its radical insistence on the care, protection, and even flourishing of the most needy within the community.

Chapter 25 begins with another law about judicial proceedings regarding the carrying out of punishments appropriate to fit the crime. While the particular crime is not mentioned in 25:1–3, the punishment is flogging, often used in the ancient Near East as a means of disciplining workers and children or as a punishment for harming another's property, which allows us to see why it follows the commands regarding wages and allowances of eating off another's land in chapter 24. What is of significance here is the limit imposed on the number of lashes (v. 3), which is unique among ancient Near Eastern laws regarding flogging. It is also noteworthy that the floggings take place in sight of the judge to ensure that the flogging is done in a restrained way.

Before moving on to the issue of levirate marriage in verse 5, there is an interesting additional verse stuck in between the section on flogging and the one on marriage, a verse that contains the prohibition against muzzling an ox "while it is treading out the grain" (v. 4). The concern reflected in this law over humane treatment of animals that work on behalf of humans indicates that the welfare of the human world is also dependent on and inseparable from the welfare of the natural world. The text returns once again to the issue mentioned above: that all members of Israelite society (even the nonhuman ones) should be allowed access to the basic necessities of life. While this law is not mentioned again in OT writings, it is referenced twice in the New Testament (1 Cor. 9:9; 1 Tim. 5:18). These NT references suggest that in early Christianity

> Moses writes as the situation demands, so that his book is a picture and illustration of governing and of living. For this is the way it happens in a dynamic situation: now this work has to be done and now that. No man can so arrange his life (if he is to act in a godly way) that on this day he uses only spiritual laws and on that day only temporal. Rather God governs all laws mixed together.
>
> Martin Luther, "Preface to the Old Testament," in *Martin Luther's Basic Theological Writings*, ed. Timothy Lull (Minneapolis: Fortress Press, 1989), 124.

the general principle of those who work hard should be properly rewarded still held sway.

Deuteronomy 25:5–10 addresses the issue of levirate marriage, where if a married man dies childless, his brother is required to marry the widow and father a child who will be considered the son of the deceased (vv. 5–6). A well-known example of levirate marriage is seen in Genesis 38:6–9, where Judah's daughter-in-law, Tamar, is remarried to her husband's brother after her husband dies. This law of levirate marriage, we must note, not only works to ensure that the name of an Israelite man is carried on after his death (cf. Num. 27:4; 2 Sam. 14:4–7), but it also serves to protect the widow, for with an heir, she will continue to have access to her dead husband's land inheritance. But as both the story of Tamar in Genesis 38 and the passage in Deuteronomy 25 attest, resistance by the brother to fathering a child by his deceased brother's wife was a common occurrence, because a son for the deceased brother likely meant less land for the living brother. In Deuteronomy 25:7, permission is granted to the widow to take her brother-in-law to court if he refuses the levirate marriage. If he continues to refuse her, the widow then is called on to "pull his sandal off his foot" and "spit in his face" (v. 9). This public shaming would give this family the reputation of not providing for its widows, thus making it more difficult for the family to contract marriages for their sons. At the same time, such actions by the widow would allow her to be released from her deceased husband's family.

The law of levirate marriage is also referenced in the Gospel narratives by the Sadducees who ask Jesus about a woman who marries seven brothers and about which one of the men will be her husband in the resurrection (Matt. 22:23–33; Mark 12:18–27; Luke 20:27–40). Belief in resurrection was a contested notion among the Jews of Jesus' day, and the Sadducees—who did not believe in life after death—wanted to expose the problems inherent in such a belief

> Let the elders who rule well be considered worthy of double honor, especially those who labor in preaching and teaching; for the scripture says, "You shall not muzzle an ox while it is treading out the grain," and "The laborer deserves to be paid."
>
> (1 Tim. 5:17–18)

Jesus said to them, "Is not this the reason you are wrong, that you know neither the scriptures nor the power of God? For when they rise from the dead, they neither marry nor are given in marriage, but are like angels in heaven. And as for the dead being raised; have you not read in the book of Moses, in the story about the bush, how God said to him, 'I am the God of Abraham, the God of Isaac, and the God of Jacob'? He is God not of the dead, but of the living."

(Mark 12:24–27)

when it is linked to a practice like levirate marriage. In his response, Jesus affirms that the Mosaic law in Deuteronomy is a guide for life in this world; at the same time, he claims that God's life and vision are bigger than this world alone, and in life with God that extends beyond the bounds of death, earthly institutions and limitations will no longer apply.

While we have observed how the absolute rule of the patriarch over his household has been diminished through several of the Deuteronomic laws (cf. 21:10–21; 22:13–30), we also see in 25:11–12 that this shift in authority from the father or husband to the elders also has its downside for women. The command in verses 11–12 has to do with a woman who intervenes in her husband's fight with another man in order to help him. If she grabs his genitals, the text reports, she is to be punished with the loss of her hand and should be "shown no pity" (v. 12). This punishment by mutilation is only one of two places in the Bible where such punishment is endorsed (cf. Exod. 21:22–25 for the other example). Defense of her husband does not warrant sexually shaming another man in public. This law shows the primacy of protecting male sexuality within Israelite society.

Verses 13–16 deal with business ethics and honest weights and measures. It is stated here as a moral injunction to measure goods accurately. Once again we see that all aspects of life are under the umbrella of obedience to God's commands "so that [the Israelites'] days may be long in the land" (v. 15).

Chapter 25 concludes with a deeply troubling section regarding the Amalekites. Even amidst the attention paid in the Pentateuch to Israel's wars with other nations, along with the claims that they will be victorious when God endorses the war, there is a level of brutality

> Israel's experience with the Amalekites must have been particularly bitter to have led to a determination to wipe them out. Acts of hostility by other nations did not elicit such a response, not even those of Egypt. . . . The account in Exodus provides no explanation for the determination, but Deuteronomy does: this was a sneak attack on a defenseless weak lagging at the rear of the migrating Israelites, an attack which showed that Amalekites lacked even the most elementary decency. Conceivably, the Israelites thought that the Amalekites had genocidal intentions . . . and regarded the command to wipe them out as measure-for-measure punishment.
>
> Jeffrey Tigay, *The JPS Torah Commentary: Deuteronomy* (Philadelphia: Jewish Publication Society, 1996), 236.

expressed toward Amalekites that is not seen in relationship to other peoples. Both in Deuteronomy 25:19 and in Exodus 17:14 the phrase "blot out the remembrance of Amalek from under heaven" is used. The narrative of Israel's battle with Amalek is recounted in Exodus 17:8–16, where the Amalekites attack Israel shortly after the exodus, and the conflict with Amalek shows up in several other places, such as Numbers 24:20, 1 Samuel 15, and Esther 3:1.

Even with the contextualization of why Israel would find the Amalekites such a serious threat, the call to wipe them out and blot out their name under heaven has for centuries stuck in the throats of biblical readers. Indeed, this passage and similar ones have been disowned by many modern theologians, Jewish and Christian. "This is no God that I know," wrote Jewish philosopher Martin Buber in response to the passage.[37] How do we reconcile love of widow, stranger, and orphan with this talk of annihilation? The short answer is: we don't. But here are some things we can say: When the text was put in its final form, the Amalekites were likely no longer in existence; therefore, the threat to Israel was, at that point, theoretical rather than actual. Further, if we remember that Deuteronomy was put together in its final form when Israel was in exile, we can

37. As quoted in James Kugel, *How to Read the Bible: A Guide to Scripture, Then and Now* (New York: Free Press, 2007), 448.

acknowledge that the Israelites hearing these words would not have the power to blot out the Amalekites even if they had still posed a threat. What we are left with, then, is another example of the ideological rhetoric of the Deuteronomist. Even Martin Luther cautions against seeing what he insists is God's vengeance as human vengeance.[38] Still, the problem of God's sanctioning the blotting out from under heaven others of God's good creation leaves us with an irreconcilable tension: the God of Deuteronomy who sanctions the utter annihilation of a people is the same God who is, as Daniel Berrigan suggests, "the original Good Samaritan."[39]

FURTHER REFLECTIONS
The Command to Remember

As we have witnessed from the first chapter of Deuteronomy on, God's people are called to remember a lot of things. One of the most insistent commands to remember is this:"Remember that you were a slave in the land of Egypt, and the LORD your God brought you out from there with a mighty hand" (5:15). As we have discussed, this injunction forms the foundation of Israelite identity and Deuteronomy's revolutionary ethic of remembering the poorest of the poor,

---

The process of remembering brings with it an obligation to ethical discernment: which memories do we want to affirm and further develop and which do we want to repudiate and transform? We cannot forget the commandments to exclude the Ammonites or blot out the memory of Amalek because their presence in the Torah reminds us of how easy it is to respond to vengeance with more vengeance, or injustice with more injustice. But we can also consciously cultivate memories that encourage us to stop the cycle of violence and domination.

Judith Plaskow, "Contemporary Reflections," in *The Torah: A Women's Commentary*, ed. Tamara Cohn Eskenazi and Andrea L. Weiss (New York: URJ Press, 2008), 1188.

---

38. Luther, *LW* 9:249.
39. Berrigan, *No Gods but One*, 78.

the dregs of society who are all-too-often forgotten in the structures of communities, both ancient and modern. What we have in chapter 25 is yet another call for Israel to remember, but this time to opposite effect: remember what Amalek did to the Israelites; blot out the remembrance of them; do not forget (25:19).

As Jewish feminist theologian Judith Plaskow notes, there are times when we need to lift up the memories that the text works to suppress, such as the memory of Moses' sister, Miriam. While the Deuteronomist invokes her name in Deuteronomy 24:8–9, he only references her disobedience, lifting her up as a negative example for Israelites to avoid following. Plaskow suggests, however, that when we read Deuteronomy's sparse treatment of Miriam, we should remember not only her disobedience; just as important are her courage and initiative in helping save her brother (Exod. 2:1–10).[40]

Through critical engagement with the text we remember and lift up suppressed narratives. At the same time, critical engagement with "texts of terror"[41] (a term used by feminist biblical scholar Phyllis Trible in reference to texts that talk about harm done to women but also, it seems, applicable to passages that advocate acts of genocide) that remain part of the narrative, such as the blotting out of the Amalekites, requires that we remember them in order to denounce their misuse to justify acts of genocide in the present.

So how might such a text be used in a potentially productive way? Rabbi Arthur Waskow reminds us that the Amalekites were descendants of Esau. "So Amalek is part of our own family—the residue of rage that sprang from the grief and anger Esau felt. Amalek is always a possibility within us, as well as in others. The Torah is teaching that we must blot out every urge to become Amalek, our own as well as others'—by turning that urge toward compassion."[42] Remembering our kinship with others as well as our common human culpability can prevent us from applying this terrifying text in ways that perpetuate harm.

40. Judith Plaskow, "Contemporary Reflection," in Eskenazi and Weiss, eds., *The Torah*, 1188.
41. Phyllis Trible, *Texts of Terror: Literary-Feminist Readings of Biblical Narrative* (Minneapolis: Fortress Press, 1984).
42. Rabbi Arthur Waskow, "Amalek Today: To Remember, to Blot Out," the Shalom Center, September 8, 2001, https://theshalomcenter.org/node/299.

26:1–26:19
Conclusion of the Law Code

The final chapter of this section devoted to law begins with Moses instructing the people on what to do once they enter the land promised them by God. Here in chapter 26 we no longer have a recitation of laws but a concluding exhortation that returns to the key theological themes of the text: the call for Israel to acknowledge God's persistent care; the reminder that the land God is giving them is sheer gift; and the insistence that fundamental to Israel's right relationship to God is the practice of attending to the needs of the stranger, the widow, and the orphan.

> In many ways, "law code" is a wholly inadequate designation for the phenomenon which we have observed in Deuteronomy 12–26. This is not a list of legal sentences. It is law pressed into the service of theological preaching.
>
> J. Gary Millar, *Now Choose Life: Theology and Ethics in Deuteronomy* (Grand Rapids: Wm. B. Eerdmans Publishing Co., 1998), 144–45.

This law code section ends where it began: with instructions for worshiping God. The focus on how to worship in chapter 12 suggests that worship should be Israel's first act in the new land. Chapter 26 returns to the theme of worship, reminding Israel yet again that their very existence is grounded in the gratuitous divine choosing of Israel to be God's treasured people. Right relationship with this God entails worship, honor, and thanksgiving to God at the first and the last.

Deuteronomy 26:1–15 is an expanded version of the instructions for offering firstfruits in 18:4 and for tithing in 14:28–29. As they settle into the land, the Israelites shall offer their firstfruits back to God in the temple, a place God has chosen as a dwelling place for God's name. To give of the land's *first* fruits is also an acknowledgment of the gift nature of the land. At the same time, in bringing their offering to the Lord, the people are reminded that their identity began

> O come, let us sing to the Lord;
>   let us make a joyful noise to the rock of our salvation!
> Let us come into his presence with thanksgiving;
>   let us make a joyful noise to him with songs of praise!
>
> (Ps. 95:1–2)

in wandering, in living as a people *without land*: "'A wandering Aramean was my ancestor'" (v. 5). Even as they anticipate reaping the fruits of this new land, Moses frames that moment with repeated reminders of Israel's own history and identity: You were enslaved; you cried out to the Lord for deliverance. Just as important, Israel is called on to remember that the Lord heard them and brought them out of Egypt "with a mighty hand," with "an outstretched arm," "with a terrifying display of power," with "signs and wonders" (v. 8). Here is a clear witness to God's responsiveness to the cries of anguish of God's people. In response to God's faithfulness, in response to God's gift of the land, Moses tells Israel that they shall bring their offerings to the temple with gratitude, acknowledging God's faithfulness, seen in the fulfillment of the promises God made to their ancestors.

The words uttered in verses 5–10 by Moses are often referred to as a "credo" and along with 6:20–25 are understood as a confession of faith. Within the landscape of contemporary Christianity, there are certainly those who are critical of the collective reading of creeds or confessions of faith, arguing that recitations of ancient statements of faith fail to be meaningful or relevant for twenty-first century people of faith. In the 1990s, historian of Christianity Jaroslav Pelikan offered a defense of creeds and ancient confessions of faith during an interview with radio host Krista Tippett. Pelikan states,

> [The law in Deuteronomy] is not presented as a code but is integrated with the ongoing story of the people of God, unlike the law codes of the ancient Near East (or of contemporary societies). Law for Israel is always intersecting with life as it is lived—filled with contingency and change, complexity and ambiguity.
>
> Terence E. Fretheim, "Law in Service of Life: A Dynamic Understanding of Law in Deuteronomy" in *A God So Near: Essays on Old Testament Theology in Honor of Patrick D. Miller*, ed. Brent A. Strawn and Nancy R. Bowen (Winona Lake, IN: Eisenbrauns, 2003), 191.

> My faith life, like that of everyone else, fluctuates. There are ups and downs and hot spots and cold spots, and boredom and *ennui* and all the rest can be there. And so I'm not asked on a Sunday morning, "As of 9:20, what do you believe?" And then you sit down with a three-by-five index card saying, "Now let's see. What do I believe today?" No, that's not what

they're asking me. They're asking me, "Are you a member of a community which now, for a millennium and a half, has said, 'We believe in one God'?"[43]

Indeed, Pelikan's understanding of the role of the creeds in Christian community relates closely to the intended role of the creeds and confessions within the book of Deuteronomy, especially with respect to their ability to link us to the wider community of faith, both historically and contemporarily. While the function of the confession of faith in chapter 6 is catechetical, intended to teach and instruct the Israelites and their children on who they are, whom they worship, and how they are to live, the function of the confession in chapter 26 is liturgical, focusing on how Israel will thank and praise God for their new life in the land. While this credo section is not a prayer, it is reminiscent of psalms of thanksgiving (cf. Pss. 18, 30, 34), where the sufferer cries out and the psalmist recounts how God responded to the cries. Just as in the Psalms, the operative stance here is one of gratitude, and Israel is called to "celebrate with all the bounty that the LORD [their] God has given to [them] and to [their] home" (v. 11). Israelites shall remember their movement from suffering to redemption to a promised life of blessing in the new land. It is also clear here that enjoying the land of milk and honey is inextricably bound to the enjoyment of the relationship of the covenantal relationship with God.

> I sought the LORD, and he answered me,
>   and delivered me from all my fears.
> Look to him, and be radiant;
>   so your faces shall never be ashamed.
> This poor soul cried, and was heard by the LORD,
>   and was saved from every trouble.
>
> (Ps. 34:4–6)

When one reviews in this section the events that occurred in Israelite history to get them to this point, one notes that references to

---

43. Jaroslav Pelikan, "The Need for Creeds," Speaking of Faith with Krista Tippett, March 20, 2008, http://being.publicradio.org/programs/pelikan/transcript.shtml.

what happened at Sinai are missing from the narrative. For example, Israel's reception of the Ten Commandments is not mentioned. These omissions give the reader pause, especially since throughout Deuteronomy the events at Sinai play a pivotal role (cf. 6:20–25). Instead the focus here is on the much-anticipated, imminent entrance into the land. It's so close that even Moses can taste it. In verse 9 he says, "[God] brought us into this place and gave us this land." The laws that filled chapters 12–26 expanded on the Ten Commandments and offered wide-reaching guidance for Israel as they anticipate their new settled life in the land. Therefore, it is a fitting way for the law code section of the book to conclude: with instructions to Israel on how to express their gratitude.

We note that once again in verses 12–15 "the Levites, the aliens, the orphans, and the widows" are singled out as recipients of an every-three-year tithe, the second act of obedience required on Israel's entrance to the land (after the first requirement of worship). The tithing signals a return in chapter 26 to another fundamental theological theme of Deuteronomy: the insistence that faithful, obedient living is bound up with sustained attention to the most vulnerable in society. Thus we see again the vision for a new life in the new land: that the fundamental disposition of God's people will be to ensure that God's blessing will be facilitated through attention to the needs of all.

> Poverty contradicts the very meaning of the Mosaic religion. Moses led his people out of slavery, exploitation, and alienation in Egypt so that they might inhabit a land where they could live with dignity. In Moses' mission of liberation there was a close relationship between the religion of Yahweh and the elimination of servitude.
>
> Gustavo Gutiérrez, *A Theology of Liberation* (Maryknoll, NY: Orbis Books, 1988), 167.

Chapter 26 begins with a reference to God's dwelling among the people (v. 2) connoting God's intimate presence among the Israelites. In verse 15, however, Moses beseeches God to "look down from [God's] holy habitation," which highlights God's transcendent nature. To have both immanent and transcendent descriptions of God in the same chapter suggests that God is with Israel as it enters

> For there is no distinction between Jew and Greek; the same Lord is Lord of all and is generous to all who call on him.
>
> (Rom. 10:12)

the new land but is neither contained by the land nor limited to a relationship with the Israelites alone. Rather God is also the Lord of all.

The final verses of this section on the law bring to a conclusion Moses' setting forth of the statutes and ordinances that begins in 5:1–2. We recall that in chapter 5 Moses stresses the contemporary nature of the covenant when he tells the people that God's covenant is "not with our ancestors" but with all who are alive "today." Again in 12:1, Moses introduces the expanded set of statutes and ordinances that Israel is to observe when they enter the land. Finally Moses concludes his task of setting forth all the commands needed for new life in the land in 26:17: "Today you have obtained the LORD's agreement: to be your God; and for you to walk in his ways, to keep his statutes, his commandments, and his ordinances, and to obey him." We hear in this verse of God's renewal of the covenant. Verse 18 continues with a renewal of Israel's commitment: "Today the LORD has obtained your agreement: to be his treasured people, and to keep his commandments."

> "I will be your God, and you shall be my people."
>
> (Jer. 7:23)

God pledges to be Israel's God, and Israel pledges to be God's people and to obey God's commands.

The final verse of chapter 26 offers reflection once again on Israel's chosen status, asserting that God has placed Israel "high above all nations" and expects Israel to be a people "holy to the LORD [their] God" (v. 19). Genesis 18:19 reveals that the story of Israel begins with Abraham as a story of a people charged "to keep the way of the LORD by doing righteousness and justice." Moving through the Pentateuch's story of Israel, we see that Israel's particular way of living is intended to reflect God's character in the world. These concluding verses of chapter 26 reference once again Israel's special status, and similar to 7:6 the Deuteronomist emphasizes here the way in which Israel is set apart from other nations. And Israel shall receive praise and honor from other nations, not because of any innate superiority but rather because of its God and the distinctive way in which Israel is called to live:

"For what other great nation has a god so near to it as the LORD our God is whenever we call to him? And what other great nation has statutes and ordinances as just as this entire law that I am setting before you today?" (Deut. 4:7–8). With these words of covenantal renewal, the covenant between God and Israel is concluded "literally, legally, liturgically."[44] But neither the story of Israel—nor the Deuteronomic narrative—ends here. What follows in the final chapters is more exhortation by Moses, more calling on Israel to fulfill its covenantal responsibilities and more detailing what will happen to Israel if they do not obey the commands.

---

44. Miller, *Deuteronomy*, 186.

27:1–28:68

The Conclusion of Moses' Second Address: What Will Israel Choose, Blessing or Curse?

Chapters 27–34 contain the final words and actions of Moses. In chapter 27, Moses continues the process of giving up power that began in the very first chapter of Deuteronomy, when he appointed tribal leaders to take on the responsibility of adjudicating disputes within Israel. Now in chapter 27, Moses stands before the people not as a solitary leader but as one who is passing on the duties to the next generation, first to the elders in verse 1 and then to the Levitical priests in verses 9–10.

Since the people will enter the promised land without Moses to lead, guide, and teach them, the people are instructed to write down on the stones "all the words of this law" (v. 3). And when they enter the new land, they are also instructed to make an altar, offer sacrifices, and eat the sacrificial meat in a spirit of rejoicing (v. 7). Biblical scholar Dennis Olson suggests that when we put together the directions to write down Moses' words alongside the ceremony

Rabbi Kushner encourages us to examine Moses' reaction to the fact that everyone he's leading will enter the Promised Land and he won't: "He doesn't go off and sulk. . . . He gathers the people at Mount Nebo and prepares them for what they will face in the future. In the Jewish tradition, we speak of him as Moses *Rabeinu*—Moses, Our Teacher—not Moses, our Political Leader; not Moses, Who Freed the Slaves. Moses, Our Teacher. He dedicates himself to getting the people to embrace the ideas that they have to live by when he's no longer around to remind them."

Harold Kushner, *Overcoming Life's Disappointments* (New York: Knopf, 2006), 288, as cited in Bruce Feiler, *America's Prophet: Moses and the American Story* (New York: William Morrow, 2009), 290.

described in verses 2–8, we see that "Israel is to enjoy a party to celebrate coming into the land and publishing the first edition of the *torah*."[1] Looking ahead to the book of Joshua, we see that the book of the law is front and center with Israel as they enter into the promised land (cf. Josh. 1:8) and that the instructions given in Deuteronomy 27 regarding the book of the law are carried out by Joshua and the people (Josh. 8:30–35).

The transition from the spoken word of Moses to the written torah—a powerfully concrete image of movement from oral tradition to text—is, in addition to holy war, another central ideological innovation of Deuteronomy. In chapter 27, Moses literally begins to step aside to make way for the written torah. At the same time we also catch a glimpse of how the leaders of the future will lead differently than Moses did, for they will always be governed by the torah that is written down and displayed for all to see (27:8).

Once again in verse 9 the Deuteronomist is focused on the life of those Israelites poised to enter the land: "This very day you have become the people of the LORD your God." While in the Exodus

> Moses, who spake with God as with his friend,
> And ruled his people with a twofold power
> Of wisdom that can dare and still be meek,
> Was writing his last word, the sacred name
> Unutterable, of that Eternal Will
> Which was and is and evermore shall be.
> Yet was his task not finished, for the flock
> needed its shepherd and the life-taught sage.
> Leaves no successor; but to chosen,
> The rescuers and guides of Israel,
> A death was given called the Death of Grace,
> Which freed them, from the burden of the flesh
> But left them rulers of the multitude
> And loved companions of the lonely. This
> Was God's last gift to Moses, this the hour
> When soul must part from self and be but soul.

George Eliot, "The Death of Moses," *Complete Poems: The Personal Edition of George Eliot's Poems* (New York: Doubleday, Page, & Co., 1901), 434.

---

1. Dennis Olson, *Deuteronomy and the Death of Moses: A Theological Reading* (Minneapolis: Augsburg Fortress, 1994), 116.

narrative the Israelites become the people of God through the covenant at Sinai, here in Deuteronomy 27, as the people are poised to cross over the Jordan River into the land God has promised them, the words of Moses and the priests echo the Shema of 6:5: they proclaim that Israel is called to hear [*sem*] and obey [*sem*] the law; this is how they become the people of God "today."

In accordance with his words in Deuteronomy 11:29, in 27:11–13 Moses says that on entering the promised land at Shechem, the twelve tribes of Israel shall separate into two groups: one group climbing verdant Mount Gerizim to receive the blessing of the people, the other group climbing the desolate Mount Ebal to receive the curse. With the first reference to the mountain of blessing and mountain of curse in 11:29 and a return to the two mountains in 27:11–13, this division of Israel into those who receive the blessing and those who receive the curse functions to frame the collection of laws in chapters 12–26.

It is also curious to observe that Mount Ebal, where the laws of Moses are to be translated into written form (27:4), is the setting for the curses rather than the blessings (27:13). The close proximity of the law and the curses foreshadows the preoccupation in Deuteronomy 28 with curses that will befall Israel if they disobey the law.

In his commentary on chapter 27, Martin Luther notes that Moses "ordained blessing before cursing; for blessing comes first, so that it will be stronger, better, and more desirable to the people, but that the curse will be hateful." Moses, Luther writes, "would rather have left [the cursing] out altogether, so that it would not strike the people."[2] But include them Moses did. In fact, there are no explanations of blessings paired with the curses in chapter 27 as there are in chapter 28. And once we get to chapter 28, the curses literally outnumber the blessings by a considerable amount. It seems that the accent on curses in chapters 27–28 underscores the life-or-death implications of Israel's obedience to God's commands; in addition, the extended attention paid to the curses in these chapters likely was intended to discourage disobedience by elucidating the disastrous consequences that follow such behavior.

---

2. Martin Luther, *LW*: 259.

Contrary to the very public nature of the crimes and punishments addressed in chapters 21–25, the curses described in 27:11–26 focus on potentially private acts committed away from the eyes of the Israelite judicial system.[3] At the same time, however, just like the laws in chapters 21–25, the violations listed in chapter 27 also threaten the foundations of Israel's social structure (e.g., right worship, honoring one's parents, etc.). The recitation of this list of curses begins with the phrase "Cursed be anyone," suggesting that anyone is capable of committing crimes like these that are difficult to detect. In his commentary on the passage, Martin Luther references Augustine as he reviews the curses. On the topic of sin as the great equalizer, Augustine writes, "There is no sin one man has done which another man could not do; for we are all the same flesh of the same mass, of the same badness, ruined and cursed through the first sin of Adam.[4] In using this quote from Augustine, Luther acknowledges that anyone (and everyone) in Israel was at risk of disobeying God's commands.

> Indeed, the word of God is living and active, sharper than any two-edged sword, piercing until it divides soul from spirit, joints from marrow; it is able to judge the thoughts and intentions of the heart. And before him no creature is hidden, but all are naked and laid bare to the eyes of the one to whom we must render an account.
>
> (Heb. 4:12–13)

Whether it is the act of depriving aliens or widows of justice (v. 19) or the transgression of sexual boundaries through incestuous relationships (vv. 20, 22), these curses, affirmed by the Israelites through the recitations of "Amen!" after each listing, suggest that even though such actions might evade the judicial processes, God will nevertheless be a witness to such transgressions. God's judgment, we hear at the close of the chapter, reaches to "anyone who does not uphold the words of this law" (v. 26). This reference likely pertains not just to the laws listed here but also to the entire scope of the laws laid out in Deuteronomy 5–26.

---

3. Patrick Miller, *Deuteronomy,* Interpretation: A Bible Commentary for Teaching and Preaching (Louisville, KY: Westminster John Knox Press, 1990), 195.

4. Augustine, *De Correptione et Gratia,* ch. 7, PL 44:923–25, as quoted in Luther, *LW* 9:261.

Chapter 28 begins with a conditional clause, *if* Israel will obey, *then* they will be blessed (vv. 1–2). The chapter also begins with a recitation of blessings that will come to the Israelites if they obey "all [God's] commandments [Moses is] commanding them today" (v. 1). Of note is the few number of verses in chapter 28 that are actually dedicated to blessing (vv. 1–14) compared to the verses dedicated to curses (vv. 15–68). Further, the blessings in verses 2–14 seem almost too good to be true. To envision a life that is blessed in the field and at the table, kept free from any enemy invasion, blessed with children and wealth—taken together, the list of blessings presents an image of an idealistic future where an obedient Israel is showered with goodness in every aspect of life. Everything Israelites could hope for is covered in the list of blessings. After a few short verses of a life overflowing with blessing, however, the focus shifts to curses.

> **Human inheritance is both blessing and curse.**
>
> Kathleen Norris, *Amazing Grace: A Vocabulary of Faith* (New York: Riverhead Books, 1998), 22.

Initially the curses in verses 15–19 present mirror images of the blessings in verses 2–6. If Israel obeys God's commands, then the people's relationship with God, with other nations, and with the land will be blessed: "Blessed shall you be in the city, and blessed shall you be in the field" (v. 3). But if Israel disobeys, the relationship between God and people breaks down, and chaos in the natural and social realms ensues: "Cursed you shall be in your city, and cursed shall you be in the field" (v. 16). While the Deuteronomic narrative up to this point has been focused on *the decision* Israel must make—whether to walk in obedience to God's commands or not—the Deuteronomist turns here to a detailed examination of the consequences for the Israelites should they choose disobedience.

And the consequences, the list of curses makes clear, will be severe. In short, the curses in 28:15–68 paint a vivid picture of what life will be like for Israel if all that God has done for Israel is taken away. The entire vision for a new life in a new land that the Deuteronomist describes in previous chapters of Deuteronomy is undone through this daunting list of curses. Rather than God's giving Israel the land that flows with milk and honey, "the LORD will make pestilence cling to [them] until it has consumed [them] off the land" (v. 21) and "change the rain of [their] land into powder" (v. 24). Rather than God's ensuring victory for the Israelites as they fight their way to the promised land, "the LORD will cause [them] to be defeated before [their] enemies" (v. 25). Rather than being able to enjoy the fruits of the land, "[Israel] shall plant a vineyard and not enjoy its fruit" (v. 30). All the

> But if you will not obey me, and do not observe all these commandments, if you spurn my statutes, and abhor my ordinances, so that you will not observe all my commandments, and you break my covenant, I in turn will do this to you: I will bring terror on you.
>
> (Lev. 26:14–16a)

blessings that have been promised by God to God's covenantal partner, Israel, will be revoked.

How are we to understand this portrait of devastation presented by the Deuteronomist? It is important to acknowledge that the tradition of lists of blessings and curses is an ancient one; in fact, many ancient Near Eastern treaties concluded with lists similar to what appears in Deuteronomy 27–28. It is also the case that the list of curses in those ancient treaties typically far outweighed the list of blessings. Those who drafted such treaties wanted their contractual partners to live up to the terms of the treaties, and the list of curses served as incentive to do so. Significant parallels exist in language and in sequence to curses used in other treaties of the time. Understanding that this list is not unique to Deuteronomy—that it was a literary convention of ancient treaties—helps us gain some perspective on the devastating claims made within the chapter. It is possible that the curses listed here are more literary conventions than references to particular historical events.

At the same time, other scholars suggest that Deuteronomy likely was set in its final form during Israel's exile in Judah in the seventh century BCE. If we go with this dating of the text, many of the curses could be read as reminiscent of Israel's experience in exile. For instance, verse 36 talks about Israel's being brought "to a nation that neither you nor your ancestors have known." The verse also suggests that the ultimate curse is not exile but the practices that follow from a life of exile, primarily the worship of other gods (v.

36), which we know is part of Israel's own exile narrative. If Israel does not obey God's commands, the Deuteronomist insists, it will go from being regarded as God's treasured possession "to an object of horror" (v. 37). Life will bear precious little resemblance to the visions of blessed life in the land set forth by the Deuteronomist in the chapters preceding this one.

> Their idols are silver and gold,
>   the work of human hands.
> They have mouths, but do not speak;
>   eyes, but do not see.
> They have ears, but do not hear;
>   noses, but do not smell.
> They have hands, but do not feel;
>   feet, but do not walk;
>   they make no sound in their throats.
>
> (Ps. 115:4–7)

The list of curses continues to paint a revolting image of what the future holds if Israel disobeys. Not only will the land fail to provide the Israelites with food (vv. 38–40), but also their descendants will be taken into captivity, away from the land God had promised them. Further, the curse in verse 43 that tells of how aliens in Israel's midst will rise up suggests that those who were legally and economically vulnerable will now have the upper hand. Again, life as God intended, life as the Deuteronomist portrays it in previous chapters of the text, will not come to pass if Israel chooses to disobey.

While the deeply unsettling descriptions of curses in verses 15–44 seem to be more than adequate to understand the consequences that await a disobedient Israel, an even more ominous shift in tone occurs in verse 45. No longer is the litany of curses set in conditional terms (if . . . then); rather, the Israelites are told, "All these curses *shall* come upon you, pursuing and overtaking you until you are destroyed, because you did not obey the Lord your God" (v. 45, emphasis added). In verses 47–57 and again in 62–68, the list of curses becomes descriptive of what *will happen* to the Israelites *because* they have disobeyed. The images that fill these verses are evocative of Israel's future life of exile, where another nation "shall swoop down on [them] like an eagle" (v. 49) and "besiege [them] in all [their] towns" (v. 52), and there will be no protection from such horrible events. Israel will be reduced to "desperate straits" (v. 53), and Israelites will engage in all sorts of repugnant behavior, even eating the fruit of their womb (vv. 53, 57). Israel's life will resemble once again a life similar to what the people endured in Egypt, from being afflicted with the diseases that were present there (v. 60) to being a people with no land to call their own (v. 64). The vision is bleak and terrifying: "Your life shall hang in doubt before you. . . . In the morning you shall say, 'If only it were evening!' and at evening you shall say, 'If only it were morning!'—because of the dread that your heart shall feel and the sights that your eyes shall see" (vv. 66–67).

As chapter 28 creeps closer to its ominous close, we hear that because Israel will refuse to serve God faithfully, the Israelites will once again return to the conditions of enslavement they had in Egypt. Indeed, the closing verse suggests that it will be even worse for Israel than the first time in Egypt: "There you shall offer yourselves for sale to your enemies . . . but there will be no buyer" (v. 68). This ironic reference back to enslavement in Egypt demonstrates how this pivotal event of Israel's identity as God's covenantal partner is now invoked to signal the loss of all that Israel has been given since leaving Egypt. And especially in the closing verses of the chapter the declaration of *assured* future events points to a physical and spiritual exile from the promises of land, of flourishing, and of God.

FURTHER REFLECTIONS
Fifty-Three Verses of Curses

In the minds of contemporary readers, this massive list of curses no doubt seems unbelievably harsh, particularly when the attribution of the agent behind the curses is often God. There is an anti-exodus theme at work in the list of curses: the Deuteronomic narrative that focuses on a retelling of Israel's journey from slavery to the edge of the promised land is being reversed, moving away from the promised land and back to the life of slavery. We see that God's protection of Israel through the long and arduous journey from Egypt to Horeb to Shechem can be taken away and Israel can be forced back to an Egyptian-like life of captivity, where life is constantly threatened by

> The Exodus is told and retold, rooted in tribal memory. Then something else, an opposite event. The freedom story vanishes in the thin air of a curse. Radically, ruthlessly, the original is rewritten. One history is erased; another is contrived. Contrived—or real; this anti-Exodus, this humiliated return?
>
> Daniel Berrigan, *No Gods but One* (Grand Rapids: Wm. B. Eerdmans Publishing Co., 2010), 150.

death. Given this harsh picture of Israel's future, what are we to say about how we are to interpret the fifty-three verses of curses today?

While we have suggested that the list of curses may not refer to actual historical events, at the same time we acknowledge that the vivid portrayal of pain and horror present in the curses may reflect a writer who wrote during the exile about conditions he had actually witnessed.[5] It seems plausible that the Deuteronomist writes out of his own experiences of war, defeat, and exile when he talks of how the Lord will destroy his chosen ones, how Israel's enemies will "consume [their] livestock," "besiege [their] towns," and push them to such desperation that they "will eat the fruit of [their] womb." Thinking of these verses as possibly written after the fall of Jerusalem brings to mind the work of cultural critic Edward Said on the trauma associated with exile. Said writes, "True exile is a condition of terminal loss."[6] Living in exile often inculcates in those who are exiled a deep sadness that cannot be surmounted, for all forms of security and all tangible resources for resilience are stripped away. The resources on which Israel thought they could rely, such as its "high, fortified walls" (v. 53), no longer protect them. In the morning they wish it were evening; in the evening they wish it were morning. What's left is despair.

Thus, while we can trace the framework of such a list back to other ancient Near Eastern treaties, theologically we can see the list as much more: as a portrayal of all Israel is poised to lose after their entrance into the land given them as a gift from God. Therefore, what is also present here is not only an articulation of consequences

---

5. Daniel L. Smith-Christopher, *A Biblical Theology of Exile* (Minneapolis: Fortress Press, 2002), 96–104.
6. Edward Said, "The Mind of Winter: Reflections of Life in Exile," *Harpers*, 1984, 49.

of disobedience but the words of lament, deep expressions of grief, for all Israel could have had but lost.

To take this point about the curses acting as a form of lament for Israel a bit further, let us return to the issue of why Israel will likely endure such curses in the first place. As mentioned above, God is at times referenced as directly responsible for the blessing or curse, but other times, God is not referenced as the agent of joy or woe. For instance, the blessings in 28:3–6 recount a more general and impersonal connection between obedience and blessing while others, such as those listed in verses 7–13, attribute the blessings directly to God. It is similar with respect to the curses. Some curses seem to be the outcome of neglecting the laws of the covenant (cf. vv. 16–19, 30–34) while in others, such as in verses 20–29, curses are attributed directly to God.[7] The agony that is repeatedly expressed in the list of curses in chapter 28 resonates with a character who appears later in the Old Testament, Job, and his description of the relentless suffering he endures, where his days "come to their end without hope" (Job 7:6). So while the Deuteronomist makes repeated connections between Israel's disobedience and the curses that will befall the people, at the same time there are verses in chapter 28 that move beyond the disobedience-retribution framework to talk about Israel's suffering. Perhaps in not attributing every act of suffering to divine agency, the Deuteronomist is, like the author of the book of Job, granting permission for his readers to acknowledge that all suffering does not fit into tidy theological frameworks.

> To the "why" of suffering we get no firm answer. Of course some suffering is easily seen to be the result of our sin: war, assault, poverty amidst plenty, the hurtful word. And maybe some is chastisement. But not all. The meaning of the remainder is not told us. It eludes us. Our net of meaning is too small. There's more to our suffering than our guilt.
>
> Nicholas Woltersdorff, *Lament for a Son* (Grand Rapids: Wm. B. Eerdmans Publishing Co., 1987), 74.

In the midst of the textual support behind the claim that these curses constitute Israel's just deserts, we want to pay special

---

7. Olson, *Deuteronomy and the Death of Moses*, 121.

attention to those verses that do not attribute every calamity as originating with God. Countless Christian theologians over the centuries have taken such lists of curses as evidence of Jewish guilt, both historically and contemporarily. To cite just one example of such theologizing, Martin Luther claims in his Deuteronomy commentary that "the Jews deserved the curses of chapter 28 most, even when they shone with the most splendid-looking works without the spirit, as is evident in all the prophets, who sneer at such hypocrisy of theirs and terrify them with such curses."[8] It is because of statements like these that we should linger over the curses that are not linked immediately back to God and listen for the echoes of lament. The text resists—in however muted a fashion—the tidy theodicies that has the suffering of Israel—and indeed human suffering in general—all figured out. As theologian Nicholas Woltersdorff eloquently reminds us, "There is more to suffering than our guilt."

Where do we end up, after this seemingly endless recitation of curses, after four times more space is devoted to curses than to blessings? Is it possible to see God as ultimately more merciful than wrathful?

The book of Deuteronomy could have ended here. As was the case with many ancient Near Eastern treaties, the curses could have had the last word. But Deuteronomy continues, moving through—and eventually even past—the curses and the wrath. The narrative proceeds to Moses' third address, where he introduces Israel to a new covenant that proclaims once again that God is the beloved covenantal partner of Israel, that God has promised them land, and that God will see them through to the future.

---

8. Luther, *LW* 9: 261.

29:1–32:52

Moses' Third Address: The Covenant at Moab

29:1–30

Another Covenant

Chapter 29 begins by telling us that "these are the words of the covenant" (v. 1), words that are repeated often throughout Deuteronomy. But verse 1 ends with the claim that the words are "in addition to the covenant that [God] made with [Israel] at Horeb." Israel is now in the land of Moab, a land just east of the Dead Sea and home of Mount Nebo, the place Moses will go to die. Thus, as Israel is poised to enter the land God has promised them, it appears that Moses gathers the people together at Moab to introduce to them another covenant besides the one that God makes with them at Sinai. What's curious is that while the Moab covenant is discussed three times in the remaining chapters of Deuteronomy (29–32), it is not mentioned anywhere else in the Old Testament. What, then, is the Moab covenant, and what role does it play in the life of the ancient Israelites?

Each articulation of the Moab covenant emphasizes three themes, all of which are reminiscent of the covenantal presentations in the rest of Deuteronomy: first, there is attention given to God's past faithfulness to Israel; second, the covenant attends to the present reality of the limits to Israel's ability to obey; and finally there is a glimpse of God's future activity to overcome Israel's very human limitations. This structure is similar to the structure of Deuteronomy as a whole, from an account of God's faithfulness throughout Israel's past (chaps. 1–4) to the explanation of the law code with its repeated reference to the consequences of what happens when the laws go unfulfilled (chaps. 6–28), and finally, to its reference to a covenant that looks toward the future and offers hope (chaps. 29–32).

Some scholars believe chapters 29–30 refer to an actual covenant-making ceremony because all the people are gathered together before Moses (v. 2) for the apparent purpose of entering into covenant with God (v. 12). Indeed, the prologue in verses 2–9 is similar to the prologues to the Sinai covenant that are presented in other places in the Deuteronomic text. Verse 2 begins with a reminder to Israel of all God has done, from the pivotal rescue of Israel from slavery in Egypt to Israel's many successes in battle (vv. 7–8). The rapid rehearsal of the narrative of the wilderness experience hearkens back to Moses' speech in chapters 1–4; and now in chapter 29 the Deuteronomist is once again clear in his claim that God's faithfulness is certain and that the Israelites have seen God's wondrous acts with their own eyes (vv. 2–3). At the same time, we cannot ignore that in the middle of this recounting of God's actions on behalf of Israel is the statement that this same God "has not given [Israel] a mind to understand, or eyes to see, or ears to hear" (v. 4). This message seems clear: God has been faithful, but the Israelites, bound by their own limitations, have not yet been able to understand that. While God has yet to give Israel all it needs to see, hear, and understand, Moses nevertheless passes on to the people the words of God, who says, "I have led you for forty years in the wilderness" and has provided for all their needs (vv. 5–6). Thus these reminders of God's power and care provide grounds for hope that one day, Israel will be granted the ability to live fully as God's people, even as God continues to care for them today and into the future.

The section in verses 10–15 begins by listing all the different groups that stand assembled before Moses "today." That the list ranges from the elders to men, women, and children and even to the aliens

---

Then [Moses] repeats the kindnesses (v. 5) that for forty years in the desert their clothing did not wear out and their shoes were not used up, that they did not eat bread, and that they did not drink wine and strong drink. Thus God showed them—and they themselves were to know it— that He was theirs.

Martin Luther, *Lectures on Deuteronomy,* LW 9: 272.

and "those who cut [their] wood" and "draw [their] water" suggests that just as with the covenant at Horeb, the covenant at Moab is intended to be for all of Israel. In addition, just as with the covenant at Horeb, we are reminded that this covenantal relationship between God and Israel originates in the promise God made to Israel's ancestors (v. 13). In this section, just as in the previous references in Deuteronomy to covenant, there are repeated references to the covenant being made with the Israel of "today." But with the covenant at Moab, Moses also states that God is making the Moab covenant "with those who are not here with us today" (v. 15). This is a covenant that is oriented to Israel's future generations.

In the next section, verses 16–28, we see that the central issue of the Moab covenant is the same as the covenant at Horeb: exclusive devotion to God (vv. 17, 26), hearkening back to the Shema in 6:4–5. Once again we hear that the worship of other gods leads to curses and death for God's people. Verses 18–28 indicate that Israel will break their covenantal vow; therefore, these verses return to images of an angry, wrathful God. The text states that all the curses listed in this book will come upon those who stray from faithful relationship with God. Israel's turning from God is seen as "a root sprouting poisonous and bitter growth" (v. 18), and the Deuteronomist is insistent: God will not forgive them and will even blot out their names from under heaven (v. 19). The reference in verse 23 to the destruction of Sodom and Gomorrah only serves to reinforce the seriousness of the missteps of those who disobey.

Once again we are confronted with harsh, wrathful, and unforgiving images of Israel's God. Amid the anger and fury, however, we also catch glimpses of an expression of rejected and wounded

> Most preachers and most composers of prayers today treat the biblical doctrine of the wrath of God very much as the Victorians treated sex. It is there, but it must never be alluded to because it is in an undefined way shameful.... God is love; therefore we must not associate him with wrath. God is love; therefore he is indefinitely tolerant. Presumably it is for such reasons that the Christian churches ... have in practice turned their backs upon the biblical doctrine of the wrath of God.
>
> R. P. C. Hanson, *God: Creator, Saviour, Spirit* (London: S.C.M., 1960), 37.

> How can I give you up, Ephraim?
>   How can I hand you over, O
> Israel?
> . . .
> My heart recoils within me;
>   my compassion grows warm
> and tender.
> I will not execute my fierce anger;
>   I will not again destroy
> Ephraim;
> for I am God and no mortal,
>   the Holy One in your midst,
>   and I will not come in wrath.
>
> (Hos. 11:8–9)

divine love similar to what we see in Hosea when it talks about Israel's rejection of God. Israel's disobedience leads to a portrait of God who is not just angry and wrathful but wounded as well. God is the God of Israel's ancestors, the God who led them out of Egypt, the God who kept them alive in the wilderness. And in response, "they turned and served other gods" (v. 26). Israel, precious in God's sight, rejects God's gift of blessing, and God is grieved. This grief and anger lead God to uproot Israel from the land and "cast them into another land, as is now the case" (v. 28), a likely reference to Israel's future exilic existence.

The last verse of chapter 29 contains a cryptic reference to "the secret things" that belong to God and the "revealed things" that belong to the Israelites and their children. Interpreters are unsure of the referents of the secret and revealed things. What the verse does seem to suggest is that the Israelites, as human beings, are not privy to the ways of God. Why hasn't God yet given Israel the ability to see, hear, and understand? Why is God's projected rejection of Israel so harsh? Verse 29 suggests that those "secret things" belong to the Lord. But what we can know is this: that God chose Israel out of love, that God is passionate in God's desire for relationship with God's people, and, as we shall see in chapter 30, that even amidst talk of curses and the blotting out of names under heaven, God's faithfulness to God's people is promised to prevail.

> It was not because you were more numerous than any other people that
> the LORD set his heart on you and chose you—for you were the fewest of all
> peoples. It was because the LORD loved you and kept the oath that he swore
> to your ancestors, that the LORD has brought you out with a mighty hand, and
> redeemed you from the house of slavery, from the hand of Pharoah king of
> Egypt.
>
> (Deut. 7:7–8)

After the stern warnings in chapter 29 the tone changes in chapter 30 as the Deuteronomist offers a vision of hope for the future of God's people. The focus of chapter 30 is on Israel's promised future, on a time when the blessings and curses have already occurred (v. 1) and the people once again have the opportunity to return to a life of obedience before God. If Israel chooses to obey, "even if [they are] exiled to the end of the world," God will bring them back to the land and restore to them the blessings of prosperity in the land (v. 5).

At this stage in our reading of Deuteronomy we are well aware that Israel has been here numerous times before: they are presented with a decision, and they must *decide* to obey God. We also know that time and time again, when faced with this choice, Israel—in very human fashion—has chosen the path of disobedience. Is there any indication that this opportunity for covenant making at Moab opens for Israel new avenues for being able to choose obedience? Actually there is. Verse 6 returns to a key point that has been made multiple times throughout the pages of Deuteronomy: that obedience is ultimately a matter of the heart. Verse 6 even contains parallel imagery to 10:16,

> The fact that I'm still a sinner is precisely why I'm stuck on hope. As a person who never quite gets it right, I'm always hoping for more in this life— more chances to be gracious, kind, loving.
>
> Deanna Thompson, *Hoping for More: On Having Cancer, Talking Faith, and Accepting Grace* (Eugene, OR: Cascade Publications, 2012), xiv–xv.

where Israel is called to "circumcise the foreskin of your heart, and do not be stubborn any longer." We know that circumcision is a sign of the covenant (cf. Gen. 17:11) and is used both here and in chapter 10 in a metaphorical way to signify the change of heart that needs to occur if Israel is to obey. The key distinction between the reference to circumcision in 10:16 and the way the metaphor is used in 30:6, however, comes in who performs the circumcision. In 10:16, Moses calls on Israelites to perform the act of circumcision *on themselves*. But in 30:6, Moses tells Israel, "The LORD your God will circumcise your heart and the heart of your descendants." Thus the claim made in 29:4 that God had yet to intervene and equip Israelites to see, hear, and understand (and by implication, *obey*) is here answered with the insistence that God will indeed change their hearts, and

It is necessary only to look into what is nigh at hand and to perceive the tribulation and promise of life, as it is set before us in every word we speak and in every motion of our heart. . . . What we mean is the new orientation of all possible human activity, the step from hope to tribulation and from tribulation to hope, the eternal advance, which accompanies or does not accompany, which assists or hinders, all human progress. Set over against all human possibilities, it is the 'Wholly Other'; and because it is this, it is the possibility that is always and everywhere open—the possibility for the living, Unknown God to be what He is.

Karl Barth, *The Epistle to the Romans*, trans. Edwyn Hoskins (Oxford: Oxford University Press, 1968), 380.

then the Israelites *will* love the Lord their God with all their heart and soul (30:6) just as they were commanded to do in the Shema in 6:5 and again in 10:12. In chapter 30, the command to change the heart becomes a promise that the heart will be changed. The day is coming, Israel is told, when Israel will have divinely given capacity to fulfill the commands of God. And in this promised future, God's blessing will have specific material outcomes for the bodies of the Israelites and the land they till (v. 9). Israel will obey God, and God will delight once again in Israel (v. 9).

But what does Scripture say? The Word is very near you, in your mouth and in your heart. And to these the Savior also kindly points out the matters pertaining to the kingdom of God, that they may not seek it outside themselves or say, "Behold here or behold there." For he says to them, "The kingdom of God is within you."

Origen, as quoted in *Exodus, Leviticus, Numbers, Deuteronomy,* Ancient Christian Commentary on Scripture, Old Testament 3, ed. Joseph T. Lienhard (Downers Grove, IL: InterVarsity Press, 2001), 326.

But according to the Deuteronomist, the fact that God will make obedience possible does not let Israel off the hook regarding their present responsibility for following the law. In verses 11–14, which follow the claims that God will make it possible for Israel to obey, the focus is brought back to the present task of heeding the commandments "today." Moses' words are intended to reassure Israel when he insists, "This commandment I am commanding you today is not too hard for you, nor is it too far away"

(v. 11). It's not out of reach for Israel: "No, the word is very near to you; it is in your mouth and in your heart for you to observe" (v. 14).

What are we to make of this tension between God's creating the condition for the possibility of obedience and Moses' exhorting the people to be obedient? To respond to this question, Christian theologians like Martin Luther have turned to the apostle Paul's use of Deuteronomy 30 in his letter to the church at Rome:

> Moses writes concerning the righteousness that comes from the law, that "the person who does these things will live by them." But the righteousness that comes from faith says, "Do not say in your heart, 'Who will ascend into heaven?'" (that is, to bring Christ down) "or 'Who will descend into the abyss?'" (that is, to bring Christ up from the dead). But what does it say? The word is near you, on your lips and in your heart" (that is, the word of faith that we proclaim). . . . (Rom. 10:5–8).[1]

In his interpretation of Rom. 10:5–13, Luther, like many other Christian interpreters, notes that in his use of Deuteronomy 30, Paul does not quote Moses word for word. Especially noteworthy for Luther is Paul's omission of any reference to Moses' instructions in verses 12–13 to "hear [the commandment] and observe it." While Luther acknowledges that for Moses as well as for Paul, "the commandment is fulfilled when the Word is in the heart . . . and that happens through faith,"[2] he nevertheless argues that Christians, following Paul, must realize that it is faith of the heart and not works that save.

It is vital to acknowledge along with Luther that the words of Deuteronomy 30:11–14 are a far cry from a rigid legalism that insists all one needs to fulfill the law is to act the right way rather than the wrong way. It's an issue of the heart, and the impetus toward obedience and the ability to fulfill the law originate in the power of God. If we understand Moses' repeated focus on obedience within the wider context of God's grace that makes obedience possible in the first place, we can then push Luther and other Christian theologians

---

1. Luther, *LW* 9:279.
2. Ibid.

toward a stronger affirmation of the inseparability of faith and works. Indeed, twentieth-century theologian Dietrich Bonhoeffer met this issue head on in his explanation of what he called "cheap grace": "Cheap grace is the grace we bestow on ourselves. Cheap grace is the preaching of forgiveness without requiring repentance, baptism without church discipline, Communion without confession. . . . Cheap grace is grace without discipleship, grace without the cross, grace without Jesus Christ, living and incarnate."[3]

We risk becoming advocates of cheap grace if we only hear in Deuteronomy 30 Moses' reference to God's promise without the accompanying reference to renewed commitments to obey God's command. And Moses reassures the Israelites in 30:11 that divine wisdom and guidance are neither esoteric nor abstract, nor are they out of reach. Rather, Moses insists that God's Word has been clearly set out in this book and is and will continue to be available and accessible to all.

> Maybe that's one reason we worship—to respond to grace. We praise God not to celebrate our own faith but to give thanks for the faith God has in us. To let ourselves look at God, and let God look back at us. And to laugh, and sing, and be delighted because God has called us his own.
>
> Kathleen Norris, *Amazing Grace: A Vocabulary of Faith* (New York: Riverhead Books, 1998), 151.

This intimate portrait of the Word in verse 14 is for Christians also evocative of claims of the Word becoming flesh in Jesus Christ. In John 1:14 the claim of the Word being very near to us is affirmed and amplified in Jesus: "The Word became flesh and dwelt among us." And if, as I am suggesting here, Deuteronomy 30:11–14 becomes part of our picture of what grace looks like, we can take solace in the final words of this section that link Israel's intimacy with God's Word to their ability to observe God's command.

The final section of chapter 30—verses 15–20—is one of the few sections of Deuteronomy included in the Christian lectionary cycle. These verses represent not just the climax of Moses' third address, but it also could be argued that they represent the climax of the

---

3. Dietrich Bonhoeffer, *The Cost of Discipleship* (New York: Touchstone, 1995), 47.

entire book of Deuteronomy. Even as we have heard in earlier verses of chapter 30 about God's action to open Israel's heart and make obedience a real possibility, verses 15–20 once again set before Israel the choice between obedience and disobedience, between life and death.

As many commentators note, this call for a decision is perhaps the most powerful and explicit of such calls in the entire Bible. At the beginning of Deuteronomy, Moses tells Israel, "See, I have set the land before you" (1:8) and with these words commands Israel to do as God commands and go and enjoy the fruits of the land. In chapter 11, as Moses prepares to enumerate for Israel the additional laws needed for prosperous life in the land, he again uses this formula: "See, I am setting before you today a blessing and a curse" (11:26). The choice is

> It is probably here that the Christian church has the most to learn from the Old Testament. . . . It is [in Deuteronomy] that we see theology applied to the details of life in the most thoroughgoing and painstaking way. It is here that we see how to make godly decisions—how to choose life over death.
>
> J. Gary Millar, *Now Choose Life: Theology and Ethics in Deuteronomy* (Grand Rapids: Wm. B. Eerdmans Publishing Co., 1998), 182.

Israel's. And now, as Moses' speeches draw to a close, he invokes this formula one last time: "See, I have set before you today life and prosperity, death and adversity" (v. 15). All throughout Deuteronomy, the choice between following God's commands and choosing the path of disobedience is set before the people. Finally here in 30:15–20, Moses not only lays the choice before the people; he admonishes them to "choose life!" (v. 19).

Verse 19 widens the context for the Moab covenant. Indeed, this covenant involves more than just Israel and its descendants. Moses calls on "heaven and earth" to be witnesses to what Israel will choose. In the presence of God's good creation, Moses utters this final command to choose life. Choosing life means that the people of God and their descendants may be blessed and that they may fulfill the covenantal promises made between their ancestors and God (v. 20).

While other OT passages report on Israel's commitment to live up to its end of the covenant and obey God's commands, what is

> **That all shall be well, and all shall be well, and all manner of things shall be well.**
>
> Julian of Norwich, *Showings of Love* (Mahwah, NJ: Paulist Press, 1978), 225, *www.umilta.net/love1.html.*

particularly powerful about Moses' call for Israel to choose life in chapter 30 is that the text does not give us Israel's response. Unlike Exodus 19:8 where the Israelites proclaim, "'Everything that the LORD has spoken we will do,'" the Deuteronomist leaves Moses' final exhortation unanswered. Whether or not the people of God choose life remains an open question.

That this exhortation to choose life is set in the wider context of chapter 30's insistence that God will change the hearts (v. 6) of God's people and that the command of God is not too hard to follow (v. 11), however, gives us hope that in the end, the hearts of the people of God will be oriented toward God, and they indeed will choose life.

FURTHER REFLECTIONS
Choosing Life

The phrase "Choose life!" from Deuteronomy 30:19 is most often invoked today within the context of the debate over abortion. While abortion is certainly a significant moral issue of our day, our commentary on chapter 30 attempts to show that the context for the call to choose life is much broader than any single-minded focus on a particular moral issue. Chapter 30 concludes with Israel's teacher, leader, and prophet Moses speaking God's words to the people: "I have set before you today life and prosperity, death and adversity" (v. 15). In these final verses of the chapter, the Deuteronomist distills the admonition that is at the heart of the book of Deuteronomy: Israel will choose life by worshiping and obeying God and by following God's commands for life in the new land. How might this call to life, then, be interpreted in our current context?

In Deuteronomy, choosing life is synonymous with choosing a life of blessing. And the vision of a blessed life for Israel, we see vividly in Deut. 28:1–14, is one of abundant, vibrant, productive life in the land. For a segment of contemporary Christianity, the word "prosperity" has become endemic to what it means to choose life and be in a position to best receive God's blessing. Today's "prosperity preachers" preach a "prosperity gospel" that insists that choosing life and obeying God leads to material and financial prosperity. *Time* magazine's 2006 cover story "Does God Want You to Be Rich?" reported that 17 percent of Christians say they considered themselves part of the prosperity gospel movement while a full 61 percent believed that God wants people to be prosperous. Further, 31 percent agreed that if you give your money to God, God will bless you with more money.[4]

> **The Lord will make you abound in prosperity, in the fruit of your womb, in the fruit of your livestock, and in the fruit of your ground in the land that the Lord swore to your ancestors to give you.**
>
> (Deut. 28:11)

Prosperity preaching has many critics within and outside of Christianity. Although biblical passages like Deuteronomy 28:11 talk about God's blessings in terms of material prosperity, Christian theologians like Sallie McFague offer a different reading of what "choosing life" means for twenty-first century Christians, especially those whose lives bear many signs of such prosperity. McFague builds off of Jesus' words in John 10:10: "'I came that they may have life, and have it abundantly.'" For McFague, choosing life in our contemporary context of ecological strife and massive economic inequality must entail living differently: "We live to give God glory by loving the world and everything in it."[5]

> **It's God's will for you to live in prosperity instead of poverty. It's God's will for you to pay your bills and not be in debt. It's God's will for you to live in health and not in sickness all the days of your life.**
>
> Joel Osteen, *Live Your Best Life Now: 7 Steps to Living at Your Full Potential* (Nashville: FaithWords, 2007), 41.

---

4. David van Biema and Jeff Chu, "Does God Want You to Be Rich?" *Time Magazine*, September 10, 2006, http://www.time.com/time/magazine/article/0,9171,1533448,00.html.

5. Sallie McFague, *Life Abundant: Rethinking Theology and Economy for a Planet in Peril* (Minneapolis: Fortress Press, 2000), 4.

To live without protest under our current economic model of global capitalism, McFague insists, is to choose death over life, curse over blessing. Just as it was for the ancient Israelites whom Moses addresses in Deuteronomy 30:19, choosing life for Christians must be a choice made with eyes wide open to whether and how our moving toward abundance or prosperity affects both human and nonhuman beings. If we widen our lens beyond our own particular circumstances, choosing life must involve care and concern for all God's creation.

31:1–32:52
Leadership Transition and a Song of Woe

The opening words of chapter 31, "When Moses had finished speaking all these words to all Israel," herald a transition in the text from Moses' delivering lengthy speeches to a narrator who describes the final scenes of Moses' life. While Moses tells the people matter-of-factly that he is old and will not cross into the land with them (v. 2), we cannot underestimate the effect that the impending loss of Moses will have on the Israelites. Moses is not just any leader; as we have rehearsed many times in these pages, he has been Israel's leader, teacher, intercessor, and suffering servant. Therefore, it is no surprise that we learn in chapter 31 that Moses will be replaced not simply by another leader but by a leader, a book, and a song.

It goes without saying that losing someone of Moses' stature and significance would prove traumatic for the people. What will they do without him? In the narrative in chapter 31, Moses quickly shifts his attention away from his own fate and back toward God's enduring faithfulness to Israel. It is important to remember that even with Moses' faithfulness as their guide, the Israelites have struggled to trust in God (cf. Deut. 1:29). Therefore Moses tells all of Israel once again that God will be with them and lead them to victory in battles against other nations (31:3–6). Even though Moses' days with Israel are numbered, he wastes no opportunity to exhort Israel to be the covenantal partner God desires: "Be strong and bold" and "have no fear" of your enemies, for God is with you.

Because Moses will not be entering the promised land with Israel, he must commission Joshua, his successor, just as God commanded him to do (cf. Deut. 1:38; 3:28). Interestingly, when Moses commissions Joshua he uses the same words he used when addressing all of Israel: "Be strong and bold." That Joshua, as Israel's new leader, needs strength and courage links these final chapters of Deuteronomy to the next chapter of Israel's story, found in the book of Joshua. Three times in the first nine verses of Joshua, God commands him to "be strong and courageous" (Josh. 1:6, 7, 9). In both books, Joshua's call to courage is linked directly to Israel's journey into the land that God had promised. And at the conclusion of his commissioning of Joshua in Deuteronomy 31, Moses offers Joshua a benediction of sorts: "'It is the LORD who goes before you. He will be with you; he will not fail you or forsake you. Do not fear or be dismayed'" (v. 8), a theme also echoed in Joshua 1.

This story of commissioning offers insight into a model of leadership that still proves relevant today. The leadership of Moses—and soon of Joshua—is about strength and courage in following God's commands, qualities that are not just of the head but also of the

> "I hereby command you: Be strong and courageous; do not be frightened or dismayed, for the LORD your God is with you wherever you go."
>
> (Josh. 1:9)

heart. While Moses is often cast by later interpreters as a hero—after all, he led the Israelites out of slavery into freedom—Rabbi Harold Kushner's recent study of Moses focuses more on Moses' capacity as a leader—and as a person—to cope with failure and disappointment. Transferring the position of leader of Israel from Moses to Joshua concretized the notion that Moses would not lead Israel into the promised land. In his chapter called "It's Not All about You," Kushner lifts up Moses' humility as a leader, attending especially to his ability to stay focused on the good of the whole people rather than just on his own wants and desires:

> Humility means recognizing that you are not God and it is not your job or responsibility to run the world. Some people are disappointed to learn that; most mentally healthy people are

immensely relieved. Moses was able to surmount the problems and frustrations in his life because he understood that he
was not God and could not be expected to be, and that God's
plan for humanity did not depend solely on him.[6]

Exactly what kind of leader is Moses, and what are the characteristics of leadership that his successor, Joshua, also needs to possess? It is noteworthy that while Moses serves multiple roles—from
teacher and intercessor to prophet—neither he nor Joshua is commissioned to a particular office (such as king, priest, or prophet).
Rather, both men are called to lead God's people in responding to
God's command, which in this case is to journey into the land promised by God and to choose life in that new land.

Moses' commissioning of Joshua in verses 7–8 can be understood
as the opening scene in a three-act play where the transfer of power
between Moses and his successor is completed. Before moving to
acts 2 and 3 of the commissioning, however, the Deuteronomist
directs our attention to one of Moses' final acts as leader: the translation of the oral tradition into a written one. While in chapter 27
the Deuteronomist has Moses instructing the people to write down
all the words of the law (vv. 3, 8), in 31:9 we hear that it is Moses
who writes down the law and then gives it to the priests and elders
of Israel. Just as in chapter 27, though, the written law described in
chapter 31 is to accompany the ark of the covenant, which houses
the Ten Commandments and moves with Israel from place to place.
But in chapter 31, Moses' commands go even further than what he
instructed in chapter 27. Here we learn that the law is to be read
"before all Israel" (v. 11), including not just the men, women,
and children but the aliens as well (v. 12). Moses' words in this
section remind Israel of the intimate connection between the presence of God and the awareness of the law they are commanded to
obey (v. 11).

The transfer of power from Moses to Joshua continues in verses
14–29 with God summoning Joshua and Moses into the tent of
meeting. Within the tent, God appears "in a pillar of cloud" (v. 15)

6. Harold Kushner, *Overcoming Life's Disappointments* (New York: Knopf), 117.

and focuses first of all on Moses. "'Soon you will lie down with your ancestors,'" God says to Moses and then moves to more bad news of yet more disobedience on the part of Israel: "'Then this people will begin to prostitute themselves to the foreign gods in their midst'" (v. 16). They will abandon their God; they will break the covenant. In anticipation of imminent disobedience of the people, God commands Moses to one more important act: "'Write this song, and teach it to the Israelites; put it in their mouths, in order that the song may be a witness for me against the Israelites'" (v. 19). Even as the text reports on God's foreknowledge of Israel's dis-

> God instructs Moses to write a poem and teach it to Israel, in order that they will not forget him. "Give ear, O heavens, let me speak," the poem begins, invoking the most sacred ingredient of the desert, water. "Let the earth hear the words I utter! / May my discourse come down as the rain, / My speech distill as the dew." The poem goes on to predict the ultimate rebellion by the people against God, but says, in the end, that God will not forsake Israel.
>
> Bruce Feiler, *Walking the Bible: A Journey by Land through the Five Books of Moses* (New York: HarperCollins), 415.

obedience, at the same time God's speech to Moses in verses 14–21 also contains yet another vivid description of the richness of the promised land: "flowing with milk and honey" (v. 20). In response to God's command, Moses does what he is told and writes the song.

Verse 23 takes us to the third act of Joshua's commissioning. This time it is God who commissions Joshua; Moses is nowhere in sight. The movement in this chapter from Moses as the agent of divine action to God as central actor is a tangible sign that Moses' tenure as leader is drawing to a close. As we will hear in the closing words of the book of Deuteronomy, Moses was uniquely gifted as a servant of God, having a relationship with God that was unmatched by any other leader in Israel (34:10–12). So as Moses' years of leadership draw to a close, God steps in and plays a more direct role in the life of God's people.

After the three-act commissioning of Joshua, the spotlight returns one final time to Moses, who, having finished writing down the words of the law, gives the book of the law to the priests and commands them to place it alongside the ark. Both the book of the law and the ark are mobile, and, unlike Moses, they can and will cross over into the land with the people. It is also important to note that recording and preserving the law in written form did not relegate the law simply as an artifact of a past time and place. Rather the book becomes a witness to the way in which God's Word can transcend time and space.

But even as the book of the law becomes a witness *for* God's ongoing relationship with the people, Moses states in verse 26 that the book will also become a witness *against* Israel in its anticipated disobedience. Unlike in verses 12–13, where Moses describes the function of the law in positive terms—that the reason to have it read before all of Israel is so that the Israelites may learn to fear God and observe the commands—we hear in verse 26 the description of the law's negative function: that it will witness *against* Israel in the future.

> For "no human being will be justified in his sight" by deeds prescribed by the law, for through the law comes the knowledge of sin.
>
> (Rom. 3:20)

Just like the song Moses is commanded to write, the law will also illuminate the way in which Israel is not adhering to God's commands.

That the law will stand in judgment of God's people is a theme that resurfaces later in the Old Testament in the story of King Josiah in 2 Kings 22, whereupon hearing the words of the book of the law, he tears his clothes and says, "Great is the wrath of the LORD that is kindled against us, because our ancestors did not obey the words of this book, to do according to all that is written concerning us" (2 Kgs. 22:13). Even more prominently for Christians, this idea of the negative function of the law is taken up by the apostle Paul, who insists that the law's negative function is an important part of the larger role it plays in the lives of God's people: "What then should we say? That the law is sin? By no means! Yet, if it had not been for the law, I would not have known sin. I would not have known what it is to covet if the law had so said, "You shall not covet.". . . So the law is holy, and the commandment is holy and just and good" (Rom. 7:7, 12).

Even though Paul affirms the positive role of the law in Romans 7, centuries of theologians have focused more on what they call the negative function of the law. In particular, theologians of the Reformation like John Calvin have highlighted the negative use of law. Calvin writes, "While [the law] shows God's righteousness, that is, the righteousness alone acceptable to God, it warns, informs, convicts, and lastly condemns, every man of his own unrighteousness. For man, blinded and drunk with self-love, must be compelled to know and to confess his own feebleness and impurity.[7] Clearly the negative role of the law is theologically significant, especially as it allows us to become aware of our sin. But Calvin does not stop there. Like both Moses and Paul, he understands the law's role as positive as well as negative. The second use of the law, according to Calvin, comes in its ability to make visible the parameters of acceptable behavior; and in third place, the law positively directs the people of God in how to live according to God's will. All three of these uses are visible in Moses' complex treatment of the law throughout Deuteronomy.

Chapter 31 ends with Moses assembling the people before him one last time (v. 28) and indicating that it will not just be the song or the law that witnesses against the people of God, but all of creation will do so as well. In this final stance before the people of Israel, Moses also recites the words of the song that God commanded him to write so that all Israel would hear and be warned of their impending disobedience, which brings us to the song itself in chapter 32.

The song is rendered in poetic form, which has a decidedly different quality to it than the prose we have been interpreting thus far in Deuteronomy. This exemplary piece of Hebrew poetry, which scholars insist was written much earlier than the surrounding chapters, chronicles the disintegration of the relationship between God and Israel. And while the summary of the song in 31:16–20 suggests that it should be sung "when many terrible troubles come upon" Israel (v. 21), we shall see as we move through the verses of chapter 32 that the song of this new covenant of Moab ends not with judgment or curse but with compassion and vision for future life for the people in the promised land. In order to get to a note of hope, however, we

---

7. John Calvin, *The Institutes of Christian Religion*, vol. 1, bk. 2 (Louisville, KY: Westminster John Knox Press, 1960), 7:6.

On the whole, it's better to think of the Bible as poetry rather than as prose, at least as we generally distinguish between those two in our reading practices. You cannot skim poetry for plot, and you cannot read it in distraction. That is why poetry is read by poetry lovers: it is a nonutilitarian act, like many other acts of love. Therefore, reading the Bible "as poetry" means slowing down to ponder each phrase, to wonder why *this* word was chosen and not another, how this line or paragraph or story builds on what precedes and leads into what follows.

William P. Brown, *Engaging Biblical Authority: Perspectives on the Bible as Scripture* (Louisville, KY: Westminster John Knox Press, 2007), 41.

must first wade through the diatribe against Israel, who once again is accused of breaking faith with their God.

As we turn to an examination of the poetry itself, we recognize that the language of the song is also evocative of a lawsuit, where God charges Israel with unfaithfulness to their covenantal relationship. Scholars have divided the song into various numbers of sections; in the end, what is most important to see is that it begins with an introduction and then moves through the story of Israel's relationship with God—from God's choosing Israel, to Israel's disobeying God, to God's anger and punishment, before concluding with a turn toward God's restoration of Israel. As is likely clear from this rehearsal, the song provides a poetic review of the key themes of the Deuteronomic narrative.

In the introductory section in verses 1–3, we hear that heaven and earth are to listen to the words of Moses' song (v. 1). Just as in 30:19, the reach of this covenant at Moab extends beyond Israel alone. Verse 2 overflows with water images, such as Moses' petition "May my teaching drop like the rain." The references to water highlight the pedagogical role the song is intended to play. Just as water is essential for sustaining life (especially the lives of those who have wandered in the desert, a place of so little water), so too is Moses' song intended to guide the Israelites so that they "may live long in the land" (v. 47). We are told in 31:19 that the song should instruct in a negative way: that is, it should function to expose Israel once more as a disobedient covenant partner, a partner who will bear the wrath of an angry God. The song's introduction concludes with an attestation of God's greatness, reminding Israel that its covenant partner is deserving of honor and praise.

Interestingly, the claim in verse 3, "I will proclaim the name of the LORD," is followed by a plethora of images and names for God used in the verses to come. In verse 4, God is called "the Rock," an image used four more times in the song (vv. 15, 18, 30, 31). In the Psalms, God is often referred to as a rock, connoting strength and steadfastness.

In contrast to this image of God's faithfulness, the song of Moses casts Israel in the role of the disobedient child who has gone against its parent's will (vv. 5–7). God, also imaged here in an intimate way as the father "who created . . . made . . . and established" Israel (v. 6), is caring, nurturing, and loving while Israel fails to respond in kind. Returning to a central theme of the book of Deuteronomy, the song calls on Israel to "remember" God's loving actions toward them (v. 7). Verses 7–8 then return to a crucial aspect of reality that Israel must remember: that when God "divided humankind," God chose Israel to be God's people (v. 8). While we have heard this theme of election and chosenness multiple times before (cf. Deut. 7:7–8), what is especially noteworthy here is the reference to God's apportioning of the rest of the people of the world with other gods. It is clear that Israel is God's "own portion" (v. 9); at the same time, God is also presented as having given other peoples to other gods (v. 8). When we link Deuteronomy 32:8 together with passages such as 4:19 that support the existence of other religions and other gods, we have opened to us, biblical scholar Patrick Miller suggests, "the possibility of a dialectic between the one and the many, between the one God of Israel, the God of Jesus Christ, who for Israel and the church is the only God, and the many

> The LORD is my rock, my fortress, and my deliverer;
>
> my God, my rock in whom I take refuge,
>
> my shield and the horn of my salvation, my stronghold.
>
> (Ps. 18:2)

People of faith often see themselves as self-sufficient entities, dependent on their religious beliefs alone for guidance and sustenance. They may see people of other religions as entirely wrong or only partially correct. Such theological arguments do not provide space for mutually enriching relationships with others. By devaluing the beliefs of others, they often lead to mere "tolerance" of neighbors of other faiths. These theological arguments require responses that are likewise based in theology.

Anand Rambachan, "Finding Theological Support for Religious Diversity," *Diversity & Democracy*, vol. 11, no. 1 (2008), http://www.diversityweb.org/DiversityDemocracy/vol11no1/rambachan.cfm.

gods who are worshiped to the far corners of the earth."[8] Obviously, the Deuteronomist does not offer a full-fledged theology of religious pluralism here; nevertheless, as our lives become increasingly religiously diverse, more theological attention must be directed toward such claims, especially as a counterpoint to such passages as Deuteronomy 4:39 and 32:39 that maintain a strongly monotheistic stance. In these evocative verses of the Song of Moses, verses that are to be heard by the heavens and the earth, we find an Israel who clearly belongs only to God and at the same time other peoples who participate in God-ordained relationships with other gods. What we have here is no easy, relativistic pluralism. As we have witnessed, Deuteronomy contains some sharp critiques of the other gods Israel is tempted to worship (cf. Deut. 17:2–5; 32:16–17); at the same time, however, Deuteronomy does not advocate a narrow exclusivism.

This covenantal relationship between Israel and God is fleshed out in verses 10–14 as the song rehearses the story that Israel is called on never to forget: that God "sustained them in a desert land, in a howling wilderness waste" (v. 10). To reinforce the abiding nature of God's care of Israel during those bleak years, the Deuteronomist turns again to another parental image, this time in a maternal key: that of an eagle caring for its young. This image is also used in other poetic sections of the biblical text, such as Psalm 91:4. Overall, however, it is important to note that parental imagery for God is quite sparse in OT writings.

8. Miller, 229.

At the same time, although Moses' words elsewhere in Deuteronomy affirm God's transcendence beyond gender (cf. 4:15–16), we want to highlight the rich use of multiple names, images, and metaphors employed within the poetry to evoke a richer and more complex understanding of who this God is.

The maternal image is invoked yet again as the song turns its focus to God's providing Israel with the promised land. In verse 13, we hear that God "nursed" Israel with honey from the land. Israel, here imaged as God's son, Jacob, "ate his fill" in the land (v. 15). Once again it is important to lift up the plurality of images of God used by the Deuteronomist throughout this text. It is much too simplistic to say that Deuteronomy gives us a wrathful God. While a wrathful God is certainly a prominent image, other images like the parental ones widen the scope of how this God is viewed and understood.

But we're never too far from wrath in Deuteronomy. Here the tone of the song shifts. Jacob indeed ate his fill but "grew fat, bloated, and gorged" (v. 15). The reference to Israel's forgetting God's care after the Israelites got a taste of prosperity is reminiscent of the stern warnings given in 8:10–15, where Moses implores Israel to not forget the Lord when they have entered the land and eaten their fill. But as the Song of Moses suggests, forgetting the Lord is precisely what Israel will do. Verses 16–18 detail

> Like an eagle, the Lord spreads his wings over us, his nestlings. There the Lord is compared with the eagle guarding its young. The simile therefore is appropriate that God protects us as a father and as a hen guarding her chicks lest they be snatched away by a hawk.
>
> Jerome, as quoted in *Exodus, Leviticus, Numbers, Deuteronomy,* Ancient Christian Commentary on Scripture, Old Testament 3, ed. Joseph T. Lienhard (Downers Grove, IL: InterVarsity Press, 2001), 333.

> The Jewish compromise between the "must-speak-of-God" and the "cannot-speak-of-God" is the so-called awe of names. We abstain from every mention of the tetragrammaton by using other names for God in order not to profane it. We speak of God as Jesus did, periphrastically, as the Greatly to be Praised, our Father in Heaven, the Holy One, Ruler of the World.
>
> Karl Rahner and Pinchas Lapide, *Encountering Jesus—Encountering Judaism: A Dialogue* (New York: Crossroad), 1987, 37.

Israel's disobedient acts, most egregiously the turn from worshiping God to worshiping other gods. Israel is unmindful of its parent, the one "who gave [it] birth." The Deuteronomist continues with the parent/child imagery still longer in verses 19–27 as we hear that God will "spurn his sons and daughters" (v. 19). If we understand the poem as also using a juridical framework, these verses deliver the sentence to a disobedient Israel.

Once again, we hear that the punishment against Israel is severe. In verse 20, the Lord says, "I will hide my face from them," which is suggestive of an utter reversal of God's care witnessed to just a few verses earlier. In verse 21, the repercussions go even further as there is talk of God's deserting Israel and taking up with another nation. Christian commentators like Martin Luther have responded to this verse with the assertion, "That has happened, as the apostle bears witness in Rom. 11:11ff., since the heathen have been accepted through the Gospel." While it is certainly the case that Christians understand themselves to be grafted onto the tree of salvation, as Paul says in Romans 11:17–24, we also should not neglect Paul's subsequent claim in Romans 11:26: "And so all Israel will be saved." Historically, however, many Christian interpreters of Deuteronomy 32:21 have held a view similar to that of Luther, who concluded his commentary on this verse with these words: "And the present day Jews are irreconcilably angry with us for denying that they are the people of God and for asserting that according to this verse we are the people of God."[9] As we shall see, however, the Song of Moses concludes with a reaffirmation that the Israelites are indeed God's people on whose behalf God will act (v. 43).

> **Unlike holiness or righteousness, wrath never forms one of the permanent attributes of the God of Israel.**
>
> Walther Eichrodt, *Theology of the Old Testament*, vol. 1 (London: S.C.M., 1961), 262.

The verses that follow attest in dramatic ways to the coming actions of the angry warrior God, an image of God that biblical scholars suggest draws on ancient poetry of other warrior gods; indeed, such references also occur in other biblical poetry (cf. 2

9. Luther, *LW* 9:294.

Sam. 22:8–16). While the warrior image was a common one for the deities in Canaan and in the ancient Near East as a whole, it was expected that the warrior god of a particular tribe would typically fight on behalf of, rather than against, that god's own people. But as we see in the poetry of chapter 32 and in other places in Deuteronomy, that is not always the case with Israel's God. This God not only fights on behalf of Israel but also disciplines his own people. And like the punishment for the disobedient son in chapter 21, the discipline is the most severe possible. God will cause the land to be a source of harm to them (vv. 22–24); they will be scattered into exile; and the song even goes so far as to invoke the act referenced in 29:20: that God will "blot out the memory of them from humankind" (32:26). Once again the recounting of God's wrath unnerves us, especially in light of the vivid and repeated invocation of God as a parent earlier in the song. In these sobering stanzas, God abandons and rejects God's own children, actions that contradict other attestations of who this God is. Looking to the book of Isaiah, we also see God portrayed in a maternal way, with images that blatantly contradict the descriptions of God as a bloodthirsty warrior who hides his face from Israel:

> But Zion said, "The LORD has forsaken me,
> my LORD has forgotten me."
> Can a woman forget her nursing child,
> or show no compassion for the child of her womb?
> Even these may forget,
> yet I will not forget you.
>
> (Isa. 49:14–16)

While the Old Testament sets forth conflicting images of God in a persistently unresolvable way, it is important to observe that Israel, on the other hand, is consistently depicted as being beyond help.[10] Verse 35 reminds the reader that God is in charge and concludes with the claim that Israel's doom will come swiftly. We must admit that here again in Deuteronomy there is no getting around the wrath and vengeance of God. Just when it appears that Israel's situation

---

10. J. Gary Millar, *Now Choose Life: Theology and Ethics in Deuteronomy* (Grand Rapids: Wm. B. Eerdmans Publishing Co., 1998), 178.

could not get any worse, the Song of Moses begins to offer brief glimpses of hope. While Israel's sin will bring them great suffering, the Song of Moses suggests that when Israel is weakened, God "will have compassion on his servants" (v. 36).

FURTHER REFLECTIONS
Sin and an Angry God

We cannot deny that a central theme in Deuteronomic theology and in the Song of Moses specifically is the theme of God's wrath, which comes as a result of Israel's disobedience. Chapter 32's depiction of God's anger lives on in Christian imagination as well, perhaps most notably in eighteenth-century American theologian Jonathan Edwards's famous sermon "Sinners in the Hands of an Angry God," delivered to his Connecticut congregation in 1741. The sermon is based on Deuteronomy 32:35, words that lie at the heart of chapter 32's Song of Moses:

> Vengeance is mine, and recompense,
> for the time when their foot shall slip;
> because the day of their calamity is at hand,
> their doom comes swiftly.

Many Christians today likely want little to do with either Edwards's fiery rhetoric or with Deuteronomy's persistent recitations of the ways in which God's people will be destroyed by God's hand. To address the issue of whether or not we should continue to hold on to such notions of God's wrath, we will draw on the 1958 presentation by theologian H. Richard Niebuhr titled "The Anachronism of Jonathan Edwards," in which Niebuhr works to make Edwards's use of Deuteronomy intelligible to a modern-day audience. In this presentation, Niebuhr provides us with an insightful framework for interpreting Deuteronomy's view of the wrathful God that still holds resonance today.[11]

---

11. H. Richard Niebuhr, "The Anachronism of Jonathan Edwards," in *Theology, History, Culture: Major Unpublished Writings*, ed. William Stacy Johnson (New Haven, CT: Yale University Press, 1996), 123–33.

Niebuhr begins with the case against the preoccupation in Edwards's theology and, we will add, in Deuteronomic theology, with the wrath of God. He lays out three popular critiques brought against such theologies of wrath. First is the concern that in such theologies humanity is being demeaned for the purposes of illuminating God's power. In his sermon "Sinners in the Hands of an Angry God," Edwards proclaims to his congregation, "There is no want of power in God to cast wicked men into hell at any moment. Men's hands cannot be strong when God rises up."[12] Similarly in Deuteronomy 32:22–23, we hear that God will use God's power to "devour the earth" and "heap disasters" on the Israelites. In response to concerns about how such theologies of wrath seek to exalt the divine by belittling the human, Niebuhr reframes the issue by suggesting that such theologies actually take sin and its damning effects extremely seriously. As Niebuhr reminds his twentieth-century audience, even though we might disparage Edwards's prolonged focus on human sinfulness, we should take note that "man's inhumanity to man" has gone far beyond anything Edwards himself ever imagined.[13] The same can certainly be said for the vision of evil in Deuteronomy. Attending to the ferocity of God's wrath in Deuteronomy, then, we can see that the intensity of the divine wrath is directly related to the demonstrations of human destructiveness and harm.

> The anger of God speaks the truth. No matter how "nice" we think we are, or morally in the right, our hands, too, are full of blood; we do not exist as little kingdoms apart from our human societies full of murder, thievery, cheating, whole systems of oppression. I have come to have a certain level of trust in God's anger; it is a response to what is genuinely wrong.
>
> Kathleen Norris, *Amazing Grace: A Vocabulary of Faith* (New York: Riverhead Books, 1998), 125.

It is when Israel turns from God toward other gods and practices "abhorrent things" and "sacrifice to demons" (vv. 16–17) that God's wrath is manifest in its fiercest form

---

12. Jonathan Edwards, "Sinners in the Hands of an Angry God," Christian Classics Ethereal Library, www.ccel.org/ccel/edwards/sermons.sinners.html.
13. H. Richard Niebuhr, *The Kingdom of God in America* (Middletown, CT: Wesleyan University Press, 1988), 128.

(cf. vv. 23–26). Human capacity for sin is vast, and the on-the-ground effects of sin are all too present before our eyes.

The second critique Niebuhr discusses concerning theologies of wrath has to do with the claim that theological preoccupation with God's sovereignty leaves too little room for human freedom. In his sermon, Edwards repeatedly insists that "nothing keeps wicked men at any one moment out of hell, but the mere pleasure of God."[14] In response to concerns that such claims deny the reality of human freedom, Niebuhr suggests that Edwards's insight into the message from biblical passages like Deuteronomy 32 is that God's will is to be the will of God's people. Just as we discussed in the commentary on chapter 30, there is definitely tension within the Deuteronomic text over the relationship between divine and human agency. And while Deuteronomy is emphatic in its claim of God's sovereignty over all things and over the future of Israel, at the same time there are several places in the text, such as the exhortation to "choose life!" in 30:19, where a choice is laid before the people and it is clear that they must exert their own agency to follow God's commands. Thus, accentuating God's sovereignty does not necessarily lead to a disregarding of free will.

> **Man is finite, he is given to himself as what he is. He has received his being and with it, the structure of his being, including the structure of finite freedom.**
>
> Paul Tillich, *The Courage to Be*, 2nd ed. (New Haven, CT: Yale University Press, 2000), 152.

Finally, Niebuhr turns to the criticism that theologies of wrath strike the contemporary Christian as too deterministic: indeed, according to Edwards, at any time God may cause our feet to slip, at which point we sinners could descend into hell. This is where the interplay between Edwards's theology and Deuteronomy's theology is perhaps at its most powerful. Take, for instance, the injunction in 32:39: "I kill and I make alive; I wound and I heal; and no one can deliver from my hand." In response to such terrifying images, Niebuhr suggests that rather than preaching determinism, what Edwards—and

14. Edwards, "Sinners," 642.

again we can add, Deuteronomy—depicts is the "terrible uncertainty of life."[15]

We set our feet in slippery places; there is nowhere to go to obtain a guarantee of life without hardship, suffering, and death. A fundamental point for Edwards and for the Deuteronomist is that our lives—indeed the lives of all of creation—are radically contingent, radically dependent on the Creator. The God who gives life and the God who takes life away is the God who is made known in the Bible. Very often in our contemporary minds, however, Niebuhr suggests that we have replaced the biblical God with something much more nebulous—something like a "Supreme Being" or "Sacred Power," where divine sovereignty is replaced with "chance" as the reason why our feet have not yet slipped.

It is important to assert that just as with Edwards's sermon, the Song of Moses in Deuteronomy is intended to serve a negative function; that is, it is intended to sound the call of judgment against God's people who have gone astray. And those who hear this as judgment on the way in which they have lived are called to make a change, to turn away from their sinful ways. In Deuteronomy, Israel is issued a choice: to choose the way of blessing or the way of curse, and Moses implores them to "choose life!" Similarly, Edwards's sermon ends with a call to his congregants to choose life, which in his theology is to choose Christ, to be born again.

> **O sinner! Consider the fearful danger you are in: it is a great furnace of wrath, a wide and bottomless pit, full of the fire of wrath, that you are held over in the hand of that God, whose wrath is provoked and incensed as much against you, as against many of the damned in hell.**
>
> Jonathan Edwards, "Sinners in the Hands of an Angry God," Christian Classics Ethereal Library, www.ccel.org/ccel/edwards/sermons.sinners.html.

Finally, as we noted in the introduction, while there is clear scriptural assertion that God *is* love (1 John 4:8), there is no corresponding scriptural claim that God *is* wrath. What this means is that God's anger, wrath, and vengeance are all ultimately put to use in the

---

15. Niebuhr, *Kingdom of God*, 130.

And now you have an extraordinary opportunity, a day wherein Christ has thrown the door of mercy wide open, and stands in calling and crying with a loud voice to poor sinners; a day wherein many are flocking to him, and pressing into the kingdom of God.

Jonathan Edwards, "Sinners in the Hands of an Angry God," Christian Classics Ethereal Library, www.ccel.org/ccel/edwards/sermons.sinners.html.

service of God's love. This is why the Song of Moses and the book of Deuteronomy, and even the Bible as a whole, do not give divine wrath the last word.

Scripture's final vision is this: that there will be a new heaven and a new earth, where "death will be no more; mourning and crying and pain will be no more, for the first things have passed away" (Rev. 21:4). Back in Deuteronomy, the people of God are, like us, still living in the land where death too often reigns, struggling to trust in those promises of God for a new land, a new life.

But then in verses 40–42 we are confronted yet again with images of God as a vengeful and bloodied divine warrior. Though we hear more about God's vengeance, God's anger is now directed toward the despairing Israelites' enemies. As we have stated before, there is no getting around these images. They play an integral role in Moses' song

In addition to hoping for more in this life, I also hope for more beyond. I hope that the promises of God are true; that there is more to life beyond this earthly one; and that in that life beyond there will be no more crying, no more dying, only light, only love, only joy.

Deanna Thompson, *Hoping for More: Having Cancer, Talking Faith, and Accepting Grace* (Eugene, OR: Cascade Publications, 2012), xv.

and in Deuteronomy as a whole. If we put these images in the context of the entire chapter, however, we see God's vengeance being meted out against a haughty and disobedient Israel; at the same time, we catch glimpses in the song of a God who acts on behalf of the people when they have been brought low and "their power is gone" (v. 36). But when they're powerful and forget their dependence on God, God acts against them.

While we cannot avoid and should not neglect the significance of the image of God as divine warrior within Deuteronomy, at the same time we must see this image as one alongside many other images of God. Within the Song of Moses, parental imagery dominates in verses 4–14, giving way to divine warrior imagery in verses 19–43. Of course one of the reasons we find images of a warrior God so troubling is not just what they say about God but what they might grant to God's people in terms of taking violence into their own hands. As we move toward the end of the song, we hear that God's wrath is no longer directed against Israel but against Israel's enemies (vv. 41–43). Might it not be tempting for God's people to take the vivid imagery of God's arrows "drunk with blood" as permission for God's people to take military matters into their own hands? Indeed, if God's sword "will devour their flesh" (v. 42), why not help God out with our own swords?

Amid the disturbing, upsetting images of the bloody warrior God that saturate the second half of the Song of Moses, there is a brief but powerful rebuttal of such crusading mentality: "Vengeance is mine," says the Lord (v. 35), which means it's not ours, as the apostle Paul says in Rom. 12:19: "Beloved, never avenge yourselves, but leave room for the wrath of God; for it is written, 'Vengeance is mine, I will repay, says the Lord.'" Nothing in Moses' song suggests that God's people should vindicate themselves; rather, vengeance and vindication is relegated to God and God alone.

The song concludes in verse 43 with a reference to the land God has promised Israel and the promise that God will again make it possible for Israel to occupy the land. Then in verses 44–47 the narrative returns with Moses once again exhorting Israel to take the words of the song to heart. He also gives the words as a command to the

> You shall put these words of mine in your heart and soul.
>
> (Deut. 11:18)

Israelite children "so that they may diligently observe the words of the law" (v. 46). This language is evocative of 6:6–7 and 11:18–19, where Moses exhorts Israel to take to heart and observe the commands he is giving them that day.

What is different about Moses' exhortation in 32:46, however, is that the song remains a witness against Israel whereas in chapters 6 and 11 the language remains more positive. This takes us back full circle to the beginning of Moses' song where we heard that it would serve an important pedagogical purpose, teaching through illuminating the possible paths of disobedience open to Israel (32:2). And verse 47 hearkens back to the powerful passage in 30:19 where Moses sets before Israel the choice between life and death. This is no insignificant matter, we hear yet again; Israel's choice is inseparably linked with blessing or curse, and the song is meant to witness to the pressing need for Israel to choose life.

The chapter ends with a foretelling of Moses' imminent death. God commands Moses to ascend Mount Nebo and view the land of Canaan, the land Israel will enter after Moses' death. Verse 50 also contains a startling imperative use of the verb "to die," where God commands Moses, "You shall die there on the mountain." While this scene is rendered with more detail in the final chapter of Deuteronomy, in these verses God tells Moses he is dying before Israel gets to Canaan due to the same reason his brother, Aaron, died when he did, "because both of [them] broke faith with [God] among the Israelites at the waters of Meribath-kadesh" (32:51; cf. Num. 20:10–12; 27:12–14). Earlier in Deuteronomy, however, the reason given for Moses' death outside the promised land is the result of the people's sin (1:37; 3:23–29; 4:21). As we can see, there is an unresolved tension throughout the Deuteronomic text between Moses' living and dying for the sake of others and living and dying because of his own human limitations. And as we will see, this tension remains unresolved to the end.

> Moses and Aaron gathered the assembly together before the rock, and he said to them, "Listen, you rebels, shall we bring water for you out of this rock?" Then Moses lifted up his hand and struck the rock twice with his staff; water came out abundantly, and the congregation and their livestock drank. But the LORD said to Moses and Aaron, "Because you did not trust in me, to show my holiness before the eyes of the Israelites, therefore you shall not bring this assembly into the land that I have given them."
>
> (Num. 20:10–12)

The conclusion of chapter 32 also brings with it the conclusion of talk of the covenant at Moab. Before moving on to Moses' final words of blessing for Israel and the poignant scene of Moses' death, let us consider the relationship between the covenant at Horeb and the Moab covenant laid out in chapters 29–32. In the Horeb covenant, the focus is on the agency and actions of the people. The first twenty-six chapters are insistent in their exhortation that Israel "keep all the decrees and commandments" and "observe the commands diligently" (cf. 6:2–3). In chapters 29–32, which deal with the Moab covenant, in contrast, divine agency and action take center stage. The prime example of this, we recall, comes in 30:6 where the previous command to Israel to "circumcise your heart" (10:16) becomes a divine promise: God will ultimately bring about the Israelites' change of heart. This accent on divine agency and promise in the Moab covenant is suggestive of another difference between the covenants at Horeb and Moab: the Moab covenant contains a stronger sense of hope in God's promised future. Even though God's people have been and always will be sinful and rebellious (cf. 31:16–22, 27–29), God ultimately remains devoted to and works on behalf of Israel in order to secure blessing for them (32:36, 43).

> Moreover, the LORD your God will circumcise your heart and the heart of your descendants, so that you will love the LORD your God with all your heart and with all your soul, in order that you may live.
>
> (Deut. 30:6)

As mentioned before, the covenant at Moab is not referenced in any other place in Scripture. That it is presented as a new covenant "in addition to the covenant at Horeb" (29:1) has led to comparisons between it and the new covenant in Jeremiah 31:33–34, where God says, "I will put my law within them, and I will write it on their hearts." While similarities exist between the covenant at Moab and Jeremiah's anticipated new covenant—such as the intimate connection between the law and the heart—there are also significant differences. Perhaps most notable is that in the Jeremiah covenant there is no longer any torah ("I will put my law within them"), written word ("I will write it on their hearts"), or teachers ("No longer shall they teach one another"), all of which are vital for the Moab covenant.

Finally, while Jeremiah introduces the covenant as one that God will make with Israel "after those days" (31:33), the Moab covenant is, like the rest of Deuteronomy, still primarily concerned with "today." When Moses exhorts Israel to choose life in 30:19, we hear this command as one that commands a response by the hearer—today.

33:1–34:12

Not Quite the Promised Land: God's Faithfulness and Moses' Death

33:1–29

Moses' Final Words: A Blessing

In contrast to the words of the Song of Moses that God commissioned Moses to write and teach to the people (Deut. 31:19), chapter 33 suggests that as a "man of God," Moses now will offer his own last words for Israel, words that come in the form of a blessing. The reference to Moses as "man of God" (v. 1) is the only time this designation is given in the Pentateuch, whereas it appears numerous places in other OT writings to refer to Moses and to other prophets (such as Elijah in 1 Kgs. 17:18, 24). Note the contrast created between the concluding verses of chapter 32 that emphasize Moses' disobedience and the opening verse of chapter 33 where Moses stands as the only man of God in the first five books of the Bible.

These final words of blessing given by Moses are reminiscent of fathers' blessings on their children, particularly Jacob's blessing for his twelve sons before his death in Genesis 49. It is important to observe, however, that even though Moses had two sons, Gershom and Eliezar (Exod. 18:3–4), his final blessing is not for his own children but rather for the tribes of Israel.

Verses 2–5 offer an introduction to the blessing that—similar to chapter 32—is also rendered in poetic verse and thought to be older in composition but later in terms of its becoming part of the Deuteronomic text. These verses recount God's history with Israel; they also reference Mount Sinai, the place where Moses first encountered God in the burning bush (Exod. 3:1–6). Some of the language here is cryptic, such as the references to the "myriad of holy ones" who were with God (v. 2). Also in dispute is the referent for the claim that "there arose a king in Jeshurun" in verse 5. Some suggest that the king referred to here is God, a term used only two other times in the Pentateuch to refer to God (Exod. 15:18; Num. 23:31). Others suggest that the term references the kings that arise in Israel after they enter the land. With the setting forth of guidelines for kingship in Israel in Deuteronomy 18:1–8, such a reference is possible in this blessing given for Israel and its future. Whichever proposal is ultimately correct, the more significant issue is that the blessing anticipates—or reflects—the future life the tribes of Israel will have in the land. In anticipation of life in the land, Moses' words of blessing focus on prosperity and protection for the people of God.

Verses 6–25 contain words of blessing to each of the tribes of Israel (except Simeon). While most such listings of the tribes proceed according to birth order (see, for example, Jacob's blessing of his sons in Gen. 49), here the listing follows geography, moving from tribe to tribe based on the location of the land they will inhabit in the future. Thus the list begins with Reuben, in whose land Israel now stands.

In the blessings of the tribes that follow, several issues are worth noting. First, the blessing of the Levites is the most distinctive (vv. 8–11), for it attests to the Levites' faithfulness and the special role given them throughout the book of Deuteronomy. When Moses will no longer be around to model obedience and teach Israel the law, Israel is directed to look to the Levites to continue those tasks. Second, the blessing to the tribe of Joseph is the longest and the most extravagant, containing repeated references to the bounty of the land on which the tribe resides. Third, the divine warrior imagery so prominent in chapter 32 lingers, especially in the blessing for the tribe of Judah, where Moses calls for help against Judah's adversaries (v. 7), and in the blessing of the Levites, where Moses' blessing includes a hope that God will "crush the loins of [Levi's] adversaries" (v. 11). In fact, the blessing concludes with vivid divine warrior imagery in which God is depicted as a celestial warrior who rides through the heavens, subdues other gods, and destroys the enemies of Israel (vv. 26–27). The final verse of blessing even contains a whiff of triumphalist language, as it depicts a militarily successful Israel who shall "tread on the backs" of their enemies (v. 29).

But just as in chapter 32, the militaristic images do not ultimately endorse the view that Israel is permitted to wage God-directed war on its enemies whenever it desires. Moses' words are clear: military victory—or indeed any kind of prosperity or happiness—is ultimately God's doing rather than Israel's. The words of Moses in the final verse of chapter 33, that Israel is "a people saved by the LORD," makes clear that Israel cannot save itself.

> In the Old Testament too there are, beside the laws, certain promises and words of grace.
>
> Martin Luther, "Preface to the Old Testament," in *Martin Luther's Basic Theological Writings*, ed. Timothy Lull (Minneapolis: Fortress Press, 1989), 119.

34:1–12
The Death of Moses

Moses' death scene at the close of Deuteronomy—indeed, at the close of the Pentateuch—is one of the most powerful in Scripture. Israel's leader for four decades, the one who suffered and interceded on their behalf (cf. 9:18–19), will not make it to the land God has promised Israel. It isn't for lack of trying: in Deuteronomy 3:25 Moses pleads with God to allow him entrance into the land. But God's refusal is firm and consistent: Moses will not be allowed in.

The final chapter of the book begins with a description of Moses' ascent up Mount Nebo, to the top of Pisgah, which is a fulfillment of God's command in Deuteronomy 3:27: "Go up to the top of Pisgah and look around you to the west, to the north, to the south, and to the east. Look well, for you shall not

> Moses is on the track of Canaan all his life; it is incredible that he should see the land only when on the verge of death. This dying vision of it can only be intended to illustrate how incomplete a moment is human life. . . . Moses fails to enter Canaan not because his life was too short but because it is a human life.
>
> Franz Kafka, *Diaries 1914–1923*, ed. Max Brod, trans. Martin Greenberg and Hannah Arendt (New York: Schocken, 1965), 195–96.

cross over this Jordan." Just as Moses' role as Israel's leader began with an encounter with God on a mountaintop (Exod. 3:1–6), so now Moses' tenure as leader and his very life both end with another mountaintop encounter with God. At the top of Mount Nebo, God "showed him the whole land: Gilead as far as Dan, all Naphtali . . . all the land of Judah" (vv. 1–3). That this survey of the geography Moses sees from the mountaintop is given using the names of Israel's tribes indicates that what the text reports that Moses saw reflects the divisions of the land of Canaan in the future, after conquest.

Throughout the book of Deuteronomy various reasons have been given as to why Moses will not be allowed into the land, ranging from his bearing the punishment for Israel's sin in 4:21 to the most recent reason discussed in 32:48–52: Moses' own disobedience. But here in chapter 34, we get a straightforward depiction of Moses' death with no references to any of the former reasons. Nor do we hear any more pleading from Moses to be allowed into the land. While some commentators suggest that in the act of showing Moses the land, God partly fulfills Moses' request in 3:25 to enter the land, the fact remains that Moses, the one called "man of God" (33:1) and "servant of the LORD" (34:5), the one whose faithfulness outshines any other in Israel, does not get to set foot in or enjoy the land God has promised God's people.

As God shows Moses the land that Israel will come to occupy, God reminds Moses that it is the land promised to Israel's ancestors, to Abraham, Isaac, and Jacob, a reference that links this final chapter of the Pentateuch to its first chapters in Genesis and to the stories of the covenant God made with those ancestors. Then, after Moses glimpses this land where God's blessings are to be poured out on Israel, "Moses, the servant of the LORD, died there in the land of Moab, at the LORD's command" (34:5). Although the Deuteronomist reports Moses' age as one hundred twenty (the typical number for a long life; cf. Gen. 6:3), the text gives no indication that Moses died of old age. In fact, it asserts that "his sight was unimpaired and his vigor had not abated" (v. 7). Thus, in a final act of faithfulness, Moses dies because that is what God commanded him to do. Verse 6 reports that God buries Moses and that his burial place is not known "to this day," which may indicate that the Deuteronomist was speaking to those who claimed to know the whereabouts of Moses' grave. Christian commentators have also speculated that Moses' unknown grave site actually indicates Moses' assumption by God into heaven. Verse 9 of the NT book of Jude references a dispute between Michael, the archangel, and the devil over the body of Moses, a likely reference to the story in *The Assumption of Moses*, an ancient book that tells of the devil falsely charging Moses as a murderer not worthy of burial.[1] For many other commentators, both Jewish and Christian, the secrecy surrounding the burial place of Moses had to do instead with concerns of idolatry, a persistent worry throughout the Deuteronomic text. If Moses' grave were to be named, there would be a risk that the homage the Israelites and their descendants would pay to Moses could morph into worship of Moses himself.

> Two godly benefits did his Lord accomplish for Moses in not making known his tomb to the children of Israel. He rejoiced that his adversaries should not know it and cast forth his bones from his tomb; and in the second place, that the children of his people should not know it and make his tomb a place of worship, for he was accounted as God in the eyes of the children of his people.
>
> Aphrahat, *Demonstration* 8.9, *NPNF*², 13:378.

For all the concern that Moses might be lauded as more than human and thus worshiped in an idolatrous way, it is important to note that the text reports the Israelites as treating his death like any other human death; they observe a period of mourning for him, and then they move on. At the same time, Moses' death certainly would have been a momentous event for the people, even if that reality does not come through clearly in the text.

The story moves briskly from the description of Moses' death and burial to Joshua's becoming Israel's new leader. Verse 9 reassures the Israelites that they are in good hands with Joshua, who was "full of the spirit of wisdom because Moses had laid his hands on him." At the same time, the text also makes it clear that while Joshua might be wise, he is no Moses. In Numbers 27:20, God instructs Moses

---

1. *Lutheran Study Bible*, New Revised Standard Version (Minneapolis: Fortress Press, 2009), 2024.

> So the LORD said to Moses,
> "Take Joshua son of Nun, a
> man in whom is the spirit,
> and lay your hand upon
> him; have him stand before
> Eleazar the priest and all
> the congregation, and
> commission him in their sight.
> You shall give him some of
> your authority, so that all the
> congregation of the Israelites
> may obey."
>
> (Num. 27:18–20)

to give Joshua *some* of his authority. Joshua is to lead according to the Mosaic interpretation of God's commands (cf. Josh. 1:7–8) rather than through any direct communication with God. Joshua does not speak with God as Moses does— that is, face to face (34:10). We remember that the Levites will also share in the governing (cf. 31:25–26); in addition, there will be judges and kings in Israel. It is clear that while Israel is in capable hands with Joshua, Moses' death represents the end of an era of unrivaled leadership for Israel.

This is where the book ends: with a eulogy on the distinctiveness of Moses as a servant of God. The eulogy begins with the claim that "never since has there arisen a prophet in Israel like Moses, whom the LORD knew face to face" (v. 10). While the accent here is on Moses' prophetic role, throughout the book of Deuteronomy it is apparent that Moses played many other key roles besides prophet. In addition, that Moses knew God "face to face" harkens back to Exodus 33:11 and the claim that "the LORD used to speak to Moses face to face, as one speaks to a friend. Then he would return to the camp; but his young assistant, Joshua son of Nun, would not leave the tent." This linkage between a face-to-face relationship with God and the metaphor of friendship with God captured the theological imagination of patristic scholar Gregory of Nyssa, who found in Moses a spiritual model of what it means to live faithfully in response to God's commands:

> This is true perfection: not to avoid a wicked life because like slaves we servilely fear punishment, nor to do good because we hope for rewards, as if cashing in on the virtuous life by some business-like and contractual arrangement. On the contrary, disregarding all those things for which we hope and which have been reserved by promise, we regard falling from God's

> friendship as the only thing dreadful and we consider becoming God's friend the only thing worthy of honor and desire.[2]

For Gregory, Moses embodies his own repeated admonition throughout Deuteronomy to "take to heart" the commands of God, to follow the law with his heart for the purpose of honoring his relationship with God, who has promised him blessing.

Verses 11–12 continue recounting the ways in which Moses is unmatched among other prophets in Israel. Indeed, he is "unequaled for all the signs and wonders that the LORD sent him to perform," as well as the "mighty deeds" and "terrifying displays of power" that he has performed. What is noteworthy here is that the descriptions of what Moses did use is language that in the rest of Deuteronomy applies only to divine activity. It is God who performs "signs and wonders" against Egypt in 6:22 and 7:19; the "mighty deeds" of God made it possible for Israel to flee Egypt (cf. 11:2). But in the final words of the book of Deuteronomy, Moses shares the stage with God as one who possesses such awesome power.

Even with the high praise bestowed on Moses through the liturgy, the shadow of Moses' denial of entrance into the land lingers over the final words of the text. As Franz Kafka suggests, one way to interpret Moses dying outside the land is to understand him as a prototypical human being.[3] Moses' inability to cross over reflects an incompleteness that is endemic to all of our lives. We can see in the life and death of Moses the reality that entry into the promised land for all of us is always up ahead, just out of reach.

But that is not all there is to say about the death of Moses, for we cannot ignore the role God plays in this story. We have to acknowledge that if anyone deserves to cross over into the land of milk and honey, it is Moses. He not only persists in leading a disobedient Israel as they create idols to worship and lose faith in their God, but he even goes so far as to risk his own life to intercede before God on Israel's behalf (cf. 9:18–19). Even so, Deuteronomy ends with

---

2. Gregory of Nyssa, *The Life of Moses* (Mahwah, NJ: Paulist Press, 1978), 137.
3. Franz Kafka, *Diaries 1914–1923*, ed. Max Brod, trans. Martin Greenberg and Hannah Arendt (New York: Schocken, 1965), 195–96.

Christians are quick to claim a comedic faith, highlighting not the hilarity of Christian existence, but the ultimate victory won by Jesus over sin and death providing the experience and hope of resurrection life. When faced, however, with the reality of unexplainable suffering, destructive disasters, our own dastardly deeds, and all the persistent banalities and confounding complexities of everyday life, does a comedic confession require qualification by a down-to-earth dose of the tragic?

Wesley Vander Lugt, "Christian Theology and Tragedy: Wrestling with the Woundedly Embroiled," Transpositions: Theology, Imagination and the Arts, http://www.transpositions.co.uk/2011/11/christian-theology-and-tragedy-wrestling-with-the-woundedly-embroiled/.

the story of God commanding Moses to die before he gets to enter the land. And in the end, the text does not provide an explanation. Moses' death is inexplicable, just as in the story of Job, where the cause of Job's suffering is ultimately left unexplained (cf. Job 38–41). Even with all its theological sophistication, Deuteronomy cannot give us a final, satisfactory answer as to why Moses doesn't get into the land. He just doesn't, which is tragic, just as our own incompleteness has its own tragic dimensions for each one of us.

FURTHER REFLECTIONS
Moses as Enduring Model

Even though Moses' story is ultimately a tragic one, tragedy should not have the last word in a commentary on Deuteronomy. Indeed, the text refuses to end on a tragic note, concluding instead with grand words of praise for Moses' intimate relationship with God and for his unsurpassed role as God's prophet. In other words, even in his broken, incomplete, limited human condition, he served as a vehicle for God's redemptive, saving action in the world. This double note of tragedy and hope that defines Moses' life is likely at the heart of why he continues to live on in the theological imaginations of Jews and Christians to this day.

One of the most powerful connections between Moses and modern-day America came in the life and death of a man many called a modern-day Moses: Martin Luther King Jr. The parallels between King's life and Moses' life are many: from King's own reports of being called by the voice of God (in his kitchen rather than on a mountain), to the ways he suffered on behalf of "his people" through the bombings of his home, to his many incarcerations, and to his speaking the hard truth to people who refused to take his words to heart. Where the comparison becomes eerily solidified, though, is through the speech King gave the night before he was assassinated. He was in Memphis, Tennessee, offering his support to a sanitation workers' strike. The civil rights movement was divided over whether causes like the rights of sanitation workers were part of the civil rights struggle. While King was in Memphis marching with the workers, violence started to erupt among some of the marchers. In addition to the fracturing of the movement, King continued to receive threats on his life. On April 3, 1968, King decided at the last minute to give a speech before the sanitation workers and those marching with them. In what was to be his final speech, King cast himself as a contemporary Moses, one who was able to see the promised land of civil rights and a living wage for all, but also one who knew he was not going to get to enter that land himself.

That King was assassinated the next day was a great tragedy, not only for the struggle for civil rights but also for our country and the world. Millions were devastated by his death, wondering how the civil rights movement could continue on without him. While we cannot dismiss or neglect the sorrow and feelings of despair King's death provoked, we also must pay attention to the voices,

---

I don't know what will happen now. We've got some difficult days ahead. But it really doesn't matter with me now—because I've been to the mountaintop. I don't mind. Like anybody, I would love to live a long life, but I'm not worried about that now. I just want to do God's will. And He's allowed me to go up to the mountain. And I've looked over. And I've seen the promised land. I may not get there with you. But I want you to know tonight that we as a people will get to the promised land. So I'm happy tonight. I'm not worried about anything. I'm not fearing any man. Mine eyes have seen the glory of the coming of the Lord!

Martin Luther King Jr. "I've Been to the Mountaintop," April 3, 1968, American Rhetoric, http://www.americanrhetoric.com/speeches/mlkivebeentothemountaintop.htm.

like that of the Deuteronomist, that take us beyond the tragedy of a life stopped short of the promised land—voices like that of Andrew Young, one of King's closest friends and advisors, who said this about continuing the civil rights struggle without Martin Luther King Jr.:

> But we never had to face the world without him. His spirit has been more powerful in death than it was in life. And I suspect that's the way it was with Moses, too. When you come to the end of a God-ordained time, something new has to take over. . . . [King was, like Moses] humanity. But humanity in the hands of God. And that's what made the difference—that he put himself in God's hands. And that's what Moses did. One of the things that strengthened Martin's leadership is that he realized he didn't have to be perfect. God has always used frail human beings. And God was using him.[4]

Thus with Moses' life and with the lives of other Moseses through-out history like Martin Luther King Jr., we hold the tragic elements of their lives—and their deaths—together with the ways in which they participated in God's redeeming action in the world.

Moses may not get the land, but he gets the promise. This is the lesson of Mount Nebo and the poetic twist at the end of the Five Books that help make them such a hymn: the land alone is not the destination; the destination is the place where human beings live in consort with the divine. Ultimately, it doesn't matter that what the Bible describes is impossible to see. It doesn't matter because Moses wasn't seeing as we do. At the end, he wasn't even looking at the land. He was looking where we *should* look. He was looking at God.

Bruce Feiler, *Walking the Bible: A Journey through the Five Books of Moses* (New York: HarperCollins, 2001), 428.

---

4. Quoted in Bruce Feiler, *America's Prophet: How the Story of Moses Shaped America* (New York: HarperCollins, 2009), 269.

Final Thoughts

When I was first asked to write the commentary on Deuteronomy for this series, I was tempted to ask for a different book. There were many books of the Bible I would have jumped at the opportunity to think more deeply about, but Deuteronomy? The book of the law? It certainly was not at the top of my list. I let the invitation sit awhile and finally decided it was an excellent opportunity to engage with an entire book of Scripture and wrestle theologically and existentially with the passages I would just as soon avoid as well as those I have come to love.

As a theologian in the Lutheran tradition, I work within the inherited legacy of the law/gospel distinction, a distinction I am always keen to clarify: indeed for Luther, it is not a distinction between the Old Testament and the New Testament. That there is gospel in the Old Testament and law in the New Testament is central to Luther's understanding of the biblical text, but it is often overlooked by Christian interpreters of Scripture who prefer a Marcionite interpretation of the Old Testament.

Before immersing myself in the thirty-four chapters of Deuteronomy, I only had a surface-level appreciation that gospel exists in OT books like Deuteronomy. Turning back to what Luther and John Calvin had to say about the role of the law and commandments in Deuteronomy and other places in the Old Testament, I appreciate much more deeply the reverence these theologians had for such OT Scripture. Even as they emphasized faith alone and grace alone, the Reformers also highlighted the importance of obedience to God's commands, a key Deuteronomic theme. In reflecting on Luther's respect for the law, theologian George Lindbeck once commented that Luther nowhere said that an inability to fulfill commands is any reason for not trying.[1] That Deuteronomy is the quintessential book of the law, then, should not discourage contemporary Christian readers from seriously engaging its claims, themes, and insights for its relevance to lives of faith lived today.

One of the gifts of working on this commentary was sharing the project with my church community, Gloria Dei Lutheran Church in Saint Paul, Minnesota, during my sabbatical a few years ago. Work on the commentary was in its early stages, and the four sessions we had at church on Deuteronomy were critical to helping me frame the major theological issues I saw arising from the text. What was particularly noteworthy was how captivated many people were by the thought of digging into Deuteronomy repeatedly throughout that year. After our first two sessions, one parishioner told me that she had only three things on her calendar for the new year: a night at the opera and our two remaining sessions on Deuteronomy. In the first two sessions we dove right into addressing our Marcionite tendencies of viewing the OT God as inferior to the NT God, into dealing with the view of God as supporter of Holy War, into thinking through Christian interpretations of Deuteronomy in ways that honor and respect our Jewish neighbors' interpretations of the text, and so on. As we finished up our discussion on these engaging topics, one church member came to me and said, "It's amazing to study Deuteronomy and find that it contains everything that's most important to our faith." I thought of pointing out to her that Deuteronomy doesn't mention anything about Jesus, but instead I let her comment sink in, realizing that she was giving voice to Luther's insight that there's gospel—that is, a saving message—in Deuteronomy just as there is in the New Testament.

To push this issue even deeper, I was cognizant that as a Christian theologian I could easily fall into the long, pervasive legacy of supersessionist interpretation of OT texts generally and Deuteronomy most specifically. I live in a religiously diverse neighborhood in Saint Paul where orthodox Jews pass our house on foot every Saturday en

---

1. George Lindbeck, *The Church in a Postliberal Age* (Grand Rapids: Wm. B. Eerdmans Publishing Co., 2003), 29.

route to Sabbath services. I teach at Hamline University, an institution grounded in the United Methodist tradition but consciously
and deliberately multifaith in its orientation both inside and outside
the religion department. And I'm a Lutheran, someone who stands
in the tradition of Luther, who, for all his exegetical insights into
the value of OT commands, was one of the worst purveyors of anti-
Jewish sentiment in the entire Christian theological tradition. So it
was imperative for me in creating a commentary on Deuteronomy
not only to dig into the resources offered by Christian theologians
but also to be attentive to the reality that, as Walter Brueggemann
states, Christians constitute a "secondary listening community"
with respect to OT texts like Deuteronomy. I have striven to follow
an approach similar to Brueggemann's, where theological commentary on Deuteronomy makes the text and its claims "available for
Christian theological usage, but with the clear and modest recognition that they are not exclusively available for Christian theological
usage, and with an awareness that Christian theology may be allied
with and instructed by the ways these same texts are taken up by
others."[2]

Practically speaking, this approach meant that my research
included immersing myself in Jewish commentaries on Deuteronomy, attending Torah study on Deuteronomy at a local synagogue,
talking about the tough issues raised in Deuteronomy with a colleague and friend who also happens to be a rabbi, and having several
conversations with colleague and dear friend Earl Schwartz, who
teaches courses at Hamline in Judaism and happens to be the wisest
person I know. As I told Earl about my new commitment to move
the contemporary Christians with whom I work, live, and worship
beyond Marcionite views of the Old Testament and books like
Deuteronomy toward an understanding of the gospel that comes
through passages like Deuteronomy 30:6, Earl took out his Hebrew
prayer book and said, "Let's try replacing the word *torah* with 'the
good news.'" He then read the prayer in English with the new wording. "It works; it works," he said as he looked up, smiling. That sacred
moment at the coffee shop illustrates an aspect of my vocation that

---

2. Walter Brueggemann, *Theology of the Old Testament: Testimony, Dispute, Advocacy*
(Minneapolis: Fortress Press, 2005), 93.

working on this commentary has revealed: helping Christians move toward deeper appreciation of the gospel present in the Torah and affirming with John Calvin the following idea:

> Now since God of old bound the Jews to himself by this sacred bond, there is no doubt that he set them apart to the hope of eternal life. . . . Adam, Abel, Noah, Abraham and other patriarchs cleaved to God by such illumination of the Word. Therefore I say that without any doubt they entered into God's immortal kingdom. For theirs was a real participation in God, which cannot be without the blessing of eternal life.[3]

The words of Deuteronomy are the Word of God for both Jews and Christians, and as we Christians interpret God's Word in twenty-first-century contexts, it is vital that we do so with an ear to the wisdom and insight our Jewish brothers and sisters bring to their readings of the text.

While I do not expect this commentary or its author to have much influence over the scant attention Deuteronomy receives in the three-year lectionary cycle, I do hope that the commentary encourages church groups and Bible studies to take up more active reading and reflection on this important book. While it contains multiple passages about God and the life of faith that are unsettling, Deuteronomy also offers vigorous defense of the alien, the widow, and the orphan; pregnant resources for a theology of religious pluralism; surprising interconnections between grace and the requirement to live a certain way; and counterimages to a tidy theology of retribution that open the way for other interpretive insights. Finally, it is worthwhile for Christians to consider yet again the role of Moses and his faithfulness to God. May we, like Moses, trust that "even if you are exiled to the ends of the world, from there the LORD your God will gather you, and from there he will bring you back" (Deut. 30:4).

---

3. John Calvin, *Institutes* 2.10.7, as quoted in Peter A. Lillback, "Biblical Horizons: Calvin's Covenantal Response to the Anabaptist View of Baptism," in *The Failure of the American Baptist Culture*, ed. James B. Jordan (Geneva Divinity School, 1982), 185, http://www.biblicalhorizons.com/miscellaneous/calvins-covenantal-response-to-the-anabaptist-view-of-baptism/.

For Further Reading

Berrigan, Daniel. *Deuteronomy: No Gods but One.* Grand Rapids: Wm. B. Eerdmans Publishing Co., 2009. This free-verse commentary critiques the warrior God imagery and the ideology of holy war of Deuteronomy along with offering incisive comparisons to our current context.

Chittister, Joan. *The Ten Commandments: Laws of the Heart.* Maryknoll, NY: Orbis Books, 2006. An accessible, thoughtful, creative contemporary meditation on the meaning and relevance of the Ten Commandments for Christians, Jews, and Muslims today.

Christian Classics Ethereal Library, www.ccel.org. Calvin's sermons and biblical commentary on Deuteronomy are available here, as is Jonathan Edwards's sermon, "Sinners in the Hands of an Angry God."

Gregory of Nyssa. *The Life of Moses.* Translated by Abraham J. Malherbe and Everett Ferguson. San Francisco: HarperSanFrancisco, 2006.http://books.google.com/books?id=wAJ6fwFAligC&printsec=frontcover&dq=gregory+of+nyssa+life+of+moses&source=bl&ots=iQ62nN_K4I&sig=M0ABHp4ORyIVZt2n_TNJtgtzGY&hl=en&ei=QY8OTKe0KYjaNvLyucoM&sa=X&oi=book_result&ct=result&resnum=5&ved=0CDMQ6AEwBA#v=onepage&q&f=false. An ancient mystical reading of the life of Moses and the lessons to be drawn for one's spiritual journey toward God.

JPS Torah Commentary: Deuteronomy. Commentary by Jeffrey H. Tigay. Philadelphia: Jewish Publication Society, 1996.

Contains complete traditional Hebrew text and commentary that draws on classical and modern sources.

Lienhard, Joseph T., ed. *Exodus, Leviticus, Numbers, Deuteronomy.* Ancient Christian Commentary on Scripture: Old Testament 3, Downers Grove, IL: InterVarsity Press, 2001. Well-put-together volume of patristic commentary on the Pentateuch, with a useful introduction explaining common patristic ways of interpreting the Old Testament.

Luther, Martin. *Lectures on Deuteronomy,* in *Luther's Works,* vol. 9. Saint Louis: Concordia Publishing House, 1960. Luther regarded his little-known commentary on Deuteronomy from 1525 among the best of his scriptural commentaries.

———. Selected writings of Martin Luther online: http://www.iclnet.org/pub/resources/text/wittenberg/wittenberg-luther.html. Useful online resource for access to many of Luther's most well-known works.

Millar, J. Gary. *Now Choose Life: Theology and Ethics in Deuteronomy.* Grand Rapids: Wm. B. Eerdmans Publishing Co., 1998. Contains brief summaries of the most relevant biblical scholarship, followed by in-depth, accessible analyses of the theological claims and ethical implications of Deuteronomy.

Olson, Dennis T. *Deuteronomy and the Death of Moses: Theological Reading.* Minneapolis: Augsburg Fortress, 1994. A thought-provoking analysis of the theme of the death of Moses as it appears throughout the entire book of Deuteronomy.

Soulen, R. Kendall. *The God of Israel and Christian Theology.* Minneapolis: Fortress Press, 1996. A sustained critique of Christian supersessionism and a constructive theological proposal for an understanding of the Christian God as inseparable from the God of Israel.

van Wijk-Bos, Johanna W. H. *Making Wise the Simple: The Torah in Christian Faith and Practice.* Grand Rapids: Wm. B. Eerdmans Publishing Co., 2005. Using feminist resources as well as her experience of living in Europe during Nazi occupation, van Wijk-Bos calls Christians back to the Torah, especially through her sustained attention to the Torah's concern for the most vulnerable.

Index of Scripture

Index of Subjects